Information Literacy

Infiltrating the agenda, challenging minds

EDITED BY

GEOFF WALTON AND ALISON POPE

CP

CHANDOS
PUBLISHING

Oxford Cambridge New Delhi

Chandos Publishing
Hexagon House
Avenue 4
Station Lane
Witney
Oxford OX28 4BN
UK
Tel: +44 (0) 1993 848726
Email: info@chandospublishing.com
www.chandospublishing.com

Chandos Publishing is an imprint of Woodhead Publishing Limited

Woodhead Publishing Limited
80 High Street
Sawston
Cambridge CB22 3HJ
UK
Tel: +44 (0) 1223 499140
Fax: +44 (0) 1223 832819
www.woodheadpublishing.com

First published in 2011

ISBN: 978-1-84334-610-4 (print)
ISBN: 978-1-78063-265-0 (online)

British Library Cataloguing-in-Publication Data.
A catalogue record for this book is available from the British Library.

Typeset by RefineCatch Limited, Bungay, Suffolk
Printed in the UK and USA.

Printed in the UK by 4edge Limited - www.4edge.co.uk

Contents

List of figures and tables

Figures

Tables

Acknowledgments

The editors would like to thank the following people without whom the Staffordshire University Information Literacy Community of Practice and, therefore, this book would not have been possible. First of all, Steve Wyn Williams (Director of Academic Policy & Development, Staffordshire University) for putting the idea in our heads! Dave Parkes, (Associate Director, Information Services, Staffordshire University) for backing the project. Julie Adams for her unstinting work for the Community in creating the SUILCoP web pages and generally in being a wise and thoughtful third partner in the venture. Helen Wells and the IS marketing team for handling bookings and creating the necessary documentation. Paul Bossons' team for technical advice and help. Last but by no means least, we would like to thank all of the presenters and delegates who made all of the SUILCoP events enjoyable, productive and engaging learning experiences.

On a personal level, Alison would like to thank her Mum and Dad for their constant support and particular pride in this project and her Fellowship work. You have always been so proud of whatever I have achieved but now it is my turn to be proud of you. Many thanks are also due to Ian and James for putting up with it all.

Geoff would especially like to thank his wife Caroline for her unwavering support and immense encouragement in all his professional and academic endeavours. Geoff would also like to thank Tony Jones and Penny Vincent for inspiring him to play music again and proving that there is life beyond information literacy!

Alison Pope and Geoff Walton
Staffordshire University
February 2011

About the authors

Kirsty Baker BA (Hons), PG Dip (Open University)
Kirsty has worked at the Open University Library for over twelve years, initially as a Subject Information Specialist (Education and Social Sciences) before moving to the Information Literacy Unit when it was established in 2002. Kirsty has been involved in the development of a range of online IL skills development materials including SAFARI, the Open University's generic IL skills tutorial; an IL skills website for OU researchers; and an online guide to using the OU Library. She has been involved in the development of content and an assessment strategy for the OU short course 'Beyond Google: working with information online', and has worked as a moderator and script marker for the course. She has written a section for the OU Continuing Professional Development course 'The evolving information professional: challenges in a digital world' and developed the assessment model for the course. She has also developed Info-Rate, an online diagnostic test for IL skills which provides students with feedback and pointers for further IL skills development work. Kirsty has a special interest in accessibility, and was the project officer for the Library's ENABLE project which considered the accessibility of the OU Library service; both the physical building and the online library service.

John Crawford BA, MA, PhD, FCLIP, FRSA, FSA (Scot)
John was Library Research Officer at Glasgow Caledonian University where he was the director of the Scottish

Information Literacy Project and University Copyright Adviser. In December 2009 John retired from this role but he has every intention of continuing to be active in information literacy and promote the 'gospel of information'.

John holds degrees from London, Strathclyde and Glasgow Caledonian universities and is a fellow of the Royal Society of Arts. He has authored some 80 journal articles, book chapters, conference papers, etc. and two books on the evaluation of library and information services. His research interests include evaluation of library and information services and library and information history. He became interested in information literacy in 2002 and it has been his main research focus since then. He served on the Council of the Chartered Institute of Library and Information Professionals (CILIP) from 2002 to 2007 and during this time served as chair of its Professional Practice Committee and was a member of its Executive Board.

Bob Glass BA, MCLIP, FETC, Dip MST, FHEA
(Manchester Metropolitan University)
Bob has worked with the department since 1991. A qualified librarian, Bob is the undergraduate programme leader for Information & Communications and teaches on Common Undergraduate Degree Routes and MA/MSc courses. While at MMU he has been involved in student support and guidance, website development and curriculum development/ planning. Bob has worked in further and higher education including sessional work at Wirral Metropolitan College, Liverpool John Moore's University and North West Academic Libraries (NOWAL). He has extensive experience in teaching technical subjects and library-based competencies. He was Learning Area Co-ordinator (Information Literacy) for the LearnHigher CETL. He has taught and presented extensively

at universities and conferences in the UK, Europe, Africa and the USA.

Nancy Graham BA (Hons), MA (University of Birmingham) Nancy Graham currently works as the Subject Advisor (Medicine), Library Services at the University of Birmingham. She has worked on several projects focused on re-usable learning objects (RLOs) to support information literacy teaching, including project managing the Eduserv funded Birmingham Re-Usable Materials (BRUM) Project in 2006. The aim of the BRUM Project was to create 15 RLOs and make them available online for academics to use with their students to support information skills teaching.

Nancy has also managed two University of Birmingham alumni funded projects. The ReJiG (Re-purposing from Jorum into GEL) used existing study skills RLOs from the national learning object repository Jorum and adapted them for use on Birmingham's study skills web pages. The ReLO (Reusing Learning Objects) project outcomes included a logbook to be used for documenting the process of reusing and re-purposing existing RLOs used by librarians.

After a 2009 LILAC conference symposium, Nancy set up the IL RLO Share wiki (*http://ilrloshare.wetpaint.com*) as a means of collating information on and links to existing information literacy RLOs. In 2010, Nancy organised a one day event at the University of Birmingham, CaRILLO (Creating and Reusing Information Literacy Learning Objects), allowing librarians to share experiences of and ideas for creating and reusing learning and teaching material.

She recently began work on the JISC/HEA funded DELILA (Developing Educators Learning and Information Literacies for Accreditation) Project, along with project partner LSE. DELILA will focus on openly releasing existing information and digital literacy learning objects using Creative Commons licences through local and national repositories.

She has published on the BRUM Project and presented at several conferences, including LILAC, on the topic of information literacy RLOs.

Jill Griffiths BA Hons, MPhil (Manchester Metropolitan University)

Jill is a lecturer within the Department of Information and Communications and Research Associate within CERLIM at Manchester Metropolitan University. Jill holds degrees in Information and Library Management from Manchester Polytechnic and Master of Philosophy in Information Science from Manchester Metropolitan University.

Since joining MMU in 2000 Jill has worked on a wide variety of research projects, funded both nationally and by the European Commission focusing on Information Behaviour (academic use of electronic information sources, seeking behaviour and identification of information needs), distributed delivery of library and information services and information retrieval systems performance and usability. Current work includes students' information literacy with her colleague Bob Glass and user experience with activity data systems. Jill has also collaborated on two reuseable learning objects, Collect This!!! and Analyse This!!!, designed to assist students with data collection and analysis.

Jill teaches and supervises at undergraduate and postgraduate levels and has run workshops for PhD students and international visitors. She has published widely and has presented at many conferences and workshops, including as an invited speaker at the 17th Conference of Greek Academic Libraries: Academic Library Evaluation as a measure of Institutional Quality Assessment.

Christine Irving BA (Hons), MSc, MCLIP
Christine was the Scottish Information Literacy Project
Researcher/Project Officer based at Glasgow Caledonian
University (2004–2010). She worked on the development of
a National Information Literacy Framework (Scotland) with
cross-sector partners linking primary, secondary and tertiary
education to lifelong learning including the workplace and
adult literacies agendas. Christine is a strong advocate of
information literacy, researching and promoting the
understanding and development of information literacy in
all education sectors: in the workplace, the wider community,
politicians and government officials.

In 2006 she carried out a small exploratory study – The
role of information literacy in addressing a specific strand
of lifelong learning: the work agenda. On the basis of
this preliminary data, further research was subsequently
carried out with John Crawford into The role of information
literacy in the workplace: an exploratory qualitative study.

She holds a BA (Hons) in Information Management from
Queen Margaret University, Edinburgh and an MSc in
Lifelong Learning and Development from Glasgow
Caledonian University. She has a longstanding interest in
information, people's interaction with information and
lifelong learning. She has authored and co-authored several
journal articles and conference papers. Previous projects
she has been involved in include a Scottish cross-sector
project on Information Handling Skills where she was
one of three authors of online interactive material for
lifelong learners/post 16 year olds. As a result of this work,
in 2004 she co-authored an Information Handling Skills
national qualification at Intermediate 2 for SQA (Scottish
Qualifications Authority) and the accompanying assessment
(NAB). She is a chartered member of the Chartered Institute
of Library and Information Professionals (CILIP) and is a

LIRG (Library and Information Research Group) committee member. Following the end of the project Christine is engaged in writing about her recent research into information literacy in early years.

Gareth Johnson BSc (Hons), MSc, MCLIP, FHEA (University of Leicester)

With an original background in biomedical science, retail and web design, Gareth switched to working in and for Yorkshire and the Midlands Higher Education libraries in the late 1990s. During this time he has served as a subject specialist, research and innovation officer, open access advocate and project manager. Currently he manages the document and distance learning supply, course packs and copyright and institutional repository teams at the University of Leicester.

He first developed an interest in creating videos for entertainment and education in 2007, and has subsequently lectured on the subject across the UK. He is about to create his 200th short movie. These films have been used by librarians and trainers around the world, and hopefully inspired some to make their own too.

Professionally Gareth has served on a number of local and national committees, including the CILIP Editorial Panel, UCRG National & Forum for Interlending Committees; and is currently a CILIP Councillor. He has authored 20 publications, over 30 book reviews and has also contributed to three other academic texts. He is a frequent, popular and engaging workshop facilitator on a broad range of professional issues.

His notable other passions in and outside of the office include film creative writing, effective communication, semantic web, public speaking, intrepreneurship, cult televisual sci-fi and fantasy, LARPing, preserving and smallholding. He is also a member in good standing of the Goose Club of Great Britain.

Alison Pope BA (Joint Hons), LLB (Hons), DipLib, MCLIP, FHEA (Staffordshire University)

Alison is Learning and Information Services Manager at Staffordshire University. She manages a team of librarians, skills tutors, information professionals and information consultants working within Information Services and is based at the Stoke campus of the university. She also acts as subject support librarian working with the Law School. A Learning and Teaching Fellow at the university from 2005–2009 and a Teaching Excellence Fellow from 2010, Alison has been closely involved in the development of the university's Learning and Teaching strategy to integrate information literacy elements into the curriculum. She was co-editor (with Geoff Walton) of *Information Literacy: Recognising the Need* (Oxford: Chandos, 2006). She has spoken at many conferences including Librarians Information Literacy Annual Conference (LILAC), British and Irish Association of Law Librarians (BIALL) and the Association of Law Teachers (ALT), and published articles on the topic of information literacy and its integration into the curriculum with Julie Adams, Martin Hannibal, Geoff Walton and Keith Puttick. She is co-editor of *Information Literacy: Infiltrating the Agenda, Challenging Minds.* In June 2007 the Assignment Survival Kit project which she and Julie Adams led received the Chartered Institute of Library and Information Professionals (CILIP) University, College & Research (UC & R) Award for Innovation. You can find this learning support tool at *www.staffs.ac.uk/ask.*

Keith Puttick LLB (Hons), MA, Cert Ed (HE), PG Dip Ed (HE) Barrister-at-Law, (Staffordshire University)

Keith lectures in Employment, Social Welfare Law and Public Law at Staffordshire Law School. He is a co-author of *Employment Rights* (with Richard Painter); *Civil Appeals* (ed. Sir Michael Burton: Foreword Lord Woolf); *Butterworths Family Law/SFLS* (ed. John Fotheringham); and *The Challenge of Asylum to Legal Systems* (ed. Prakash Shah). He is a regular contributor to the *Journal of Immigration, Asylum and Nationality Law* and *Industrial Law Journal*, and has been General Editor of *Welfare & Family* for 16 years. He has organised the bi-annual Work & Welfare conference series since 1997, and with support from the Department of Business & Enterprise, TUC, Disability Alliance, East London Mosque & London Muslim Centre he commissioned the student project People Diversity & Work, the pilot for Enquiring Minds.

Katharine Reedy BA, MA, DipLib, MCLIP, PG Cert AP, FHEA, (Open University)

Katharine has worked at the Open University Library for ten years, in a variety of roles. These include faculty liaison and course support for the Maths & Computing, Technology and Arts faculties, developing and promoting the OU Library's service to students and tutors (Associate Lecturers) as part of the Learner Support team, and working with the Arts faculty to integrate information literacy skills and library resources into courses. She contributed to the Arts faculty IL policy, has written activities for the iKnow (information skills at work) website and co-authored the booklet *Integrating Information Literacy Skills into the Curriculum*, now in its second edition. She joined the Information Literacy Unit in 2009, where her responsibilities include developing and maintaining the OU Library's resource bank of information literacy activities, supporting OU tutor peer-to-peer library training and delivering library staff development. She has presented at LILAC and other conferences on a number of occasions, has published several articles (details of which are available via *http://academia.edu/KatharineReedy*) and recently gained fellowship of the Higher Education Academy. As well as the embedding of IL into the curriculum, her current interests include digital literacy, learning design and the use of new technology for learning and teaching.

Ben Scoble BSc, MSc (Staffordshire University)
After gaining a BSc in Geography from Lancaster University, Ben Scoble had sights on developing a career in project management with British Telecom. However, the lure of academia was too strong and Ben returned to Keele University to complete both a PGCE and an MSc in IT. Several years then followed with Ben being employed by Keele University in numerous roles that included running Widening Participation projects; researching student recruitment and retention; running student volunteering; and teaching on the PGCE programme. After gaining such a wide variety of skills and experiences, Ben found a perfect application for them in his role as a Learning Development Specialist for Staffordshire University. In this current role, Ben investigates pedagogy and technology with the goal of supporting the application and implementation of technology-supported learning in higher education. Outside of work, Ben considers himself to be an urban farmer, putting in many hours of physical work on his local allotment plot. However, this is not a reaction to his day job as Ben dedicates just as much free time to updating his allotment blog, YouTube channel and contributing to social networks.

Chris Wakeman BSc, BEd (Hons), MA, EdD (Staffordshire University)
Having spent eleven years as an aeronautical engineer with Rolls Royce Motors Ltd., Chris retrained as a secondary school teacher during the 1980s, attaining a Bachelor of Education degree with 1st Class Honours from the University

of Wolverhampton, prior to taking up his first teaching post in Llandudno, North Wales during 1989. Chris went on to spend seven years in schools, completing a Master of Arts Degree in Education with the Open University before being appointed as a Ministry of Defence (MoD) lecturer and the Subject Leader for Mathematics at Royal Air Force (RAF) Cosford during 1996. During his time with the MoD, Chris was part of the initial project team that was set up to establish Distance Learning provision for the training of RAF engineering technicians and was sponsored to complete his Doctorate in Education with the Open University between 1998 and 2002. After working as a visiting lecturer on the University of Wolverhampton (UoW) PGCE programme during 2000/2001, Chris was later appointed as the Subject leader for Education Studies at the UoW where he remained for four years before taking up his current post as a Curriculum Development Adviser at Staffordshire University. Chris was a member of the review team that was set up by the Quality and Assurance Agency (QAA) to revise and update the Education Studies benchmark statements during 2007/8 and was the chair of the British Education Studies Association (BESA) during 2008/9. With research interests in 'emotional intelligence' and 'blended approaches to learning', Chris is currently joint Managing Editor of the *Innovative Practice in Higher Education* online journal and a member of the editorial board and a peer reviewer for *Educationalfutures*, the journal of the British Education Studies Association.

Geoff Walton BA (Joint Hons), MA, PhD, MCLIP, FHEA (Staffordshire University)
Geoff is Academic Skills Tutor Librarian and has recently become Senior Researcher in the Institute for Applied Creative Thinking (I-ACT) in the Faculty of Arts, Media and

Design at Staffordshire University. As subject librarian he now supports the Business School. He is SLA Europe Information Professional 2010. As Senior Researcher in I-ACT, Geoff, as well as carrying out his own research, is responsible for fostering a research community within the faculty and for identifying funding opportunities across a range of subject areas. He recently completed a PhD which analysed the development of a blended approach (a mix of face-to-face and online pedagogical methods) to delivering information literacy to first-year undergraduates. He is particularly interested in the cognitive processes involved in becoming information literate. His research interests also include developing the Assignment Survival Kit (ASK), developing a process for online peer assessment, investigating the role of information literacy in lifelong learning and the experience of non-traditional undergraduate students. In his previous role as RiT Project Co-ordinator, Geoff was involved in identifying synergies between research, teaching, learning, information literacy, elearning and inquiry-based learning. Geoff is information literacy training officer for the CILIP Community Services Group Information Literacy sub-group. He is also joint Managing Editor of the new online journal *Innovative Practice in Higher Education* which will be launched in the spring of 2011. In 2010 Geoff became a Teaching Excellence Fellow at Staffordshire University.

Andrew Whitworth PhD, BA, PGCLTHE, CMALT (Manchester University)
Andrew lectures in the School of Education at the University of Manchester, and is Programme Director for the MA: Digital Technologies, Communication and Education. His research is concerned with the intersection of technology, democracy and individual and organisational learning. In

2009 he published *Information Obesity* (Chandos, Oxford), which analysed the history and present state of ICT skills and information literacy education from the perspective of critical theory. His course unit, Media and Information Literacy, was named as an exemplar in the field in the 'Learning Literacies in a Digital Age' (LLiDA) Project, and with the backing of the Higher Education Academy, was converted into an open educational resource for use by postgraduate research students across the UK (see *http://madigitaltechnologies.wordpress.com/infoliteracy*). He has worked as a trainer for the UKeiG and conducted professional development workshops on elearning and information literacy across the UK and elsewhere. He is originally from Sussex and now lives in Yorkshire.

Introduction

Alison Pope and Geoff Walton

Abstract: What are the challenges facing academics, librarians and information professionals in the second decade of the 21st century and how, if at all, do they differ from those faced in the immediately preceding decade? Will information literacy be perceived as an essential item that cannot be cut, or rather as an expensive luxury commodity? Can HE institutions afford to ignore the need for information literacy? Faced with the rigours of economic recession, can we send students out into the job market with a less than an excellent knowledge of how to find, evaluate and use information? What will be the UK Coalition Government's line on this? In the US, Barack Obama has highlighted the need for educational institutions to contribute to the development of a society which can use and understand the information all around it.

As academics, librarians and information professionals we are all aware that tough times are ahead and this chapter highlights a number of issues for debate. Even the most committed of us recognises that if essentials like social security support are under review, what chance might there be for something as ephemeral as information literacy? This is not only an economic question but a question of professional status in the academic arena. In response to this uncertainty and tight budgets, departments make changes: at the stroke of a word-processing key previously well-attended and successful embedded information literacy teaching sessions may be removed or reallocated to other colleagues. Priorities shift and curricula are reviewed. How can we be ready for these tough times? How can we ensure that we continue to provide the kind of added value which our students need on the employability market?

Key words: information literacy, employability, economic recession, curriculum design, political agenda.

Welcome to this collection of papers from Staffordshire University Information Literacy Community of Practice (SUILCoP) which reflects the illustrious history and ongoing endeavours of this seminar series from July 2006 to present (August 2010) (please see Appendix 1). We hope you find these papers as stimulating and enjoyable to read as we did. Much food for thought is included within these covers, some controversy and, of course, many practical tips on the subject of information literacy and related topics. Just to whet your appetite, Keith Puttick gives a scholarly overview of a research-informed teaching project underpinned by precepts of information literacy and run in the context of an undergraduate law module, Nancy Graham surveys the current literature and thinking on re-usable learning objects, Gareth Johnson explains how to make use of an audio visual approach to information literacy and John Crawford and Christine Irving most pertinently look at IL issues in relation to employability. Elsewhere Drew Whitworth examines the idea of information obesity; Ben Scoble looks at the coffee house culture of 17th and 18th century Britain and its uncanny parallels with the social media aspects of the present day Internet; Chris Wakeman examines enquiry based learning including problem-based approaches, webquests, dialectic approaches to delivery and facilitation and their influence on student information literacy; and Katharine Reedy and Kirsty Baker from the Open University (OU) look at how the OU Library has responded to the need for consistent and coherent embedding of information literacy skills in the undergraduate curriculum by developing an Information Literacy Levels Framework. We hope there is something for everyone and that this volume will give you a flavour of what it has been like to take part in the Staffordshire University Information Literacy Community of Practice between 2006 and 2010.

Before you go on to digest the material within the chapters themselves, in this short introduction we aim to give a broad overview of SUILCoP itself; the context, its history and a brief outline of the community of practice, i.e. those who attended the seminars. Finally, we issue a 'call to arms' and ask some challenging questions regarding the future of, not just IL, but the profession librarianship itself as we face an uncertain future.

In order to properly understand how this collection of work on the subject of information literacy in HE institutions in the very early 21st century came to be, it is perhaps necessary to give a little background. Very late in 2004 our line manager, David Parkes, Associate Director Information Services, sent out an e-mail exhorting all the library and information professionals within his team to try for one of the new University Learning and Teaching Fellowships. The scheme had recently been re-vamped and the institution was keen to encourage staff members from outside the traditional academic sphere to apply for these two-year honorary positions. Briefly, the Fellowships were designed to identify and celebrate those individuals within Staffordshire University who had demonstrated an excellent contribution to students' teaching and learning. If successful, each Fellow would need to carry out a project that would be of benefit to the university as a whole. We both applied completely independently and were delighted to be chosen after a rigorous selection procedure in which we had to outline the details of the projects we had in mind. It turned out that both our projects were to concentrate on information literacy; Geoff's revolved around analysing the use of VLEs (especially discussion boards) in order to construct a blended information literacy teaching and learning programme, and Alison's focused on attempting to get the university to take a strategic approach to information literacy.

Since the two of us had been appointed from the same university department it transpired that the selection panel had decided that we were to be given an additional task: to put Staffordshire University 'on the map' in our chosen area of research, namely information literacy. No small task and especially within the two-year time frame with a small budget which was also to be used to fund our respective projects. Despite maintaining our independent research projects we began to address this issue. What could we do that would quickly achieve this end result?

It was rapidly decided that hosting a conference at which national, if not international, experts would speak on the topic of information literacy would be the easiest way to do this. If you have read our collection of papers 'Information literacy: recognising the need' (Walton and Pope 2006) you will know that the one-day conference which we hosted in May 2006 certainly managed this. While the warm glow of post-conference euphoria was still upon us we were very susceptible to a suggestion from the Fellowship co-ordinators that maybe we could continue this success via the development of some sort of Community of Practice. In just a couple of meetings involving some scribbles on scraps of paper the idea and framework for Staffordshire University Information Literacy Community of Practice (SUILCoP) was born.

We would hold three afternoon seminars or workshops each academic year, one each term. Each year would have an overarching information literacy theme and at each session we would host an external expert and also provide the opportunity for speakers from Staffordshire to present. Funding for the seminars would come from our very small Fellowship budget. We hoped to attract interested academics, information professionals and librarians. We could provide light refreshments and travel expenses for external speakers. We advertised the sessions on the web, in the professional press and by contacting people who had attended the 2006 conference and requested to be kept on our mailing list. Very soon we had the first session booked and a series of forthcoming dates identified.

In 2006/7 our theme was 'Collaboration, curriculum and courses', in 2007/8 'Space, strategy and support', in 2008/9 'Development, dialogue and design' and, most recently in 2009/10 'Obesity, overload and opportunity'. The speakers and their topics can be seen in the Appendix to this collection of papers.

The choice of theme was driven by what seemed to us to be topical at the time and also, to be frank, by the speakers we could secure. This collection of papers is a record of the contributions of some of those speakers. Although it is retrospective, the ideas which are discussed here are just as relevant now as they were then and they give us the opportunity to think more widely about where information literacy is now and its potential direction in the immediate and long-term future.

But who were the community of practice?

Of course we cannot name names here but what we will do is give you an overview of those involved.

Some 51 different organisations have been represented at SUILCoP events. In all, 70 per cent of delegates were drawn from HE (new universities, red brick and research universities across the UK), 23 per cent from FE (both local partner colleges and some from as far afield as Scotland) and 6 per cent from other institutions (British Council, NHS and information-related companies). The vast majority of delegates were information professionals, but we are pleased to say that a diverse range of academic staff attended from time to time. In the main, delegates were external to Staffordshire University. Many of the delegates came back to SUILCoP on more than one occasion, which most definitely enabled the seminars to develop a community atmosphere of mutual support and ideas sharing.

However, since those halcyon days pre-Coalition Government a chill wind, in the spectral form of the Comprehensive Spending Review (CSR), has begun to blow through the public sector, including HE, and it is to this anxiously awaited future that we now turn.

Change of key: change of outlook

What are the challenges facing academics, librarians and information professionals in the second decade of the 21st century and how, if at all, do they differ from those faced in the immediately preceding decade? At the time of writing (August 2010) the 'Browne Report' has not yet been published but HE institutions are almost holding their collective breath in anticipation of its suggestions. Will information literacy be perceived as an essential item which cannot be cut or rather as an expensive luxury commodity? Can HE institutions afford to ignore the need for information literacy or will it be swept aside as something less attractive (and therefore perhaps less worth investing in) to potential students than swish accommodation or state of the art catering facilities? Alternatively, IL might well still be recognised as a pedagogical necessity but as one delivered by academic staff who are in the self-same process of retrenchment as we are, and see it as a means for enhancing their own teaching portfolio at the expense of ours.

When institutions are faced with challenging choices to make about how budgets are allocated, how far up the pecking order will we find information literacy? How can HE institutions, understanding the rigours of economic recession, send students out into the job market with less than an excellent knowledge of how to find, evaluate and use information? What will be the Coalition Government's line on this? In the United States, Barack Obama (2009) has highlighted the need for educational institutions to contribute to the development of a society which can use and understand the information all around it. This imperative echoes the UN's statements in Prague (USNCLIS, 2003) Alexandria (UNESCO, 2005) and in the UNESCO sponsored IFLA guidelines (Lau, 2006). What will the UK's response be? The UK already has a strong foundation in the CSG Information Literacy sub-group (already in the process of becoming a CILIP group in its own right) and the final welcome realisation in CILIP that IL is important. The ongoing success that is LILAC is a testament to the energy and endeavours of this group and it is now clear that the field is maturing, for example, from the plenary address that Ralph Catts gave at LILAC in Limerick 2010, SCONUL have taken up his challenge and have begun to form a research group to measure the impact of IL in UK HE.

As academics, librarians and information professionals we are all aware that tough times are ahead. Even the most committed of us recognises that if essentials like social security support are under review what chance might there be for something which might be regarded as ephemeral as information literacy? The reality is that in response to uncertainty and to tight budgets, departments make changes: at the stroke of a word-processing key previously well-attended and successful embedded teaching sessions can be removed or re-allocated. Priorities shift and curricula are reviewed. How can we be ready for these tough times? How can we ensure that we continue to provide the kind of added value which our academic colleagues will clearly recognise and which students so obviously need to succeed on the employability market? How can we make sure that the inroads which the first years of the 21st century saw us making into the student curriculum are not all swept away and forgotten in the new perhaps utilitarian regime?

Our call to arms . . .

In 2006, in our conference proceedings which turned out to be a very good seller, we said that,

> [. . .] information literacy is part of a bigger picture; part of a jigsaw puzzle which includes other literacies (including for example, academic, media and digital), new ways of approaching learning through critical thinking, reflective practice collaborative learning and the keyskills agenda all of which contribute to independent learning. (Pope and Walton, 2006: 7)

Clearly an instrumental view but nonetheless one wedded to the HE agenda of the time.

In 2009, as our own views of IL have matured we said,

It is our assertion that information literacy extends beyond the educational and economic to encompass the social. Information and other literacies such as digital and media are the tools which enable active participation in a democratic society [. . .] It is not the role of information literacy programmes in higher education to create mini-librarians who are good at doing research or even employable economic units but rather to foster critical thinkers who can navigate their way through the information terrain and make their own informed judgements regarding which information to use for whatever purpose. (Pope and Walton, 2009: 4)

In other words it is no longer about skills but much more than that: it is about participation in society as well as gaining the skills to be a productive part of it. As Whitworth (2007) has argued, information literacy's field of interest extends to encompass the social as well as the personal.

Recently Geoff (in a co-authored work with Mark Hepworth) reaches much further than these ideas and argues that information literacy can actually empower individuals – not just give them skills:

Empowerment is underpinned by information literacy. Being able to learn effectively and independently and use the knowledge, data and information [. . .] around them is likely to result in people having more choice. When people have choice, they are usually better informed about their situation and can see alternatives in a critical light, and then may be able to choose from or create a range of solutions or strategies. This can lead to people having more options when deciding how

> to participate and interact socially, and how to use and contribute to the resources and services available. (Hepworth and Walton, 2009: 3)

Their view of information literacy is far more than simply acquiring a set of skills or even consuming information but actually becoming fully participating individuals empowered to contribute to and change the world around them. From this they have developed a new, more radical view of IL as:

> a complex set of abilities which enable individuals to: engage critically with and make sense of the world, its knowledge and participate effectively in learning to make use of the information landscape as well as contributing to it. (Hepworth and Walton, 2009: 10)

Finally, in his own doctoral research, Geoff has shown that by using pedagogically sophisticated methods of delivery a demonstrable increase in students' information literacy abilities can be achieved (Walton, 2009; Walton and Hepworth, 2011(in press)). In short, information literacy is about deep learning, participation and making a real contribution leading to an enriched and empowered population.

All good stuff, but therein lies an identity crisis aptly identified by Thornton (2010) who sees a real disconnect between how we (the librarian and information professional) see IL and how the rest of the world perceives it. Sadly, we suspect many outside those 'in the know' still regard IL as, 'a few dull lessons taken by a librarian as part of a – probably rather dull – research skills module, rather than a vehicle of empowerment and political liberation' (Thornton, 2010: 8).

To disabuse our colleagues of this view and build upon our ideas and findings, however, we librarians and information professionals have a real role to play as teachers or enablers and facilitators of learning here – because by our very nature we tend to approach our pedagogical interventions from a 'learning by doing' perspective rather than a traditional content driven mode. These new approaches fit in well with the new and fashionable drivers towards inquiry (enquiry)-based learning, research-informed teaching and other constructivist approaches.

These ideas are not necessarily new in theoretical or policy terms. As far back as Dearing (NCIHE, 1997) and QAA (2000a and b) the ongoing change of emphasis within higher education towards a student-centred approach was apparent – and it is now that these approaches are becoming more fashionable because of the need to engage a widely diverse student intake.

We must, therefore, become equal and involved. Involved in constructing learning outcomes, planning interventions and assessment: this is not only about saving our jobs and our future profession (it would be disingenuous not to recognise that we do have vested interest here) but it is, and we should shout this from the roof tops, much more about actually contributing to the fabric of a democratically aware and enriched society which will contain engaged citizens who will not be so duped by the misinformation which led us to the economic gloom and wealth-at-any-cost capitalism of the 20th century.

It is time to stop wondering whether we are librarians or teachers, it is time to shape our amorphous 'all things to all people' role to our own advantage and redefine our profession in our own terms before it is too late. What is it that academic librarians in the second decade of the 21st century do? What is it that makes them invaluable to the whole process of tertiary education? What is it that they can uniquely bring to the business of educating employable graduates and fostering a real sense of economic and political engagement?

There are already promising developments, the UC&R/ CDG event at Warwick in May 2010 being one case in point. The focus of this session was on librarians as educators – we need more of these. Again, LILAC offers a great focus for these endeavours and to share best practice.

It can be seen that because of the skills needs requirements in evidence-based practice the NHS hold IL in greater esteem and see it as a positive force for good within their domain. Is this a model we can adapt or at least use as a means for convincing others of the worth of IL?

These initiatives and ventures show that it is not all doom and gloom. We must not, in this recession, be trapped in the doldrums and become becalmed and lose the professional will to live. We need to keep focused, is IL the infra-red vision equipment that lets us see the true image of the terrain of important information clearly?

We need to avoid becoming reactive in this retreat which is imposed by the CSR. Our outlook must be both practical and idealistic in equal measure. We cannot predict the future but we believe that defining the 21st century librarian is about being a teacher and educator not a custodian and keeper of the tomes; it is about, through teaching, turning information into knowledge. Gandhi taught that in order to achieve change you should be the change you wish to see in the world. It is about bringing the process to life and making people see it is not a dry search for stuff. What we must help people realise, and we agree with Duncan Grey here, is that IL (and perhaps the role of librarian itself) is not about giving the right answers, it is about giving people the right tools to ask and answer the questions themselves. By doing this they, our learners, are in a position to find the answer to every question for themselves (Grey, 2008: xii).

The old Chinese proverb has much to teach librarians, information professionals and educators of the 21st century:

Give a man a fish and you feed him for a day. Teach a man to fish and you feed him for a lifetime.

We forget it at our peril.

References

Grey, D. (2008) *Getting the Buggers to Find Out: Information Skills and Learning How to Learn*. London: Continuum.

Hepworth, M. and Walton, G. (2009) *Teaching Information Literacy for Inquiry-based Learning*. Oxford: Chandos.

Lau, J. (2006) *Guidelines on Information Literacy for Lifelong Learning. Final draft. International Federation of Library Associations (IFLA)*. [Online] *http://www.ifla.org/VII/s42/pub/IL-Guidelines2006.pdf* (accessed 1 August 2010).

National Committee of Enquiry into Higher Education (NCIHE) (1997) ('Dearing Report') *Higher Education in the Learning Society*. London: National Committee of Enquiry into Higher Education. London: HMSO.

Obama, B. (2009) *National Information Literacy Awareness Month, 2009. By the President of the United States of America. A proclamation*. (Online) *www.whitehouse.gov/assets/documents/2009literacy_prc_rel.pdf* (accessed 28 October 2009).

Pope, A. and Walton, G. (2006) 'Information literacy: recognising the need – an introduction'. In Walton, G. & Pope, A. J. (eds) *Information Literacy: Recognising the Need. Staffordshire University, Stoke-on-Trent, United Kingdom 17 May 2006*. Oxford: Chandos, pp. 3–11.

Pope, A. and Walton, G. (2009) 'Information and media literacies: sharpening our vision in the twenty first century'.

In Leaning, M. (ed.) *Issues in Information and Media Literacy: Education, Practice and Pedagogy*. California: Informing Science Press, pp. 1–29.

Quality Assurance Agency for Higher Education (2000a) *Subject benchmark statements: hospitality, leisure, sport and tourism*. [Online] <*http://www.qaa.ac.uk/crntwork/benchmark/benchmarking.htm*> (accessed 31 March 2004).

Quality Assurance Agency for Higher Education (2000b) *Guidelines for preparing programme specifications*. [Online] <*http://www.qaa.ac.uk/crntwork/progspec/progspec0600.pdf*> (accessed 3 June 2003).

Thornton, S. (2010) *Information Literacy: Where Next?* Paper presented at the Political Studies Association Annual Conference, Edinburgh University, 30 March 2010.

UNESCO (2005). *Alexandria Proclamation on information literacy and lifelong learning. High Level Colloquium on Information Literacy and Lifelong Learning, in Alexandria, Egypt, on 6–9 November 2005.* [Online] *http://portal.unesco.org/ci/en/ev.php-URL_ID=20891&URL_DO=DO_TOPIC&URL_SECTION=201.html* (accessed 1 August 2010).

United States National Commission on Library and Information Science (USNCLIS) (2003). *The Prague Declaration. Towards an information literate society.* [Online] *http://portal.unesco.org/ci/en/files/19636/11228863531PragueDeclaration.pdf/PragueDeclaration.pdf* (accessed 1 August 2010).

Walton, G. (2009). 'Developing a new blended approach to fostering information literacy'. Unpublished PhD Thesis: Loughborough University.

Walton, G. and Hepworth, M. (2011, in press) A longitudinal study of changes in learners' cognitive states during and following an information literacy teaching intervention. *Journal of Documentation*, 67(3), n.p.

Walton, G. and Pope, A. (eds) (2006) Information Literacy: Recognising the need. Staffordshire University, Stoke-on-Trent, United Kingdom, 17 May 2006. Oxford: Chandos.

Whitworth, A. (2007) 'Communicative competence in the information age: towards a critical pedagogy'. In Andretta, S. (ed.) *Change and Challenge: Information Literacy for the 21st Century*. Adelaide: Auslib Press, pp. 85–114.

Part 1
Collaboration, curriculum and courses

2

Information literate pedagogy: developing a levels framework for the Open University

Katharine Reedy and Kirsty Baker

Abstract: This chapter will describe how Open University Library Services has responded to the need for consistent and coherent embedding of information literacy (IL) skills in the undergraduate curriculum by developing an Information Literacy Levels Framework. This articulates the skills outcomes for IL at each stage and shows progression from first-year undergraduate study through to graduation. We outline the background to development of the Framework and the rationale behind its format. We reflect on the process of developing and evaluating it, discuss how it is starting to be used in practice, and conclude with an indication of how it is being expanded.

Key words: information literacy, skills development, progression, undergraduate curriculum, skills integration, learning outcomes.

Introduction

The Open University (OU) Library's Information Literacy Levels Framework (see Table 2.1) is a document articulating

Table 2.1 Open University Information Literacy Levels Framework

	Level 1	Level 2	Level 3
Understand the information landscape	■ Able to identify a limited number of key sources of information in the subject area or context ■ Have experienced using a limited number of formats of information (for example, books, journals, websites), as appropriate to the course ■ Able to articulate the key characteristics of different information types (e.g. print/electronic, primary/secondary, freely available/subscriber only/invisible web) as relevant to the subject or context	■ Able to identify a range of key sources of information in the subject area ■ Have experienced using a range of formats of information (e.g. bibliographic records, full text, abstracts) ■ Use knowledge of key resources and their characteristics to independently select appropriate resources for the task as relevant to the subject or context	■ Able to select and use a wide range of sources appropriate to the discipline, from the library and beyond ■ Use knowledge of resources and their characteristics to independently select appropriate resources for the task ■ Aware of sources of current information for keeping up to date and able to select and use those most appropriate to needs
Plan and carry out a search	■ Able to identify the 'knowledge gap' and what information is needed to fill it ■ Able to determine appropriate keywords including synonyms	■ Familiar with the general principles of effective searching ■ Able to recognise common search features across different databases and the web	■ Able to identify and frame problems or research questions and to select appropriate information to address these ■ Able to use search techniques and common search functions with confidence.

	■ Know how to adapt a search (for example, broadening or narrowing by adding or removing keywords, or using different ones) ■ Able to plan and carry out a search in a database on a pre-defined topic using predefined resources ■ Able to find an article or book from a reference	■ Able to use a range of database functionality (e.g. truncation, phrase searching, date limits, combining search terms) within a single database ■ Able to independently carry out a simple subject search within a single database ■ Able to use judgement to appropriately adapt a search, including the decision to use a new database ■ Able to interpret database results (e.g. bibliographic or full text), and use results functionality (e.g. sorting, saving, exporting)	■ Able to search familiar and unfamiliar sources independently and confidently, refining the search as needed (e.g. broadening and narrowing)
Critically evaluate information	■ Be familiar with and begin to apply appropriate quality criteria to evaluate pre-defined information	■ Use appropriate quality criteria to evaluate a range of resources (e.g. books, articles, websites) effectively	■ Apply appropriate quality criteria to critically evaluate information from any source to determine authority, bias, etc., which sometimes may be subtle to detect

Continued

Table 2.1 Open University Information Literacy Levels Framework *(cont'd)*

	Level 1	Level 2	Level 3
	■ Use appropriate quality criteria in a broad sense to carry out initial filtering of material from searches	■ Use appropriate quality criteria to filter results	■ Use appropriate quality criteria to filter results, and also to focus on the most relevant information within documents
Manage and communicate your results	■ Know what is meant by plagiarism ■ Know what a reference is, the information required to create a reference, and that references can be created in different styles ■ Aware of the need to accurately record search results ■ Able to select appropriate references to produce a reference list and in-text citations as required for course assignments	■ Able to produce an accurate list of references for common sources using the appropriate style ■ Able to record search results accurately ■ Aware of different systems available for managing references (e.g. social bookmarking tools, card index, diary, Refworks)	■ Able to accurately and appropriately refer to the thoughts and ideas of others in your work ■ Aware of the range of tools and techniques for managing and exporting references (e.g. card index, Refworks) and able to select and use as appropriate

skills outcomes for information literacy (IL) at each stage of the undergraduate curriculum and showing progression from first year undergraduate through to graduation. In what follows we provide an introduction to the Framework, outlining the background to its development, our aspirations in creating it and the rationale behind its format. We reflect on the process of developing and evaluating it, and consider the potential issues which may arise when using it in practice. We offer some thoughts on the support which will be needed for it to be used effectively in teaching and learning and the ways in which we are addressing this. We indicate how it is starting to be used in OU courses. Finally, we look to the future and talk about how the Framework is being extended to go beyond undergraduate study.

Background

When the OU first began to develop distance learning materials in the 1970s, the majority of OU courses were designed to be self-contained. At the time it could not be assumed that all students would be able to access information outside of the course materials. As the World Wide Web began to establish itself in the 1990s, and as the amount of digitised information increased, the OU developed an online library service that could potentially be accessed by all OU students via the Internet. Take-up of the online service was gradual. In the early days of the web not all students had access to the Internet. However, as access increased, the OU began to move to online delivery of courses. This meant that module teams were now in a position to encourage students to use the online library to find information to support their studies outside of the study materials provided.

Alongside these developments, it became clear that the OU Library needed to do more to develop and support the information literacy skills of students and staff, to ensure that both groups could make effective use of the increasing amount of information being made available via the web. In 2002 the OU Library established an Information Literacy Unit (ILU) to raise the profile of IL within the University, and to encourage and support the development of IL skills for OU staff and students. Developments within higher education helped to move the IL agenda forwards, including the Dearing Report (Dearing, 1997), which stated that students needed to become more self-directed and that they should obtain support to develop necessary skills. IL skills were also included in the Quality Assurance Agency (QAA) Framework for Higher Education Qualifications (QAA, 2001) and in the subject benchmarking statements (QAA, 2007). The ILU developed an IL strategy for the University, and promoted integration of IL at strategic level, resulting in IL statements being incorporated into OU policy documents.

The OU's approach to IL has been to adopt a number of models to ensure the broadest range of users have access to opportunities to improve their information literacy skills. These include integration of IL into the curriculum, the provision of generic online IL materials, and standalone modules in IL. However, research suggests that the most effective approach for IL skills development is to embed IL activities within the curriculum. Resources are more likely to be used if integrated, and it is also argued that IL is more meaningful within the context of study: '. . . information literacy skills are not totally generic: they must be developed in the context of a specific subject or discipline because a basic understanding of any discipline is necessary to enable learners to frame pertinent questions with which to evaluate and select appropriate sources.' (Kirkwood, 2006: 329)

For a number of years, OU librarians have been working with module and programme teams to embed IL skills into new courses in response to the changes outlined above. New Curriculum models are being developed which increasingly require students to research outside their study materials and to develop key skills – including information literacy – for life and work. All course modules now have a website in the Virtual Learning Environment (VLE), which facilitates access to relevant online resources.

The requirement for IL to be fully embedded in the curriculum to promote and enhance student independent learning and progression through programmes has been part of OU high-level strategy since 2006. The current Learning and Teaching Strategy emphasises the importance of a learner-centred approach, which enables students to develop the independent and life-long learning skills they will need to function successfully in a digital world. It has specific objectives to increase information literacy development across the curriculum and to ensure that staff are equipped with the relevant skills.

A number of faculties have developed IL policies which set out in general terms how IL should be integrated into modules and degree programmes within the relevant disciplines. There is, however, still no clear map of the course design process or the point at which IL should be considered. This can result in IL skills being 'bolted on', remaining optional, and not being assessed in a valid or reliable fashion. The OU Learning Design Initiative project (Conole et al., 2008) is now starting to address these issues by developing tools and frameworks to support the pedagogical aspects of course production.

There is variation between faculties in the way in which they have adopted IL, in part due to disciplinary differences, but also because of organisational culture. In some cases a shared understanding of the term 'information literacy' has yet to be reached between academic and library staff or between academic staff across and within faculties. This is illustrated by the different types of terminology used to describe IL (for example, information handling, information skills, digital literacy) and the way in which academic colleagues perceive the relevant skills. In academics' own practice, they may have tacit knowledge of IL skills, but the processes, procedures and cognitive skills students must learn in order to become information literate, or indeed to participate effectively in academic life in general (Lea and Street, 1998), may never have been articulated.

Previous work

Our understanding of information literacy at the OU is derived both from external IL sources, and from practical experience of delivering skills material relevant to OU students. The Seven Pillars of Information Literacy statement produced by the Society of College, National and University Libraries (SCONUL, 1999) has been a major influence, as have standards produced by the Association of College and Research Libraries (ACRL, 2000) in the US, and the Australian and New Zealand Institute for Information Literacy (Bundy, 2004). Exploration and discussion of these and other definitions and standards has helped to formulate our own understanding of IL relevant to our particular context. Work carried out by Peter Godwin (2003) at Southbank University (UK) to describe the level at which IL skills should be developed as students progress through their higher education study provided a useful starting point for the development of an IL levels framework for the OU.

The OU's Centre for Outcomes Based Education (COBE) is a research and development unit supporting innovative curriculum design, and was initially set up to support module teams in the use of learning outcomes. COBE have produced a range of support materials for academic staff, including the Undergraduate Levels Framework (COBE, 2005), a set of generic level indicators to support curriculum design, which defines IL as 'finding, critically evaluating and using information'. A summary statement about IL at levels 1–3 of OU study (equivalent to years 1–3 of traditional study) is included within the Framework, providing broad-brush guidance for those involved in module development:

- Level 1: Develop your skills in finding, selecting and using information or data in defined contexts.
- Level 2: Find, critically evaluate and use information or data accurately in a range of contexts.
- Level 3: Find, critically evaluate and use information or data accurately in complex contexts.

It is apparent, though, that even where programme and module teams are enthusiastic about incorporating skills, they are often not clear about what to include or how to go about it. Feedback has indicated that the generic level indicators for IL, and for learning outcomes in general, require greater contextualisation and that course programme chairs need clearer direction on what skills-related learning outcomes they should include. An added complexity is the fact that OU students do not all follow set pathways, so prior mastery of skills cannot be assumed at any level.

In 2007 a booklet, 'Integrating IL into the curriculum' (COBE), was produced, which started to address these issues by providing guidelines for programme and module teams on how to go about integrating IL, illustrated with case studies. While well-received, this did not go into the detail of what IL skills actually look like at each level of the curriculum or how these skills should develop over the course of a student's degree programme. The IL Levels Framework aims to fill the gap.

The rationale for the IL Levels Framework

The development of an IL Levels Framework was a natural progression from the brief statement about IL at levels 1–3 provided in the Undergraduate Levels Framework (COBE, 2005). It was felt that it would be beneficial to provide a more detailed breakdown of the skills under the IL banner, and to indicate the level at which students should be developing particular IL skills. It was hoped that the IL Levels Framework could help to support a more consistent approach to the development of IL skills within the university. This would include incorporating progression in IL as students work through the different levels of OU undergraduate study to achieve a degree. The Framework would also help to coordinate the OU Library's work – taking place simultaneously – to develop a range of generic, reusable learning objects to be integrated within OU modules, ensuring that materials were developed to cover the skills outlined within the Framework.

In developing the IL Levels Framework, we adopted a generic and pragmatic approach, building on the previous IL skills work. However, we have also engaged with research which conceptualises IL using a phenomenographic approach (for example, Markless, 2009; Andretta, 2007; Bruce, 2002, cited in Vezzosi, 2006; Limberg, 2009). This stresses the importance of taking into account context, how students learn, the influence of a web 2.0 environment and the role of reflection at all stages of the process. Markless voices concerns that existing frameworks are too linear in their approach, and over-simplistic about how people engage with information in a digital world. The mechanics of how to search can be overemphasised, with insufficient focus on evaluation, reflection and the creation of new knowledge. It is the development and use of these higher order cognitive skills that ultimately leads to deep and lasting learning with the power to transform the way people think and view the world. Therefore, although we have expressed IL skills in generic terms, we are aware of the considerable evidence in the literature to support the view that IL is a situated practice and cannot be separated from the context in which it is exercised.

The IL skills described within the Framework represent the OU Library's own view of IL within the University context, influenced by the existing IL frameworks and definitions already referred to. Skills are generic rather than tailored to particular subjects. It is anticipated that different subject disciplines will take a slightly different approach to the development of IL skills, and so the IL Levels Framework is presented as flexible and adaptable within the range of disciplinary contexts at the OU.

The key aims for the IL Framework are: to help develop and integrate IL activities within course materials; to aid skills development and progression through different levels of study; and to provide academic course teams with more detailed guidance on what to include in modules and programmes. It is envisaged that the document will be used by OU librarians working with programme and module teams, as well as by faculty staff working on skills development.

IL skills are grouped within four areas: Understand the information landscape; Plan and carry out a search; Critically evaluate information; Manage and communicate your results. To create a useful working document it was felt that it should be clear and concise, hence the decision to use four areas, as opposed to the seven categories within the SCONUL Seven Pillars, for example. Within each of the areas, IL skills are described at levels 1–3 of OU study (see Table 2.1).

While we have made clear that the Framework is a starting point rather than a prescriptive set of skills and will need to be adapted to context, there is the possibility that it could be interpreted too rigidly or fail to encourage the desired metacognitive attitudes and behaviours. Nevertheless, in the OU context (with packaged course materials the norm until relatively recently), it has been important to start by defining in some detail the skills that undergraduate students should be developing.

Development of the IL Levels Framework

The IL Levels Framework was subject to a critical reading process to ensure validity, with feedback from key stakeholders within the university informing development. The early draft document was reviewed by Learning and Teaching Librarians within the OU Library whose role includes working with academic module teams to embed IL within the curriculum. This led to useful discussions, and key questions that were asked included: at what level should a student develop a particular skill; when should students be proficient in each skill (for example, referencing); and how should we approach overlap with other skill areas such as study skills and digital literacy skills? OU Library staff welcomed the IL Levels Framework, and felt that it would benefit them when working with course teams, particularly if examples of learning materials could be associated to the skills described in the Framework.

A second draft of the IL Levels Framework was circulated to staff in COBE, who responded positively to it, and provided comments which highlighted the link between IL and employability skills. As a result of this feedback it was agreed that a mapping exercise would be carried out between the IL skills and employability skills as a future development.

A small group of academics from different faculties within the OU also gave feedback on the draft levels document. This highlighted some faculty-based skills documents, including undergraduate level skills frameworks for Social Sciences and Health & Social Care, and it was a useful exercise to map the skills within the IL Levels Framework against these faculty documents. This work revealed that the IL levels Framework was largely in agreement with the faculty documents.

One academic welcomed the development of the OU Library's levels document, and suggested that this could help to develop a shared understanding of IL skills: 'This is really very useful. I think it helps both you at the library end and us at the Faculty/Programme end to have an integrated approach . . .' (Senior Lecturer, Faculty of Social Sciences).

The positive responses received from academic colleagues are a good indicator that the IL Levels Framework will prove a useful tool when considering IL development within modules and programmes. The evaluations conducted to date have highlighted potential use of the document by faculties considering skills development as a whole, or developing their own IL policies.

Putting it into practice

A natural question raised by academic staff is how the skills set out in the Framework can actually be taught in a distance-learning environment. A VLE website, known as Library Information Literacy (LIL), has been set up to house generic activities which illustrate the skills. The site is intended as a repository for a selective sample of activities, in order to provide best-practice generic models that faculties can either use directly or – more likely – adjust to suit their own context. The four headings of the IL Levels Framework have been used to group the generic activities by skill. Any activities adapted by OU faculties for their specific contexts are listed under the heading for the relevant faculty. Students will be directed to appropriate activities on LIL from the module they are studying.

A key driver is to create some efficiency savings in module production by avoiding the creation of numerous similar but slightly different bespoke activities. It remains to be seen how much reuse of activities occurs in reality, since experience to date does not indicate much enthusiasm on the part of academic colleagues either to use generic learning objects or to incorporate activities not developed for their specific context. Indeed, one might well ask what we mean by a generic activity. It is unlikely that any activity is entirely generic, filtered as it is through the lens of the person who wrote it, with their previous background and experience inevitably rooted in specific contexts. However, faculties are increasingly of the view that activities which are generic at faculty or discipline level can work well when developing skills across programmes. There is also widespread recognition that resources no longer allow for the writing of numerous individual activities at a course module level. In practice, there is a tension between the need to keep costs down by developing generic IL activities, and the view previously discussed that IL skills development works best as a situated practice. We believe that the work described here represents a compromise.

An existing initiative that inspired the creation of the LIL site is the Health and Social Care (HSC) Resource Bank, a repository of relevant online resources, which includes a 'Finding and using information' section within the Skills area of the site. The work of other university libraries, for example, the Cardiff University Information Literacy Resource Bank, has also shaped our thinking. Like Cardiff University we have concentrated on short 'bite-size' activities, of varying lengths and in different formats, 'which can be seamlessly integrated into all kinds of teaching materials and fulfil many different purposes' (Jackson and Mogg, 2007). Example learning objects available on LIL so far include introductions to different types of online resources such as ejournals, ebooks, websites, blogs, wikis, images and multimedia and how to interpret references to these ('Understand the information landscape'), and activities teaching students how to plan a search, find a journal article from a reference and use Google Scholar to find information in the OU Library collections ('Plan and carry out a search').

A template has been developed in order to achieve some consistency of look and feel between the activities on LIL. It includes guidance for OU Library staff on how to set out learning outcomes and how to test them. It also shows how interactivity can be built in (for example, by use of drag and drop activities, video clips, flash animations or quizzes) in order to actively engage learners. Training has been provided to the OU's Learning and Teaching Librarians to develop understanding of good learning and teaching practice, and how to write for the online environment. It has become clear that a different mind-set is required when creating activities as opposed to writing web pages or demonstrating resources face-to-face. The temptation to tell people everything about a topic must be resisted in favour of writing for the appropriate level and ensuring that the learner is involved in actively doing something rather than just reading text. This is consistent with a constructivist approach and increases the likelihood that deep learning will occur.

These activities have been created in parallel with the development of the IL Framework. A recent exercise, in which activities on the LIL site were mapped to the IL Levels Framework, showed that the majority of activities so far cater for Level 1 skills development, with an emphasis on searching. Future development will need to target those areas where there are gaps and to show how skills develop through Levels 2 and 3. There will also need to be more focus on higher-order skills such as evaluation and reflection.

What support might people need to use it?

Feedback so far indicates that faculties and module teams find the clarification provided by the Framework useful, and are enthusiastic about the idea of having activities to illustrate how the skills can be developed. However, these two things by themselves are not enough to ensure success. Guidance on how to use the Levels Framework in practice will be needed, in order to support OU module teams, and to encourage consistent embedding of skills across programmes and degree awards. The IL Levels Framework indicates where students should be by the end of each level, but not how to actually teach the skills during courses. We will be providing guidance which makes clear for module teams and tutors the link between the Levels Framework and the LIL resource bank of activities.

Help with assessing the skills is also a high priority, to ensure that any assessment that takes place is both valid and reliable. Assessment needs to be appropriate for the type and level of skill. Advice about assessment is being developed by the OU Library to assist module teams with integration of library resources and IL into their modules and programmes. The Cloudworks site, for finding, sharing and discussing learning and teaching ideas, experiences and issues (Open University, 2010), is also being used to share knowledge and interact with the wider community on this and other information literacy-related topics.

Moodle quizzes are starting to be used for formative and summative assessment of skills. This works well for objective testing (right or wrong answers), but is less suitable for higher-order skills such as evaluation or reflection, where outcomes are more open-ended. As Walsh (2009) says, a balance needs to be obtained between 'a test that is easy to administer with one that will truly assess the varied transferable information skills that information literacy implies'. More reflective forms of assessment, such as portfolios, may be the way forward. Usefulness will be maximised if students can take their portfolio with them into future life and work; the recent adoption of Google Apps by the OU (Sclater, 2010) brings this aspiration closer. Frequent formative assessment would fit well with the model of bite-size activities and an iterative approach to developing the skills. The online environment can facilitate self and peer assessment, reducing the burden on tutors to provide formative feedback, and encouraging students to become self-sufficient. By making explicit what the skills are and at what level they are to be carried out, students can be helped to internalise assessment criteria and develop self-regulation (Nicol and Macfarlane-Dick, 2006).

How we will test it: case studies

The next stage in the development of the IL Levels Framework is to test it in some real life situations. Level 2 study is an area requiring more attention across the OU curriculum, in order that students develop the skills they need for Level 3. Feedback from OU Associate Lecturers, who are engaged in front-line teaching of students, indicates that lack of basic IL skills hampers students when they come to more advanced study.

A new second-level Art History module is currently being developed, which will include a significant IL skills component. Although it is uncertain at this stage whether IL skills will be formally assessed, a skills audit is proposed whereby students will do some kind of self-assessment during and at the end of the module. Even if not awarded marks, students will be directed to reflect on their skills as part of assignment preparation, particularly during the later parts of the module. This module is of key importance to bridge the gap between Level 1 and the independent study expected at Level 3 and beyond. If integration of skills is successfully achieved it could act as a model for future Level 2 Arts modules. To evaluate the usefulness of the IL Levels Framework in this situation, an action research approach is being adopted, which will involve a questionnaire to key stakeholders in the Arts faculty and the OU Library. This will be followed up by interviews with selected individuals. The data collected will be analysed to identify any changes needed to the Framework as well as to understand how module teams can best be supported.

Within the Science faculty, work is being done to map skills content of existing courses to the Levels Framework, and a new Level 2 module also provides an opening to integrate IL skills in a systematic way in order to help students make the transition from first to third level study. Likewise, the Social Sciences faculty is developing a new Level 2 module with embedded IL skills which will be compulsory for students wishing to progress to Level 3. It will be instructive to compare the way the IL Levels Framework is used in all these contexts. In the longer term, we will want to evaluate the effectiveness of the Levels Framework with students, in order to determine the impact of the Framework on their OU study success.

Possible issues

There is a considerable body of theory and research which shows that context is important to students (for example, Laurillard, 2002; Biggs, 2003). Faculties will need to adapt the Framework to their particular requirements, and to express outcomes in language which resonates with the academic discourse of their disciplines, as well as with desired employability outcomes. We will need to address the question of how well the IL Levels Framework can be applied to specific disciplines and learning contexts. It will be important to communicate clearly to tutors what skills students are expected to develop, at what level and how these relate to the workplace, and to give students the words to articulate this for themselves. We may also want to acknowledge more explicitly the importance of social and collaborative learning in the development of IL skills.

Thought is being given to how to implement skills outcomes across programmes, as it is not practical or desirable to include all skills in all modules. Brown (2001) suggests that each skill be included at least twice in each degree programme. With the move towards an awards-based approach at the OU, this should become more achievable.

Future developments

The IL Levels Framework is a living document and will most likely change over time. Over the next year, the Framework will be promoted across the OU with a view to getting it adopted into the OU curriculum. The *Integrating Information Literacy into the Curriculum* booklet is being rewritten to include the IL Levels Framework. There are also plans to put the IL Levels Framework online with links to relevant activities. Further evaluation work will be needed once the Framework has been in use for a reasonable period of time: with OU librarians to find out how the document is being used; with the teams responsible for writing OU courses; and also with OU Associate Lecturers (ALs) who work directly with students. It will be interesting to consider how ALs view the IL Levels Framework, and what impact it might have on the support they provide to students. The IL Levels Framework is part of work being carried out to implement an OU-wide pedagogical approach to course development. In future, learning design tools should flag up to programme and module teams where IL fits into the course as a whole and the IL Framework will provide the detail of what skills should be covered.

Feedback from OU academics has shown that module teams place high importance on developing students' employability skills and that there is considerable overlap between IL and employability skills. Work is currently underway to map the skills described in the IL Levels Framework to employability skills. Following on from that, consideration will be given to the best way of presenting the results of the mapping exercise to module teams. This is so that they can use this information for course planning purposes to develop IL skills and also to show students how these skills are transferrable and can be highly valued within the workplace.

There is interest from academics in expanding the IL Framework to include OU Openings courses, which are introductory level modules aimed at students who want a taster of OU study. A number of faculties working on Masters level courses are also keen to see the Framework extended to included post-graduate study. Therefore, in addition to mapping the IL Levels Framework to employability skills, the next phase of this work will also develop IL skills outcomes for the stages which precede and follow undergraduate study.

Taking a broader view, information literacy can be seen as one of the tools (University of Melbourne, 2009) and enablers (Todd, 2005, cited in Markless, 2009) of life-long learning, and a holistic view needs to be taken of the way in which students interact with information. A number of institutions have adopted a 'learning literacies' approach, which sees IL as part of a wider landscape and as one of 'the range of practices that underpin effective learning in a digital age' (LLIDA, 2009). For example, at Edge Hill University, information literacy has been integrated with study skills to align it more closely with academic practice within disciplines. At the OU, a key objective is the integration of IL skills into modules and programmes to promote independent thinking and researching. We also aspire to fuller integration of information literacy skills materials into OU study skills support.

Conclusion

The overall aim of the Framework is to improve student learning and the student experience by promoting IL and embedding it within the curriculum. It is our hope that the Framework will enable those working on the ground creating OU courses to fulfil the aspirations of high-level university strategy and faculty policy, by providing a tool-set to help shape their thinking and course design. In this way, top-down and bottom-up initiatives can be brought together in a coherent way. The importance of academic literacies is increasingly being recognised, especially for students from non-traditional backgrounds who may have little or no experience of academic conventions. The IL Levels Framework has an important contribution to make to this and positions the OU Library as an equal partner in the course development process. The framework also helps to underpin good pedagogy and the ideal of constructive alignment (Biggs, 2003) by ensuring that learning outcomes, learning activities and assessment are all consistent with each other. Finally, in the words of Lord Puttnam, OU Chancellor: 'I do think anyone with an OU degree should be brilliantly familiar with information gathering on the web. The idea you will graduate from the OU without being a world-class researcher yourself, should be nonsense. We should be challenging students to find their own links, and their own information. I'm not sure we're doing this enough' (Cook, 2009: 2). The IL Levels Framework is about helping to equip students with 21st century skills and ensuring that OU graduates are able not only to survive but to thrive in the world in which they live and work.

References

ACRL (2000) *Information Literacy Competency Standards for Higher Education*, Association of College and Research Libraries, American Library Association. Available from: *http://www.ala.org/ala/mgrps/divs/acrl/standards/informationliteracycompetency.cfm* (accessed 14 March 2010).

Andretta, S. (2007) Phenomenography: a conceptual framework for information literacy education. *Aslib*

Proceedings: New Information Perspectives, 59(2): 152–168.

Biggs, J. (2003) *Teaching for Quality Learning at University: What the Student Does* (2nd edn), Buckingham: Society for Research into Higher Education and Open University Press.

Brown, G. (2001) *Assessment: A Guide for Lecturers*. LTSN Generic Centre, Learning and Teaching Support Network.

Bundy, A. (ed.) (2004) *Australian and New Zealand Information Literacy Framework: Principles, Standards and Practice* (2nd edn), Adelaide: Australian and New Zealand Institute for Information Literacy. Available from: *http://www.caul.edu.au/info-literacy/InfoLiteracyFramework.pdf* (accessed 14 March 2010).

COBE (2007) *Integrating Information Literacy into the Curriculum*. Milton Keynes: Centre for Outcomes Based Education, The Open University.

COBE (2005) *Undergraduate Levels Framework*. Milton Keynes: Centre for Outcomes Based Education, The Open University.

Conole, G., Weller, M., Culver, J., Brasher, A., Cross, S., Clark, P. and Williams, P. (2008) *OU Learning Design Initiative*, Open University. Available from: *http://ouldi.open.ac.uk/* (accessed 29 April 2010).

Cook, Y. (2009) What are we going to look like at 50?: interview with Lord Puttnam. *Society Matters*, 12: 1–2.

Dearing, R. and National Committee of Inquiry into Higher Education (NCIHE) (1997) *Higher Education in the Learning Society: The Dearing Report*. London, NCIHE.

Godwin, P. (2003) 'Information literacy, but at what level?', in Martin, A. and Rader, H. (eds) *Information and IT Literacy: Enabling Learning in the 21st Century*. London: Facet.

Jackson, C. and Mogg, R. (2007) The Information Literacy Resource Bank: re-purposing the wheel. *Journal of Information Literacy*, 1(1): 49–53.

Kirkwood, A. (2006) Going outside the box: skills development, cultural change and the use of on-line resources. *Computers & Education*, 47(3): 316–331.

Laurillard, D. (2002) *Rethinking University Teaching: A Conversational Framework for the Effective use of Learning Technologies* (2nd edn). London: RoutledgeFalmer.

Lea, M. R. and Street. B. V. (1998) Student writing in higher education: an academic literacies approach. *Studies in Higher Education*, 23(2): 157.

Limberg, L. (2009) *Information literacies beyond rhetoric: developing research and practice at the intersection between information seeking and learning: keynote address*, i3 conference, Robert Gordon University, Aberdeen, 24 June 2009. Available from: *http://rgu-sim.rgu.ac.uk/ i3conf/presentations/Limberg_i3KeynoteInfoLiteracy.pdf* (accessed 30 April 2010).

LLIDA (2009) *Learning Literacies for a Digital Age*, Caledonian Academy, available from: *http://www .academy.gcal.ac.uk/llida/* (accessed 30 April 2010).

Markless, S. (2009) A new conception of information literacy for the digital learning environment in higher education. *Nordic Journal of Information Literacy in Higher Education*, 1(1): 25–40. Available from: *https://noril.uib.no/index.php/ noril/article/view/17* (accessed 30 April 2010).

Nicol, D. J. and Macfarlane-Dick, D. (2006) Formative assessment and self-regulated learning: a model and seven principles of good feedback practice. *Studies in Higher Education*, 31(2): 199–218.

Open University (2010) *Cloudworks*, Open University. Available from: *http://cloudworks.ac.uk/* (accessed 30 April 2010).

QAA (2007) *Subject Benchmark Statements*, Quality Assurance Agency for Higher Education. Available from: *http://www.qaa.ac.uk/academicinfrastructure/benchmark/default.asp* (accessed 30 April 2010).

QAA (2001) *The Framework for Higher Education Qualifications in England, Wales and Northern Ireland – January 2001*. Available from: *http://www.qaa.ac.uk/academicinfrastructure/FHEQ/EWNI/default.asp#framework* (accessed 30 April 2010).

Sclater, N. (2010) 'OU adopts Google Apps for education'. Virtual learning blog, posted 22 January 2010. Available from: *http://sclater.com/blog/?p=399* (accessed 30 April 2010).

SCONUL (1999) *The Seven Pillars of Information Literacy*, Society of College, National and University Libraries. Available from: *http://www.sconul.ac.uk/groups/information_literacy/seven_pillars.html* (accessed 14 March 2010).

University of Melbourne (2009) *Assessment and Teaching of 21st Century Skills (ATC21S)*. Available from: *http://www.atc21s.org/home/* (accessed 30 April 2010).

Vezzosi, M. (2006) Information literacy and action research: an overview and some reflections. *New Library World*, 107(7–8): 286–301.

Walsh, A. (2009) Information literacy assessment: where do we start? *Journal of Librarianship and Information Science*, 41(1): 19–28.

3

Information literacy in the workplace and the employability agenda

John Crawford and Christine Irving

Abstract: This chapter challenges the traditional view of information literacy as being centred on education, particularly higher education, and focuses on information literacy in a range of non-academic environments, such as collective decision making in the workplace and information literacy as part of the workplace learning process. Information 'outside the academy' has to be much more broadly defined than the traditional view of print and web sources. The role of information literacy in employability skills development is discussed and the problems of promoting it as part of the skills agenda, the emphasis on IT at the expense of information literacy, problems with terminology such as media and digital literacy, and the lack of an explicitly recognised locus for information literacy in workplace learning. There is a concise discussion on information policy making issues. Organisational issues are discussed including the differing problems and needs of large and small organisations (SMEs). Existing practices in the workplace, sources used, training needs and the lack of training materials are discussed. Low pre-existing skill levels are identified in the workplace. Training issues are reviewed: who should provide it and how it should be targeted together with examples of good practice. Information skills training programmes in public libraries are concisely described with examples of good practice.

Key words: information literacy, employability, workplace, skills agenda, information policy, information usage.

A background of issues

Although studies of information literacy in the workplace and employability are of relatively recent origin, awareness of information needs in the community of work has been around for over a hundred years. Before World War One (WW1) some large provincial public libraries built up collections relevant to local economic activity on such subjects as mining and textile manufacturing and during and immediately after WW1 industrial towns in the North of England created business information bureaux in local public libraries often in conjunction with local chambers of commerce. Significantly these services were aimed at local small to medium sized enterprises (SMEs). Due to the information needs created by WW1, technical and commercial libraries were set up in large towns like Glasgow and Birmingham (Black, 2007) to meet information demands from large organisations. After WW1 there was little further development until much later in the century.

In the 1980s academic researchers began to challenge the idea that the 'academy' is the only place where learning can take place. This led to an interest in the social dimension of learning which goes beyond the formal curriculum and is primarily linked with the work of Lave and Wenger (2002) who argue that the curriculum is the daily round of tasks that has to be undertaken to sustain the community. In this analysis learning in the workplace is viewed as a form of social interaction and much of the learning comes from colleagues. Although information literacy issues are recognised through such topics as self-education, problem solving, reading books and manuals and using the Internet, information literacy is nowhere recognised as a discrete concept (Crawford and Irving, 2009). There is also recognition that a skilled and educated workforce is essential to an advanced economy as evidenced by such statements as the Scottish Government's Economic Strategy:

> The importance of learning and skills as a fundamental driver of growth is firmly established as a critical element in the creation of a knowledge-based economy that is responsive and adaptable to rapid global change and the establishment of a wealthier Scotland. A smarter Scotland needs young people who are ready to contribute effectively in the community and the world of work and go on to develop their skills through lifelong learning. Further, it needs improved skill levels across the entire population and a better match of supply and demand. (Scottish Government, 2007a)

The strategy also links economic development with a fairer, safer, healthier and greener Scotland.

Even such a brief background review highlights key issues: the SME and the larger organisations and their differing characteristics; the need to recognise the characteristics of learning in the workplace and its emphasis on social learning, rather than 'librarianly' knowledge acquisition; the role of learning and the skills agenda in economic development; and the relationship of learning and skills acquisition to wider social issues.

Information literacy in the workplace and employability defined?

The term 'information literacy' was coined in the 1970s by Paul Zurkowski, the founding president of the US Information Industry Association, a trade and industry association (Pinto et al., 2010), although much of the roots of information literacy activity lie in higher education where it developed from traditional bibliographic instruction. This is exemplified in such documents as the Association of College & Research Libraries' [US] (2000) *Information Literacy Competence Standards in Higher Education* report which enshrines the principle of 'laddering' by identifying a hierarchy of information literacy skill levels appropriate to university students. The idea that information skills can be organised in a recognisable hierarchy represents a real challenge to the anarchic world of the workplace. However, earlier, in 1989, the American Library Association's *Presidential Committee on Information Literacy* (ALA, 1989) had addressed the problems of the 'information age' in relation to the importance of information literacy to individuals, business and citizenship, widening the concept of information literacy to reflect the different functions of information in people's lives. Australia also saw information literacy in this light contributing to: 'learning for life; the creation of new knowledge; acquisition of skills; personal, vocational, corporate and organisational empowerment; social inclusion; participative citizenship; and innovation and enterprise' (Australian Library and Information Association, 2006).

In the UK The Chartered Institute of Library and Information Professionals (CILIP, 2004) saw a need to define the term in a way that was applicable in all contexts and understandable by all information-using communities in the UK: 'Information literacy is knowing when and why you need information, where to find it, and how to evaluate, use and communicate it in an ethical manner.' The writers have used this definition in a variety of contexts including workplace and employability contexts. Where interviewees are presented with this definition, they understand it immediately and begin to reinterpret it in the contexts of their own education, qualifications, work experience, personal and professional contacts and life experiences. Others working in this field have had similar experiences, most notably Annemaree Lloyd in Australia leading her to question whether information literacy is a 'generic' skill which can be learned away from the context of practice and whether the educational concept of information literacy as a 'literacy' centralised around print and computer literacy can be transferred to the workplace (Lloyd, 2009). In her study she found practitioners to be a critical source of information. She considers that information literacy should be extended to include bodily experiences like touch and smell. For her, information literacy should be viewed as 'the catalyst for learning about work and professional practice'. This challenges the view of information literacy in a higher educational context which usually interprets information sources conservatively, i.e. books, journals, technical manuals, passworded bibliographic databases and Internet sources. It seems that attempts to impose a structure on information literacy outside the 'academy' are a subject for negotiation rather than something definable. One only has to look at early years' education in nursery and primary schools to see information sources in a wide range of media that engage all the senses.

In the workplace specifically, information must also address its relationship to another information ideology, knowledge management. To what extent the two ideologies intersect is still a subject for debate although traditionally interpreted they are very different as the following definition shows.

> Knowledge management comprises a range of strategies and practices used in an organization to identify, create, represent, distribute, and enable adoption of *insights* and *experiences*. Such insights and experiences comprise *knowledge*, either embodied in individuals or embedded in organizational *processes* or practice.
>
> KM efforts typically focus on organizational *objectives* such as improved *performance*, *competitive advantage*, *innovation*, the sharing of lessons learned, integration and *continuous improvement* of the *organization*. (Wikipedia, 2010)

The use of information is only one factor among many. Information literacy, seen from a higher educational perspective, fosters the development of individual learners through the use of published and explicit sources of information. Knowledge management, on the other hand, is concerned with an individual's knowledge, much of which is tacit knowledge residing in people's heads. Ferguson (2009) notes that while the sites of information may be broader in a workplace context than they are in a higher educational institution, the focus remains on individual learning. Although it should be noted that the lessons from workplace information literacy studies show that while the learning itself is individual, information literacy workplace activity is generally collaborative. With knowledge management the focus is on the organisation's capacity to learn, not the individual's. However, as indicated above, traditional concepts of information literacy cannot be sustained in the work environment.

While information literacy and knowledge management have separate roots they increasingly have issues in common. As Lloyd (2009) highlights, information literacy 'pursues the same goals as knowledge management ... which is to develop and nurture the knowledge sharing practices and information literate workforce that are necessary if organisations are to be adaptive, innovative and robust'.

Employability defined

In 2007 the Scottish Government in their *Skills for Scotland; A Lifelong Skills Strategy* (2007b) defined the term employability as 'the combination of factors and processes which enable people to progress towards or get into employment, to stay in employment and move on in the workplace' and employability skills as: 'a term that refers to skills, behaviours, attitudes and personal attributes that are necessary for an individual to seek, gain and sustain employment and function effectively in the workplace and are transferable to a variety of contexts. Employability skills prepare individuals for work rather than for a specific occupation.' Increasingly, universities have become interested in employability skills for their graduates and establishing links with businesses. While some universities have recognised the needs of the knowledge economy and 'employers placing a greater emphasis on information handling skills, as a key competitive advantage' (Milne, 2004: 10) embedding information literacy across the universities' learning outcomes, Jackson (2010) however asks a pertinent question of universities: 'How well do we equip students for life in the information-rich world of employment? In celebrating our successes in making significant contributions to learning through information skills programmes, are we missing the point – are the information skills we teach appropriate to the workplace?' Emerging research within the workplace increasingly suggests that they are not wholly appropriate.

Information literacy and the skills agenda

Policy documents on skills development have been appearing since about 2005. The British Government's report, *Skills, Getting On In Business, Getting On At Work* (Department for Education and Skills 2005, vol. 1, p. 1) emphasised the need for a skilled workforce, and although only ICT skills are specifically mentioned there is a clear need for information literacy skills to be promoted within this context. The report notes:

> Skills are fundamental to achieving our ambitions, as individuals, for our families and for our communities. They help businesses create wealth, and they help people realise their potential. So they serve the twin goals of social justice and economic success.

Recent reports suggest that the situation is not changing much. The *Skills For Life* document (Department for Innovation, Universities & Skills, 2009: 14) notes that 'ICT has a major role to play in helping to deliver our ambition to become a world leader in skills . . . it provides a route into learning for people to improve their literacy and numeracy skills . . .' but there is no mention of information literacy. Here information literacy has yet to be specifically referred to and is rolled up with ICT skills. The terms digital literacy and media literacy are however creeping in. The *Digital Britain* interim report

(Department for Culture, Media and Sport, 2009: 63–64) states that digital life skills are needed by all – 'education and training for digital technologies . . . underpins everything we do in the 21st Century'; digital work skills are needed by most and digital economy skills are needed by some. The *Report of the Digital Britain Media Literacy Working Group* (Ofcom, 2009: 29) goes further describing it as an entitlement: 'In order to participate fully in a Digital Britain, people should have the opportunity to develop and improve their digital skills, confidences, competencies and knowledge.' It specifically recommends that digital engagement should be aligned with 'workforce employment and promotion strategies' and organisations should be encouraged to address the media literacy needs of employees. The terms digital and media literacy seem almost interchangeable.

In the world of workplace learning studies, higher skills development thinking recognises skills which are recognisably information literacy: keeping up to date, accessing relevant knowledge and experience, use of evidence and argument, research-based practice and using knowledge resources (human, paper-based, electronic) (Eraut, 2007). The systematic exploitation of the web is also mentioned. Again, information literacy is not recognised as a concept and the use of the above terms seem to be the nearest we get to information literacy. Terminology suggestive of knowledge management also appears, but again it is not specifically referred to (Brown, 2009).

Organisations and information

While there is no doubt that information literacy is a major issue it is doubtful if it is generally well understood. A recent survey, commissioned by Microsoft, of 500 top UK decision makers found that by 2017 ICT and information literacy will be viewed as second only to team working and interpersonal skills as the most important success factor for business. Indeed, around a quarter of those surveyed ranked it as the number one skill set for future success (Microsoft Research, 2008: 11). However, action suffers from a lack of overarching policy making as Oppenheim (cited in Orna, 2008) suggests. This is because governments find it difficult to define information, as it is dynamic and innovative and has social and economic implications. Information policy making has been largely left to market forces and there is no UK Cabinet minister with overall information responsibilities. Since the potential of IT for handling and manipulating information became clear it has influenced government thinking about information policy which relegates actual information to a subordinate role. There is virtually no input from information professionals into Government policy making. Nor is the picture much better in the workplace. A survey of nearly 1000 chief executives in 1996 in the UK showed that, while 60 per cent claimed that their company had an information policy, only 20 per cent were aware of the company having an information budget, half had no formal information provision and the majority did not know who was responsible for the information resource. In 2005 the situation seemed little better. A survey of 119 information management and IT professionals showed that 44 per cent of respondents did not have a document and information management strategy (Orna, 2008).

The 'subject' area which the organisation covers also appears to be a factor. Crawford (2006) found that conceptions of and commitment to information literacy are heavily influenced by subject with staff working in health and social care areas having a high commitment to information usage while this was less marked in areas broadly defined as business and science and technology. Crawford and Irving (2009) also found that the public sector with its emphasis on skills, qualifications and continuing professional development (CPD) is an environment which appreciates the value of information even if implementation can be defective. Ahlgren's (2007) study found the public sector to be a more positive training environment and that the private sector focused only on efficiency and techniques.

There is a something of a divide between the large organisation and the SME. The large organisation may have a library or someone charged with information responsibilities. It may have an Electronic Resource Data Management (eRDM) system or intranet which staff can refer to. There will be members of staff with academic and professional qualifications who will be to some extent information aware, at least at their own operational level. Large organisations have training and CPD programmes into which information skills training programmes can be introduced. No such assumption can be made about the SME. Ahlgren (2007), in a study of a manufacturing SME, found that the emphasis was on technique acquisition and that workplace learning focused on short-term training for immediate work-related payback. Long-term skill acquisition was not considered important, an environment unconducive to the development of information literacy training. Information skills development and utilisation in the SME is a major issue. The focus is on the ability to use computers and standard software applications but not on how to structure, find, evaluate and use the information accessed via a computer. SME employees use the Internet as their primary source of information for business-related matters and spend an hour a day on average looking for information on the Internet. An estimated 6.4 hours per employee are spent looking for information in the workplace each week in the UK, but 37 per cent of the searches prove unsuccessful. In financial terms, an estimated £3.7 billion is spent on time wasted looking for information that cannot be found, but little attention has been paid to helping SMEs with navigating the Internet as a source of valuable business information (De Saulles, 2007).

Inside the organisation

Within the organisation there is a lack of systematic structured thought about how information literacy should be used and managed. Should the initiative for information policy be led by senior management or should top management entrust subordinate groups with responsibility for new developments? One of the world's leading environmental consulting services, Environmental Resources Management, led by senior managers, has embarked on a knowledge sharing programme to support the organisation's business growth. This resulted in information literacy training being embedded in the organisation's intranet (Cheuk, 2008). Many organisations in practice have an information policy which is implicit, rather than explicit and has no formal management recognition. Each organisation has an implicit policy but it is usually founded on its staff, internal sources such as intranets and eRDMs and the Internet and a small range of printed sources and contacts, both within and outside the organisation (Crawford and Irving, 2009). In relation to staff information literacy skills, Irving (2006, 2007a, 2007b) in an interview-based, pilot study found that people generally think they have the skills and competencies they need for their information-related activities and that although generally employers are not explicitly looking for information literacy skills and competencies by name, they are assuming that employees will come with these skills – particularly for professional positions. Scottish Government Information Service staff are tackling these issues through inclusion in staff induction, evaluating their information literacy skills training and developing an explicit information literacy strategy which has already had some success, but its authors recognise that the support of senior management is essential to move into the delivery phase (Foreman and Thomson, 2009).

The unstructured nature of information-seeking behaviour in the workplace is also a challenge. Information problems found in the workplace are viewed as messy and 'open-ended'. Employees often have to define their own tasks or create their own interpretation constructs to solve an information problem (Kirkton and Barham, 2005). It is all very different from the structured world of higher education with 'laddered frameworks' which attribute specific information literacy skills to successive higher education levels. A substitute perhaps can be found in the skill levels and qualifications required for particular posts. Qualifications and skills appropriate to particular posts affect the nature of information-related activities and the level at which they are framed, as do training needs and the search for higher level qualifications which encourages learning, either CPD based, or independent learning based. Existing CPD training programmes may offer pointers to the future. Adult literacy programmes which include computer and Internet training also offer an opportunity for more extensive training.

There is also the question of whether all or designated categories of worker should be involved, which often comes down to computer access, something which manual level staff may not have. Cooke and Greenwood (2008) found that job function is the most critical factor in determining whether employees will have reasonable workplace access to ICT. While manual staff are keen to learn, the attitude of line managers is crucial if skill levels are to progress beyond basic IT competency. The danger of a digital divide was one of the authors' main conclusions.

Information needs and sources used

De Saulles (2007) found that information seekers tend to be confident about their information-seeking skills and can use search engines such as Google at a basic level, but are not aware how to refine searches or where to find information that Google does not point to, such as paid-for company information sources. Keenan and McDonald (2009), in an extremely practical study based on a training programme, found that workplace attendees on an information literacy training course were unaware of advanced Internet searching; Boolean operators were seen as interchangeable and the concept was difficult to explain; people overestimate their searching skills and underestimate the skills of information professionals. Crawford and Irving (2009) found that people are the principal source of information used in the workplace and that the traditional 'library' view of information as deriving from electronic and printed sources only is invalid in the workplace and must include people as sources of information. Advanced Internet searching was not understood but advanced Internet training (the use of a search engine's advance search facility and or Boolean terms) can greatly extend employees' information horizons. Most people interviewed in the study used only a limited range of sources which, apart from colleagues, consisted of an intranet or eRDM, a limited range of Internet sources and a few printed sources. eRDMs and intranets themselves were a limiting rather than an extending factor as people tend to rely on them rather than using a wider range of searching tools. Indexing of items added to eRDMs also tends to be extremely poor as staff assigning the indexing terms of items scanned in know nothing about indexing and use terms which are vague or too general. Cheuk (2008: 138) lists some points which reinforce the above findings:

- The use of outdated information because it is convenient to do so.
- Not aware of existing resources within the organisation which can address a business issue.
- Do not know how to use the tools and make the best use of information services to access the information required.
- Assume Google is the best search engine to look for information.
- Unable to manage personal e-mail boxes resulting in e-mail overload.
- Do not want to share information for fear that information shared will be misused or abused by others.

The overall picture is one of low skill levels and a need for training.

Training issues

Clearly there are training issues to be addressed which raises the question of who should deliver them. Chambers of Commerce and employers' organisations such as the Confederation of British Industries (CBI) are possibles but in practice show little interest in offering information literacy training. Part of the problem is that employers themselves are unsure about their employees' training and learning needs. Robert Gordon University Business School obtained EU funding to develop training programmes for SMEs in the Aberdeen area but found that local businesses are unsure of their training needs (Scottish Information Literacy Project, 2009). Trade unions are another possibility and trade union learning representatives are very willing to engage with the information literacy training agenda but are hampered by lack of funds at a time when trade unions have other priorities. A promising area is public library training programmes which, while not providing workplace training, do sometimes offer employability training in which information literacy skills training can find a part.

Inverclyde Libraries in the West of Scotland has run employability training courses funded by the Fairer Scotland Fund. The courses are aimed at people with poor employability and ICT skills. Basic computing skills are taught and an identifiable Internet skills component included to help learners to meet their health, finance and employability needs. The course content was designed by the tutors and the Community Learning and Development Team and based round a relatively brief document which, after introducing the learners to the essentials of Windows, Microsoft Word and e-mail, offers an introduction to the Internet which then leads onto health literacy and financial literacy with a list of useful websites (Crawford and Irving, 2010, 2012).

Caerphilly Library Services has offered the Gateways to Learning programme; 56 libraries participated and 2000 people took part in taster sessions. Information literacy training was delivered on a one to one basis with a focus on areas of interest that the learner selected. The training community learning programme has also been adapted for use in a comprehensive school and an 'Information and computer skills for later life' course aimed at the over 50s. A key finding of the project was that courses had to be framed around subjects of genuine interest (Evans, 2009) which corroborates a key finding of Crawford and Irving (2009). Courses must be highly focused on the target audience and tailored to meet their needs. Generic courses which do not directly engage with learner needs are unlikely to be successful. A course aimed at SMEs which contain convincing examples of how information has benefited a company's performance is more likely to impress than one which does not. Parallel work on the schools sector shows the benefit of using case studies/exemplars of good practice (Irving, 2009).

There is a considerable dearth of suitable training materials and building up 'stocks' should be a priority. Most information literacy training materials have been produced by and for higher education and are unsuitable for the workplace and employability training environments as they tend to focus on more formal and traditional information sources. Crawford and Irving (2012) found that community learning tutors were entirely unaware of the materials librarians produce while librarians were equally ignorant of the good work being produced by community learning tutors. Some collaboration would be mutually beneficial.

There is also the question of who does the training and how the trainers themselves should be trained. Both Inverclyde and Caerphilly have used a combination of community tutors and library trainers and while some library assistants will be keen to participate, others will see training as an additional burden for which they are neither properly trained nor rewarded.

Examples of good practice

There is relatively little literature describing actual examples of good practice. Keenan and McDonald (2009) have described an information literacy course they ran for an Australian company earlier in the decade. It consisted of:

Overview

History of the Internet and World Wide Web
   How the Internet works

Accessing and navigating the Internet

Web browsers

   Internet Explorer layout
   URLs and accessing a website
   Adding Favourites

Preparing your search
Analysing the questions
Identifying search terms
Identifying synonyms and truncation
Connecting search terms
Searching tips and hints

Using search engines

What are search engines
Searching with Google
Advanced search on Google
Searching on Vivisimo and Dogpile
Advanced searching on these and other examples

Searching on pass worded databases was also included. This is a useful format and addresses some of the issues discussed above such as advanced Internet searching.

The learning objectives of the course for attendees to focus on were:

- Consider what they are really looking for – how do you know they have found 'it' when you don't know what you are looking for?

- Be focused and disciplined with their time.
- Get an understanding of the breadth of the information resources available to them and how to use them.
- Understand the difference between Internet based/non refereed sources of information and Internet based refereed sources of information.

The course was highly customised to meet the practical needs of attendees, again a recurring theme in other work. A particularly useful feature is a checklist of questions which attendees found extremely helpful:

- What is the question?
- What is the level of information?
- What type of information and amount?
- When do I need the information by?
- Where have I already looked?

The course worked because it was highly personalised and customised, people could see results of searching on different search engines and they had access to information professionals who could discuss other resources and search strategies. Although the course was successful within the organisation, attempts to sell it to other organisations including Government departments were not successful for reasons mainly to do with hardware issues.

Cheuk (2008) also discusses a company programme for an organisation with over 3000 staff in 40 countries. This is an intranet based resource called Minerva which defines information literacy in the workplace as allowing employees to experience information literacy in seven ways or 'Faces' (informed by Christine Bruce's seven faces of information literacy) which can be compared with Keenan and McDonald. While it is a more sophisticated model there are points in common:

- Face 1: using information/knowledge management systems, ICT tools, e-mails.

- Face 2: knowing the existence of and ability to use specific sources (e.g. experts, databases, intranet, journal subscriptions, website).

- Face 3: awareness of a process to find and use information (e.g. to understand customers' needs, to evaluate a business problem).

- Face 4: organising and controlling information so it can be retrievable (e.g. design database structure, design intranet sites, manage folders in the local file server, manage personal e-mail boxes).

- Face 5: learning or gaining new knowledge through interacting with information.

- Face 6: gaining new insights and thinking about an issue in a new or different perspective.

- Face 7: using information wisely for the benefit of the organisation and society.

These dimensions are in turn linked to the organisations' programme of cultural change. It is interesting that people are identified as an information source and that academic models lie at the back of this. To roll out the programme, 50 knowledge champions were recruited and 3000 staff received 60 minutes training. The involvement and support of senior managers has been a key theme.

More recently the Open University has been piloting generic learning materials called iKnow – Information and Knowledge at work, offering bite-sized learning materials which can be done 'in just a few minutes at your desk or on the move' to help 'save time in finding, using and organising information at work' (Open University, 2010). The small pilot study revealed that the 'bitesize' and 'mobile' nature of the materials allowed greater flexibility in the training process, and would be quite easy for staff to schedule into their working day. There was a consensus that they would 'definitely' want to see a greater availability of workplace learning materials in these formats. There were several suggested improvements which will be addressed including self-assessment and PDP tools to enable the learner to check their learning and a review of the content as it was felt to be 'still quite academic' (Parker, 2010).

This brief review of the literature and issues shows what an important area this is and how little practical developmental activity has taken place. Much of the literature is still academic in style, reviewing the ideas of other academics. There is still a dearth of reporting of actual practical programmes of information literacy training in the workplace and employability environments from which new systematic theories and further programmes could be developed. Exemplars of good practice which might impress employers are particularly lacking.

References

Ahlgren, L. (2007) 'Learning in small and medium sized enterprises in Scotland.' [Centre for Lifelong Learning] Conference proceedings 22–24 July 2007. *The times they are a-changing: researching transitions in lifelong learning.* CRLL, CD format.

American Library Association (1989) *Presidential Committee on Information Literacy: final report.* Chicago: ALA. Available at *http://www.ala.org/ala/mgrps/divs/acrl/ publications/whitepapers/presidential.cfm* (accessed 27 October 2010).

Association of College & Research Libraries (2000) *Information Literacy Competence Standards in Higher Education.*

Chicago: ACRL. Available at *http://www.ala.org/ala/ mgrps/divs/acrl/standards/informationliteracycompetency .cfm* (accessed 27 October 2010).

Australian Library and Information Association (2006) *Statement on Information Literacy for all Australians.* Available at *http://www.alia.org.au/policies/information .literacy.html* (accessed 27 October 2010).

Black, A. (2007) 'Arsenals of scientific and technical information': public technical libraries in Britain during and immediately after the World War 1. *Library Trends,* 55(3): 474–90.

Brown, A. (2009) *Higher Skills Development at Work.* London: ESRC, TLRP.

Chartered Institute of Library and Information Professionals (2004) *Information Literacy Definition.* London: CILIP. Available at *http://www.cilip.org.uk/get-involved/ advocacy/learning/information-literacy/Pages/definition .aspx* (accessed 27 October 2010).

Cheuk, B. (2008) Delivering business value through information literacy in the workplace. *Libri,* 58: 137–43.

Cooke, L. and Greenwood, H. (2008) 'Cleaners don't need computers': bridging the digital divide in the workplace. *Aslib Proceedings,* 60(2): 143–57.

Crawford, J. (2006) The use of electronic information services and information literacy: a Glasgow Caledonian University study. *Journal of Librarianship and Information Science,* 38(1): 33–44.

Crawford, J. and Irving, C. (2009) Information literacy in the workplace: a qualitative exploratory study. *Journal of Librarianship and Information Science,* 41: 29–38. Available at URL *http://lis.sagepub.com/cgi/content/ abstract/41/1/29?etoc* (accessed 27 October 2010).

Crawford, J. and Irving, C. (2012) Information literacy in employability training: the experience of Inverclyde Libraries. *Journal of Librarianship & Information Science.* (Forthcoming).

De Saulles, M. (2007) Information literacy amongst UK SMEs: an information policy gap. *Journal of Librarianship and Information Science*, 59(1): 68–79.

Department for Culture, Media and Sport (2009) *Digital Britain.* London: DCMS. Available at *http://www.culture .gov.uk/what_we_do/broadcasting/5944.aspx* (accessed 27 October 2010).

Department for Education and Skills and Department for Work and Pensions (2005) *Skills, Getting On In Business, Getting On At Work*, 3 vols. London: Department for Education and Skills.

Department for Innovation. Universities & Skills (2009) *Skills For Life.* London: DIUS.

Eraut, M. (2007) University – work transitions: what counts as knowledge and how do we learn it? In Eraut, M. et al *Making teaching more effective: articles from the Learning and Teaching conference 2006.* Brighton: University of Brighton Press.

Evans, G. (2009) Information literacy in public libraries: the lifelong learning agenda. Powerpoint presentation. Available at *http://www.slideshare.net/cirving/information-literacy-a-public-library-view* (accessed 27 October 2010).

Ferguson, S. (2009) Information literacy and its relationship to knowledge management. *Journal of Information Literacy*, 3(2): 6–24. Available at *http://ojs.lboro.ac.uk/ojs/ index.php/JIL/article/viewArticle/PRA-V3-I2-2009-1* (accessed 27 October 2010).

Foreman, J. and Thomson, L. (2009) Government information literacy in the 'century of information'. *Journal of*

Information Literacy, 3(2): 64–72. Available at *http://ojs .lboro.ac.uk/ojs/index.php/JIL/article/view/PRA-V3-I2-2009-5/1421* (accessed 27 October 2010).

Irving, C. (2006) *The role of information literacy in addressing a specific strand of lifelong learning: the work agenda.* Research article for Learning and Teaching Scotland. URL [consulted January 2008]: *http://www.caledonian.ac.uk/ ils/documents/InformationLiteracyintheworkplacearticle .pdf* (accessed 27 October 2010).

Irving, C. (2007a) *The role of information literacy in addressing a specific strand of lifelong learning: the work agenda.* MSc Work Based Learning Project, Glasgow: Glasgow Caledonian University. Available at *http://www.slideshare.net/cirving/ the-role-of-information-literacy-in-addressing-a-specific-strand-of-lifelong-learning-the-work-agenda-2729283* (accessed 27 October 2010).

Irving, C. (2007b) 'Information literacy in the workplace: a small exploratory study.' Paper presented at *Information: Interactions and Impact (i3)*, The Department of Information Management, Aberdeen Business School, The Robert Gordon University, Aberdeen. Available at *http://www.gcu.ac.uk/ils/events.html* (accessed 27 October 2010).

Irving, C. (2009) Collecting case studies/exemplars of good practice to enrich The National Information Literacy Framework (Scotland). *Library and Information Research*, 33(105): 10–18. Available at *http://www.lirg .org.uk/lir/ojs/index.php/lir/article/view/206/271* (accessed 27 October 2010).

Jackson, A. (2010) 'Just enough education to perform: information skills, professionalism and employability.' Paper presented at LILAC 2010 *http://www.lilacconference .com/dw/programme/parallel_sessions_detail_4.html#13* (accessed 27 October 2010).

Keenan, P. and McDonald, N. (2009) 'The stuff beyond Google. Presentation C1.' Available at *http://www.information-online.com.au/sb_clients/iog/bin/iog_programme_you_may_be_right_C1.cfm?vm_key=25283991-1422-0982-EBD7F567186A51B* (accessed 27 October 2010).

Kirkton, J. and Barham, L. (2005) Information literacy in the workplace. *Australian Library Journal*, available at *http://alia.org.au/publishing/alj/54.4/full.text/kirton.barham.html* (accessed 27 October 2010).

Lave, J. and Wenger, E. (2002) 'Legitimate peripheral participation in communities of practice,' in Harrison, R, et al. (eds) *Supporting Lifelong Learning, Perspectives on Learning,* London: Routledge.

Lloyd, A. (2009) Informing practice: information experiences of ambulance officers in training and on-road practice. *Journal of Documentation,* 65(3): 396–419.

Microsoft Research (2008) *Information Age.* January 2008.

Milne, C. (2004) 'University of Abertay, Dundee,' in SCONUL, *Learning Outcomes and Information Literacy.* London: Higher Education. Available at *http://www.sconul.ac.uk/groups/information_literacy/papers/outcomes.pdf* (accessed May 2010).

Ofcom (2009) *Report of the Digital Britain Media Literacy Working Group.* Ofcom. Available at *http://stakeholders.ofcom.org.uk/market-data-research/media-literacy/medlitpub/media_lit_digital_britain/* (accessed May 2010).

Open University (2010) iKnow – Information and Knowledge at work. Available at *www.open.ac.uk/iknow* (accessed 27 October 2010).

Orna, Elizabeth (2008) Information policies: yesterday, today and tomorrow. *Journal of Information Science,* 34(4): 547–565.

Parker, J. (2010) E-mail to Christine Irving, 29 April.

Pinto, M. et al. (2010) Thirty years of information literacy (1977–2007): a terminological, conceptual and statistical analysis. *Journal of Librarianship and Information Science*, 42(1): 3–19.

Scottish Government (2007a) *Government Economic Strategy*. Edinburgh: Scottish Government. Available at *http://www .scotland.gov.uk/Publications/2007/11/12115041/5* (accessed 27 October 2010).

Scottish Government (2007b) *Skills for Scotland; A Lifelong Skills Strategy*. Edinburgh: Scottish Government. Available at *http://www.scotland.gov.uk/Publications/ 2007/09/06091114/0* (accessed 27 October 2010).

Scottish Information Literacy Project (2009) 'Project blog', 19.02.09. Available at *http://caledonianblogs.net/ information-literacy/2009/02/19/visit-to-robert-gordon-university-business-school/* (accessed 27 October 2010).

Wikipedia (2010) *Knowledge Management*. Available at *http:// en.wikipedia.org/wiki/Knowledge_management* (accessed 27 October 2010).

4

Information literacy in the context of contemporary teaching methods in higher education

Chris Wakeman

Abstract: This chapter will explore contemporary Higher Education (HE) facilitation methods and their influence on student Information Literacy (IL) skills. Central to the discussion will be 'enquiry-based learning' including problem-based approaches and webquests, each of which has become an integral part of HE practice. Dialectic approaches to delivery and facilitation will also be considered including Socratic methods, which are now commonly used in many HE schools and faculties. The principal aim of the chapter is to broaden commonly held beliefs relating to information literacy to include wider aspects of information access and exchange in the context of contemporary classroom culture. The ability to recognise a need for information, to critically evaluate information and its sources, and then to use that information effectively in order to construct new concepts or create new understandings, is now a fundamental part of HE classroom practice during which contemporary HE students increasingly engage in dialectic processes in the quest for effective learning. In essence, this chapter will seek to expand the concept of information literacy beyond the accepted principles and frameworks established by the Australian and

New Zealand Institute for Information Literacy, to include the day-to-day aspects of IL that are often overlooked or unrecognised.

Key words: information literacy, contemporary HE culture, enquiry based learning, dialectic approaches, Socratic methods.

Introduction

The perception of Information Literacy (IL) as a 'library or study skill' has more recently been broadened to embrace the wider concepts of lifelong learning, research and proficiency in the use of Information Communication Technology (ICT). Even so, the development of IL competence through the processes of contemporary Higher Education (HE) teaching methods often goes unrecognised and despite a major shift towards enquiry-based and dialectic approaches to delivery, IL is still considered as the preserve of the university library or learning centre rather than an integrated and inseparable part of the HE curriculum.

The authors of the *Australian and New Zealand Information Literacy* (ANZIIL) *Framework*, 2nd edition, 2004, begin to acknowledge the relationship between IL and teaching method, stating that: 'The responsibility of educators promoting information literacy is to engage in best practice in *all* areas of teaching and learning' (page 27). They go on to note that:

> The most effective strategy for 'embedding information literacy into the total educational process' starts with incorporating best practice assessment where information literacy is included in the objectives and

learning outcomes of units of study and assessment tasks. (page 27)

The notion of embedding IL into undergraduate curricula, and more specifically into module programmes and assessment tasks, had already been explored by Hepworth (1999), who outlined plans for such provision in the School of Applied Science at Loughborough University. Further works by Hepworth are cited by Johnston and Webber (2003) who themselves describe approaches to IL teaching in HE. They draw attention to Hepworth's continuum of IL teaching (page 342) though they seem to be at odds with his proposal that the best approach to IL teaching is to integrate its delivery into that of another discipline, instead favouring a credit-bearing IL package that is separate from disciplinary modules and programmes. Despite their preference for a discrete IL programme of study, Johnston and Webber go on to highlight what they perceive as 'problems associated with current practice' (page 342). One such problem is what they describe as the 'prescriptive agenda' set by leading bodies such as the Association of College and Research Libraries (ACRL). The assumption by the ACRL they suggest is that 'the skills have been mastered for good once each unit can be labelled as complete' (page 342).

They go on to describe this as a 'tick the box' approach to education in key skills which leads to a 'surface learning approach' that is largely based on memorising rather than a 'deep approach' in which the student intends to make sense of the content and develop personal understanding. Perhaps more ominously, Johnson and Webber highlight concerns regarding the personnel delivering IL teaching, focusing in particular on librarians. They suggest that librarians themselves need more education about learning and teaching and in some cases leave much to be criticised from an educational perspective (page 342).

Storey-Huffman (2008) writes about models of IL integration and recommends what she calls a 'specific disciplines model' (page 1). She describes an approach through which each discipline on campus would develop an IL component that would highlight IL theory and concepts specific to the discipline in question. She goes on to suggest that in this model subject tutors would work closely with librarians to develop a team approach, identifying the specific assignments and activities that represent the outcomes and learning objectives for both the discipline and the ACRL standards. This methodology would seem to alleviate some of the concerns expressed by Johnston and Webber who, as noted above, refer to a perceived lack of educational knowledge in the case of some librarians. Despite the merits of the Storey-Huffman approach, it could be argued that this does not represent integration in the fuller sense as although what she suggests would make IL teaching more discipline specific, the model still advocates a separate unit for IL delivery rather than full integration into existing modules of study.

So where are we at present in the debate which surrounds IL teaching and the best forms of delivery? There appears to be two distinct schools of thought, on the one side of the fence are those who see IL as a distinct and generic subject which should be taught by a central team regardless of the discipline or subject background of the participant; and, on the other side of the fence, are those who propose integration, in its various forms, which range from full assimilation into existing module programmes at the one extreme to separate but discipline specific IL units at the other.

Despite the two contrasting schools of thought, the consensus appears to be moving towards the former and more complete approach to integration, which advocates would contend is already an integral and fundamental aspect of many contemporary methods of delivery in Higher Education. It is from this premise that this paper shall now describe two contemporary approaches to learning delivery which fully cover the IL agenda.

Enquiry based learning and the IL perspective

Enquiry based learning (EBL) has become a fashionable approach to delivery in many Higher Education institutions. The concept of EBL is wide and varied and the term should be considered as an umbrella statement for a host of approaches that are founded on student enquiry and in which the student has ownership of their work, which may become increasingly self-directed. Group work is often the platform for EBL delivery, though independent learning may also be a principal feature.

For the purposes of this piece of writing, it is appropriate to focus on a specific approach to EBL, which has become known as the 'WebQuest'. WebQuests offer opportunities for EBL in its purest form and can be adapted for large groups, small groups or individual students. Timescales for the WebQuest may vary from hours to days to weeks, sometimes continuing throughout a module programme. Above all, the contemporary Higher Education student enjoys and embraces the WebQuest experience and few would argue against the fact that if learning is enjoyable and fun, whatever the age of the participant, then it is far more likely to be motivating, engaging and lead to the more desirable forms of deep learning (see Biggs, 2006). Information literacy skills are integral and deeply rooted within the WebQuest culture and a well designed WebQuest will address all six core standards from the ANZIL framework (2004)[1] in a meaningful and discipline specific way.

The term 'WebQuest' first emerged in 1995 when two practitioners[2] at San Diego State University (SDSU) first introduced the WebQuest method with participants on their 'Master' and 'Distance' programmes. In the intervening years practitioners in all fields of education have embraced the WebQuest methodology, applauding its pedagogical and andragogical merits and in particular, its contribution to the development of IL skills. WebQuests, of course, take many forms, but in HE, the accepted format would seem to be a research or problem orientated package which stimulates participant curiosity, encouraging them to search for and manage new information and to use this knowledge to construct new concepts or create fresh understandings. Ethical and moral issues concerning the use and application of new knowledge are an integral part of the WebQuest as is a growing understanding of cultural, legal and social issues relating to the outcomes of the quest.

Take a simple WebQuest designed for level 2 undergraduate students working in groups of three. The discipline specific nature of WebQuest design makes it difficult to provide a generic overview of how WebQuest activities should be introduced; in this example the WebQuest is firmly rooted in the area of Educational Psychology, and practices in other subject disciplines may differ. In the context of this piece of work there is neither the time nor space to provide the whole WebQuest in the form it would be presented to students, for this reason the example given will focus entirely on the 'WebQuest task' which is included as Figure 4.1. In this case, the timescale for completion of the WebQuest task was 2½ hours.

Figure 4.1   WebQuest task

At the outset of today's session you will be asked to place yourself in a group with 2 other participants in order to undertake a 'WebQuest'.

1. Once you are in your group you will pick the name of an Educational Psychologist from a vessel which will be brought around by your tutor (one per group).
2. You will have 2½ hours to research the educational psychologist assigned to your group and you should aim to find out the following information:
   - Nationality, date of birth/death, education, disciplinary background.
   - Area(s) of work (i.e. intelligence, memory, social psychology, personality etc.) and major findings attributed to the person concerned.
   - Major publications.
   - A paragraph indicating why *you* consider this educational psychologist to be important in the context of this module and to which areas of the programme the person's work relates.
   - Links to resources that are relevant to the Educational Psychologist concerned and may be of use to participants on this module.
3. Your findings from the WebQuest should be produced in word format on a single side of A4.
4. *Once you are happy with your work, you should access the folder which has been set up on the module VLE site under your Educational Psychologists name. You should upload your A4 sheet with your findings to the folder and return to the lecture room for the close of the session.*

The merits of the exercise from a learning perspective should be clear. Each individual group researches a single Educational Psychologist, but the final resource for student use is significantly larger. Sixty students in the wider group would mean twenty groups, and consequently a resource focusing on twenty Educational Psychologists which students can then access for the purposes of their studies – the synergy generated through the WebQuest is in the order of 20:1.

More importantly, the IL skills which students need to use and develop throughout the task pervade all aspects of the ANZIL framework, permeating all six strands as students endeavour to accomplish the task. There is little doubt that WebQuests, as a form of EBL, provide excellent opportunities for the development of IL skills.

Dialectic facilitation approaches: an alternative approach to IL development

Dialectic approaches or techniques based on dialogue have become a popular facilitation style in contemporary university settings. Mackeracher (2004) suggests that 'learning is a natural and dialectical process' (page 5) and advocates dialectic teaching as an essential and fundamental aspect of HE facilitation.

As in the case of enquiry-based approaches, the term 'Dialectic Teaching' should be considered as the higher level construct under which many variations of the dialectic theme co-exist. One such approach which has become known as 'Modern Socratic Dialogue' (MSD) is commonly used on post-graduate programmes or during sessions where student numbers range from 15–20 participants. MSD with larger cohorts is possible, though as the number of participants grows 'sampling' becomes an integral part of the practice.

MSD is underpinned by a method which encourages participants to reflect and think independently. It is often practiced in small groups led by a facilitator, but skilled participants may become independent and operate within the Socratic culture without external influence. Delivered and coordinated in the right way the Socratic method enhances self-confidence in one's own thinking and develops skills in listening, articulation and information literacy within a collaborative framework that is centred upon critical philosophy. The example provided as Figure 4.2 is typical of a contemporary MSD. The worth of MSD participation and engagement is unambiguous. Information literacy is just one of the skill sets that learners will develop along with a range of related abilities.

Referring to the structure and function of MSD, Marinoff (2009) provides further clarification by considering how to prepare for the dialogue. He states that: 'Reference to published work is not permissible in a Socratic Dialogue; reference to concrete personal experience is what counts and suffices for the purpose' (page 3). What Marinoff suggests, strengthens the belief that MSD brings a new dimension to information literacy. The information literate person in this context will not be the individual who can search out traditional sources of information using tried and tested techniques but the person who can operate within the self-contained environment of the dialogue. Rational discourse, adept listening skills and an ability to generate new concepts and ideas from the information that exists within the group will be the staple diet of the information literate MSD participant who will need to demonstrate high levels of emotional competence to remain within the rules that govern the MSD.

MSD brings a new dimension to the ANZIIL principles and standards. Certainly the MSD model is aligned to the overarching principles that underpin the ANZIIL framework; the MSD participant engages in independent constructivist learning during the dialogue and, one hopes, derives satisfaction and personal fulfilment from using information intelligently during the event. There is an expectation also, that MSD participants demonstrate social responsibility through a commitment to lifelong learning and community participation. Nonetheless, the dialectic nature of IL in the

Figure 4.2 A contemporary 'Modern Socratic Dialogue'

During today's session you will be asked to participate in a 'Modern Socratic Dialogue' (MSD). The following information should be helpful in ensuring that the MSD is successful in terms of each participant's learning. The development of transferable dialectic reasoning and information literacy skills is integral to the MSD process.

The focus for the MSD will be on the following philosophical question:

'What is education?'

Rules for the MSD

- A Modern Socratic Dialogue is a collective inquiry *NOT* a traditional debate with one side winning and the other losing.
- To get the maximum benefit out of the MSD you should draw upon your own experience and think for yourself throughout the activity.
- Do not speak hypothetically.
- Express your doubts.
- Strive for consensus.

Why are we holding a Modern Socratic Dialogue (MSD)?

A MSD is a collective attempt to find the answer to a fundamental question. The question 'What is education?' will be at the centre of the dialogue, but rather than examining existing philosophical explanations, the MSD will be characterised by the concrete experiences of you, the participants, who will ultimately engage in systematic reflection as the basis for developing shared judgements about the question. The MSD aims for consensus. Each participant's thoughts need to be explicated in such a way that participants fully understand each other as the communal enquiry evolves. In essence, each participant in the MSD should gain a deep and meaningful insight into the central question fuelled by self reflection on one's own professional practice and values.

What will be the learning outcomes?

Each partaker in the MSD will have opportunities to develop skills in self-reflection, critical reasoning and dialectic information literacy. Participants should also build an awareness of the moral and ethical implications of their contributions and aim to develop emotional competence and dexterity.

MSD context is not reflected by the ANZIIL core standards (2004), which fail to recognise that IL skills may be developed through dialectic activity. This is somewhat at odds with what is written elsewhere in the ANZIIL (2004) document where it is acknowledged that information is often transmitted in 'other ways' (page 1) and 'communicating ideas and information is integral to information literacy' (page 1).

The Association of College and Research Libraries (ACRL) (2010) Information Literacy Competency Standards for Higher Education offer a greater level of encouragement by including a whole section on 'information literacy and Pedagogy' (page 2). Though the linkage between IL and pedagogy that forms the focus of the ACRL perspective is centred on traditional concepts of IL, they do acknowledge that a well designed HE programme will help to create a framework for the development of IL skills, by enabling 'student centred learning environments where inquiry is the norm' (page 3). They go on to acknowledge that 'thinking critically is part of the process' (page 3) but fall short in recognising explicitly the clear linkage between IL skills development and contemporary dialectic approaches to teaching and learning. It seems that the ACRL perspective on pedagogy and IL skills development is centred on the traditional 'problem-based learning' (PBL) model which seeks to engage participants in accepted information searching processes using conventional means and sources.

A new dimension . . .

So where do the 'new' and contemporary approaches to HE facilitation lead us in terms of IL skills development? It seems clear that over the past five years teaching models and styles of delivery have evolved to meet with current agendas towards widening participation and student retention. In turn, this has added a further dimension to the concept of information literacy which as yet is not reflected in the accepted standards and frameworks offered by the ANZIIL and the ACRL. Linkage between IL and pedagogy has been recognised but this is focused around established concepts of IL and relates largely to problem based and enquiry focused models of facilitation. As noted earlier in this chapter, WebQuests form one such approach which may be either problem or enquiry focused and offers huge potential for the development of traditional IL skills as an integral part of the process.

Dialectic teaching, however, is somewhat different. Whether it is through focus groups, collaborative discussion or modern Socratic dialogue, the approach brings a fresh dimension to IL skills development. It brings to the table a new IL skills set which will appeal to learners who have a preference for an auditory style and which is dependent for success on an authentic set of abilities based on etiquette, emotional competence, good listening skills and articulation. The amount of knowledge and information that is brought to the dialogue is finite but the synergy generated through the dialectic process is considerable. Information literacy in this context is developed through the senses and processed through the cognitive and affective areas of the neo-cortex as the learner seeks fresh meaning and understanding based on the information received. In essence, this rich form of learning offers unlimited potential for the development of the information literate student in a non-traditional sense.

Conclusion

The established frameworks that structure the development of IL skills in Higher Education have served a useful purpose in defining the principles and core standards that portray the traditional image of the information literate student. In one sense these frameworks are a reflection on the conventional teaching models and approaches to learning that the HE student would have experienced prior to the widening participation (WP) agenda, when delivery paradigms were largely structured around traditional information-gathering techniques and were focused in and around the university library. The changing student profile in the post WP era has brought much new knowledge and information into the HE arena, and much of this valuable resource exists in the form of life experience or is grounded in global culture rather than the traditional form which could be accessed through literature. This has led to a new pedagogy and in turn a fresh angle on IL which includes the contemporary approaches and methods that are needed to access, assimilate and utilise this new information source and make it an integral part of the teaching, learning and information gathering process. In this light, the time is right to revisit the models and frameworks that demarcate the parameters of the IL spectrum to include this latest sphere of pedagogic activity and redefine the IL skill set which the contemporary HE students require if they are to reach their potential within the current environment.

Notes

1. The six core standards defined by the ANZIIL underpin Information Literacy acquisition, understanding and application by an individual (see ANZIIL framework, 2nd edition, page 11).
2. Bernie Dodge is widely credited as having first developed the WebQuest concept in February 1995. It is also acknowledged that SDSU/Pacific Bell Fellow Tom March contributed to this work during the early stages.

References

Association of College and Research Libraries (2010) *Information Literacy Competency Standards for Higher Education. http://www.ala.org/ala/mgrps/divs/ acrl/standards/informationliteracycompetency.cfm#ildef* (accessed 10 February 2010).

Australian and New Zealand Institute for Information Literacy (2004) *Australian and New Zealand Information Literacy Framework (2nd edition)*. Adelaide: Library Publications, University of South Australia.

Biggs, J. (2006) *Teaching for Quality Learning at University (2nd edition)*. Maidenhead: Open University Press.

Hepworth, M. (1999) *A study of undergraduate information literacy and skills: the inclusion of information literacy and skills in the undergraduate curriculum.* 65th IFLA Council and General Conference proceedings, Bangkok, Thailand, 20–28 August 1999.

Johnston, B. and Webber, S. (2003) Information literacy in higher education: a review and case study. *Studies in Higher Education*, 28(3): 335–52.

Mackeracher, D. (2004) *Making Sense of Adult Learning (2nd edition)*. Toronto: University of Toronto Press.

Marinoff, L. (2009) *The Structure and Function of a Socratic Dialogue. http://www.appa.edu/groupfacil.htm* (accessed 25 January 2010).

Storey-Huffman, R. (2008) 'How to Integrate Information Literacy into Higher Education Curriculum.' *http://www .big6.com/2008/04/11/how-to-integrate-information- literacy-into-higher-education-curriculum/* (accessed 7 January 2010).

Part 2
Development, dialogue and design

5

'Enquiring Minds' and the role of information literacy in the design, management and assessment of student research tasks

Keith Puttick

Abstract: This chapter considers the Enquiring Minds (EM) project at Staffordshire University, and the role that information literacy (IL) principles and standards can play in improving the quality of students' research. Clearly, an essential pre-requisite is institutions' commitment to embedding IL principles in the curriculum, while at the same time creating more (and better) opportunities to deploy research and research-related skills and putting Enquiry-Based Learning (EBL) at the heart of the student experience. However, if progress is to be made it will be essential for lecturers – working with groups like information specialists – to factor IL principles and competency standards effectively into research task design, guidance, and assessment criteria. While it is clearly essential to bring IL requirements into learning outcomes (a vital step in changing behaviour, and raising the quality of students' research), it is also necessary to recognise the limitations of learning outcomes. Consequently, there is considerable value in ensuring that IL standards are adapted and deployed to meet the needs of particular tasks, with task designers supplementing learning outcomes with effective guidance. As EM research has suggested, some EBL schemes or types of project work may require close guidance on specifics like taking 'preliminary steps', using 'a range of different enquiry methods', or 'communicating research results effectively'. The chapter concludes by emphasising the value of embedding IL principles in the curriculum – something that has considerable potential for improving students' research, and empowering them to become independent learners and 'producers of knowledge'. However, this will necessitate more effective ways of assessing IL aspects of learning outcomes, and rewarding good practice in conducting effective searches, authentication, and critical evaluation.

Key words: enquiry, student research, information literacy, IL competency standards, information specialists, EBL.

Introduction

Besides developing undergraduate students' research and research-related skills, and providing adequate opportunities to deploy those skills, what more can be done to improve the quality of students' research; and what are the benefits to be gained by bringing information literacy (IL) requirements into the curriculum? These are issues that the Enquiring Minds (EM) project at Staffordshire Law School has been considering since 2007. As considered in this chapter, a key dimension to this is the role that the assessment of IL requirements can play in the process of embedding IL in programmes, and in improving the quality of students' research outputs.

The Enquiring Minds (EM) project

EM is a Research Informed Teaching (RiT) funded project that has been looking at ways to improve the quality of students' research. Work began in 2007 following an initial pilot *People, Diversity and Work* when a group of four final-year students successfully undertook a major piece of research and presented their findings at the national conference *Empowerment, Welfare & Work* that year. The high quality of that research reinforced the case for pursuing a more ambitious agenda for student research (Puttick et al., 2008: 3–5). However, it also highlighted the need for more to be done to build on the positive improvements made to our undergraduate skills programmes, and to equip them with the range of skills now expected of graduates by the Quality Assurance Agency for Higher Education (QAA, 2007; 2008). This is also a prerequisite to the introduction of many of the enquiry-based learning (EBL) options, including project work, which QAA standards expect, and which promote higher order learning outcomes (Spronken-Smith et al., 2008:1). The value of EBL approaches is clear, whether tasks are undertaken within the 'information frame', and enquiry that is exploring existing knowledge; or it is in the so-called 'discovery frame' which entails enquiry that builds on such knowledge, contests it, or is developing new areas of enquiry (Levy, 2009).

Just one of the many challenges for institutions in enhancing their provision, or developing new programmes is that researchers now operate in a digital age in which they have access to a multiplicity of resources for accessing, manipulating, recreating, and communicating information. As the Melville Report has made clear, the use of Web 2.0 technologies is accompanied by the problem that information literacies, including searching, retrieving and critically evaluating information from different sources, are what it called 'a significant and growing deficit area' (Melville Report, 2009: 7). Accordingly, one of their key recommendations was that Higher Education institutions, colleges, and schools must 'treat information literacies as a priority area and support all students so that they are able, amongst other things, to identify, search, locate, retrieve and, especially, critically evaluate information from the range of appropriate sources – web-based and other – and organise and use it effectively . . .' (Melville Report, 2009, paras 39–40, 42, 73).

In the face of a daunting array of source materials that information systems generate, what strategies can lecturers and information specialists develop to try to ensure that student researchers access what is needed, effectively and efficiently? In addressing this central question, it has become increasingly clear that teaching institutions like ours should recognize that IL is a graduate attribute (Webber and Johnston, 2006), and so should be developing effective strategies at the level of awards and modules for incorporating IL principles and appropriate competency standards into task design, pre-task guidance, and both formative and formal assessment (Walton, 2005; Puttick, 2009).

IL, the teaching-research nexus and EBL

In the bigger picture, besides addressing some of the challenges presented by information gathering and management in the digital age, what are the wider advantages to be gained by embedding IL principles in the curriculum?

As well as helping to address the 'literacies deficit', and meet the increasingly tough standards set by QAA (QAA,

2007) and other external bodies, we believe that by incorporating IL requirements more effectively in programme delivery and assessment, not only will undergraduates gain the skills and confidence needed to become better, more autonomous learners – a vital factor in their future employability – but that students will be better placed to join the 'community of researchers' in the ways envisaged by commentators like Hasok Chang (Chang, 2005). Improving students' research skills enables them to participate in a wider range of EBL options and project work – something which, in turn, will help to build the academic learning community and bring students closer to the 'research scholar' model favoured by commentators like Hodge, Pasquesi and others (Hodge et al., 2007). Apart from exploring these and other issues around skills development and deployment, and linked matters like improvements to rewards, incentives, and assessment, the EM project's focus has been on the part that EBL approaches can play in the development of the teaching-research nexus. However, these are benefits that have to be progressively developed. Having explored this in some depth since 2007, we would certainly agree with the observation that teaching-research links are not 'automatic', and have to be 'constructed' (Jenkins et al., 2007: 2). What is more, the issues involved do not just focus on the student side: as the Melville Report rightly concluded, there are also some significant challenges for lecturers – some of whom may need to reflect on whether their own research, teaching, and learning work equips them to make informed choices about teaching and learning methods (Melville, 2009: Area 2 Staff Skills).

In making progress in these respects, consideration also needs to be given to matters such as the creation of opportunities to showcase successful project work, and use the product of students' and lecturers' research as a resource for teaching programmes, creating a culture in which the institution also benefits by putting research more firmly at the centre of legal studies and the student learning experience (Puttick et al., 2008). As Helen Walkington and Alan Jenkins have argued, this requires that new ways of disseminating students' work should be made available (Walkington and Jenkins, 2008). This links to the point that while formal assessment is a key driver in the raising of standards, it is by no means the *only* factor that motivates students (Joughin, 2009; Bone, 2009: 239). For example, for some students the opportunity to present good work to their peer groups, or to publish and showcase it in other ways, is also an important motivating factor – a theme that project team members advanced in a paper at the Association of Law Teachers Conference in Cambridge University (Harrison et al., 2010).

Issues around the communication of research outputs, and the need to ensure that communication skills are adequately factored in to assessments, is a theme that is revisited later in this chapter. Before that, it is proposed to consider the role that externally-set standards play in the development and assessment of research-related skills like communication, analysis, and team-working.

External standards: QAA

In 2008, QAA made it clear that it expects graduates with a bachelor's degree to have developed a 'systematic understanding of key aspects of their field of study, including acquisition of coherent and detailed knowledge, at least some of which is at, or informed by, the forefront of defined aspects of a discipline'. This is amplified by the expectation that students by the time they graduate should have 'an ability to deploy accurately established techniques of analysis and enquiry within a discipline', and 'manage their own learning'. Furthermore, they should be able to:

- Apply the methods and techniques that they have learned to review, consolidate, extend and apply their knowledge and understanding, and to initiate and carry out projects.

- Critically evaluate arguments, assumptions, abstract concepts and data (that may be incomplete), to make judgements, and to frame appropriate questions to achieve a solution – or to identify a range of solutions – to a problem.

- Communicate information, ideas, problems and solutions to both specialist and non-specialist audiences (QAA, 2008: Section 4 Qualification Descriptors, para 37).

Further guidance is in the QAA Benchmark Statement for Law (QAA, 2007), revising the earlier Statement published in 2000. However, given the significant changes there have been since 2000, particularly in areas like e-learning and assessment systems, it is surprising how little was changed. As the UK Centre for Legal Education said during the 2006 consultation on proposed revisions (UKCLE, 2007), it would have been helpful to see 'an acknowledgement of shifts in pedagogical practice', and some general guidance on the standards of practice 'considered fundamental to any well run programme of study' – for example in a specification about assessment criteria. Nevertheless, the guidance in the 2007 statement is now more visibly in synch with IL and technology literacy (TL) principles and standards. This has been a developing area of interest for the EM project, and members of the project team like Chris Harrison who have been addressing some of the TL issues highlighted in the Melville Report (2009) when helping to develop new programmes like the

Staffordshire Law School's Blended Learning Legal Practice Course, or 'new generation' programmes like the distance learning LLM in Sports Law.

Among other things, the revised 2007 Law statement now expects a student to be able to demonstrate a basic ability 'to identify accurately the issue/s which require researching', as well as having the technical proficiency to identify and retrieve up-to-date legal information, and use primary and secondary legal sources (para 6.3). In addition to skills of analysis, synthesis, critical judgement and evaluation, students should be able to demonstrate a basic ability 'with limited guidance' to act independently in planning and undertaking tasks in areas of law which they have already studied; be able to undertake independent research in areas of law which they have not previously studied 'starting from standard legal information sources . . .' (para 7). In the area of 'key skills' renewed emphasis is given to communication and literacy skills, including the presentation of knowledge and arguments 'in a way which is comprehensible to others and which is directed at their concerns', as well as 'read and discuss legal materials which are written in technical and complex language'.

Interestingly, in the area of research skills there is a new emphasis on a student's ability to 'work in groups as a participant who contributes effectively to the group's task' (para 8). This is an aspect that the EM project has been interested in for some while, and which featured in a conference paper at the Learning in Law Annual Conference (LILAC) 2009, *Concepts of Culture in Legal Education* (Puttick et al., 2009).

It is in these contexts that the EM project's work has revisited the role that assessment can play in improving research and allied skills.

The EM *People, Diversity & Work* pilot

As already noted, the EM project was preceded by a pilot called *People, Diversity & Work*. This was undertaken by a team of 3rd Year Law, Advice Studies, and Broadcast Journalism students, and was commissioned by the organisers of the *Empowerment, Work & Welfare* conference in November 2007 – a conference organised in collaboration with the Trades Union Congress, the Institute of Employment Rights, ACAS, Temple Cloisters, the Engineering Employers Federation, Citizens Advice, Disability Alliance, the Child Poverty Action Group, and Carers UK – which debated, among other things, youth aspects of the government's empowerment strategy, in particular employment, and retention policies being developed by the government at the time (Empowering People to Work, 2006).

Despite its many positive features, the pilot highlighted some significant shortcomings in students' ability to plan and manage such small-scale projects as a form of 'research-based inquiry' (Healey and Jenkins, 2009: 6) – for example in terms of their unsystematic approach to preparing such projects, and utilising appropriate research methods (the project highlighted, for example, how Google remains the 'first choice' for many student researchers, even at level 3). Nor was it always clear that the task of locating relevant information, ahead of the 'question-setting' phase was always conducted in the most effective ways. A key issue concerned the lack of a realistic timetable for completing 'key stages' in the research ahead of the Empowerment conference. The value of preparing students more effectively for such small-group project options (now an important strand in our portfolio of level 3 options) became more apparent when, in discussion with EM project partners, it became apparent how other institutions – particularly in the USA – address such aspects in their skills development programme, helped by information literacy standards that offer important pointers to how such project work *should* be approached – particularly in the design stages of EBL options. This links to points made by commentators like Moira Bent and Elizabeth Stockdale, who have observed that students embarking on a new project tend in many cases not to spend sufficient time reflecting on what it is, exactly, that they are looking for; or rationalise how they propose to set about or how to go about initiating effective searches for information once the project themes have been identified (Bent and Stockdale, 2009).

This important subject is revisited later when consideration is given to the way that a number of key 'standards', including those issued by ACRL in the USA, have informed the approaches taken to the introduction of new research skills elements into Staffordshire University's CPE GDL-LLB Use of Legal Sources & Legal Research Skills module.

Bringing IL into the Law curriculum

In the context of the EM project much of the interest has been in aspects of IL which help students' recognise when information is needed, and then to manage the process of locating, evaluating, and using information for specific tasks. A key step for Law undergraduate students is in adapting information in applied skills settings as part of the process of bringing it into the student's 'knowledge base' (ACRL, 2000).

As already suggested, there is much to be learnt from the experience of teaching and learning practice in US law schools – not least in the way literacy standards feature in the assessed research and writing elements of both core and elective subjects. As well as receiving instruction in areas of skills development like research and writing skills, opportunities to research and write about subjects that have been researched feature strongly in many schools' programmes. It is also the case that US law students are probably given greater opportunities to publish their work, for example after participating in American Bar Association writing competitions or for their school journals. Typically, a student will not only complete a credit-bearing, year-long module in Legal Research and Writing, she or he will have extensive opportunities to complete enquiry-based project work as part of electives. Specific qualitative aspects of writing work is usually assessed and rewarded by free-standing credit-bearing skills elements in marking regimes. Among other features, credits may be earned by writing work for journals like the Idaho University College of Law's *Critical Legal Studies Journal*. Specifically, credits can be earned by students' online contributions to the journal (Idaho, 2009: 84).

No doubt it was President Barack Obama's involvement in such work as editor of the Harvard Law Review in 1991 – a publication that includes contributions from students as well as faculty members and outside contributors (Butterfield, 1990) – that encouraged him to support the national IL campaign in the USA, and to issue his Proclamation in October 2009 making it 'National Information Literacy Awareness Month' in the USA. In the Proclamation he observed that 'Every day we are inundated with vast amounts of information ... Rather than merely possessing data we must learn the skills necessary to acquire, collate, and evaluate information ... Our nation's educators and institutions of learning must be aware of – and adjust to – these new realities . . .' (Presidential Proclamation, 2009).

At a practical level, what does 'adjusting to these new realities' actually *mean*? Having accepted the value of IL, how does this inform the practical steps that need to be taken if we are to help our students become information literate researchers, and make discernible improvements to the quality of research outputs?

Before looking at this in more detail, it is worth looking at the steps taken so far by UK providers like Staffordshire University to bring IL principles into the curriculum.

From theory into practice: implementation

The first point to make is that any meaningful progress in this area requires a clear institutional commitment, and a strategy for implementing IL in programme curricula – and this has now been done by Staffordshire University. In doing so, the university has been giving effect to some of the ideas Alison Pope developed as part of her university Learning and Teaching Fellowship project. Not least of these has been her view about the holistic approach to dealing with IL as just one of a number of relevant 'literacies'. As she has observed, IL is 'part of a bigger picture; part of a jigsaw puzzle which includes *other* literacies (including for example, academic, media and digital); new ways of approaching learning through critical thinking, reflective practice, collaborative learning and the key skills agenda – all of which contribute to independent learning' (Walton and Pope, 2006). Taking this forward, between 2005 and 2009, a number of important initial steps were taken, including the establishment of the university's *Information Literacy Statement of Good Practice*: this was formally approved in January 2007 (Staffordshire University, 2007). In September 2007 the university then approved a revision of the learning outcome 'Enquiry' so that it encompassed a statement requiring students working at undergraduate level to embrace information literacy. As a further action, whenever the enquiry learning outcome featured in a module descriptor, students were now to be expected to 'deploy accurately established techniques of analysis and enquiry and initiate and carry out projects within (the field of study)' and 'evaluate use of information literacy, including the ethical use of information in (the field of study)'.

One of the first occasions on which this revised learning outcome was used was in the re-design of the Law undergraduate award's Skills module – a development discussed by Alison Pope in the December 2009 issue of *Legal Information Management*. As she noted in that article, the really significant aspect of this new link to the university's strategic framework was that wherever an 'enquiry' learning outcome was included in a module's descriptor, information literacy work then had to be assessed (Pope, 2009: 248) – something that has made assessment 'unavoidable'. The case for formally assessing IL elements was also made by Geoff Walton (Walton, 2005).

Notwithstanding the importance of having an institutional strategic commitment to IL, and then bringing IL into learning outcomes, there are a number of other facets to this. The main consideration is that there are still a number of more specific actions needed before IL is likely to produce any tangible benefits, or improve the quality of outputs of student researchers. Most of these link to the way skills like Research (Enquiry at Staffordshire University) are assessed – and the actions needed to be taken to accompany the process of task-setting.

In this regard *Enquiring Minds* team members have been looking more closely at assessment issues; and as will now be considered, this requires some consideration of IL competence standards and their adaptation by course providers, and those managing awards and modules within programmes.

IL competences and 'standards'

Building on a 1989 report, the American Library Association (ALA) Presidential Committee's Final Report on information literacy (Presidential Committee, 1989), which identified the 'four components' of IL – 'the ability to recognize when information is needed and to locate, evaluate and use effectively the needed information' – the Association of College and Research Libraries published standards setting out the defining characteristics of an 'information literate individual', namely someone who is able to:

- determine the extent of information needed;
- access the needed information effectively and efficiently;
- evaluate information and its sources critically;
- incorporate selected information into one's knowledge base;
- use information effectively to accomplish a specific purpose;
- understand the economic, legal, and social issues surrounding the use of information, and access and use information ethically and legally (ACRL Standards, 2004).

To help translate these ideas into practice, and help student researchers become better, more information literate people, requires a significant collaborative effort on the part of all the key stakeholders – course providers, course managers, information specialists, lecturers, and the students themselves as the Boyer Commission Report *Reinventing Undergraduate Education: A Blueprint for America's Research Universities* has indicated (Boyer Commission, 1998: 15, 24–38).

The ACRL IL Competency Standards for Higher Education (ACRL Standards, 2004), like IL standards in other countries, clearly just provide an outline that informs more specific 'indicators' for institutions and specific programmes to build on. The job of translating that guidance into workable practice points is one for institutions' programmes, taking into account the programmes' specific needs. As the Boyer Commission also observed this requires a significant collaborative effort on the part of all the key stakeholders – course providers, course managers, information specialists, lecturers, and the students themselves. It added that: 'Achieving competency in information literacy requires an understanding that this [ACRL] cluster of abilities is not extraneous to the curriculum but is woven into the curriculum's content, structure, and sequence. . . .'

IL and the limitations of 'learning outcomes'

At a practical level, when award managers and lecturers factor IL principles into their award and module learning outcomes (and then use them as the basis for formal assessment) they need to be aware of the significant limitations of 'outcomes' as an assessment tool. As we have said in several conference papers since the EM project started (Harrison et al., 2010; Pope et al., 2010), on this point we agree with much of what Trevor Hussey and Patrick Smith have said on the matter. In general, their usefulness is confined to signalling what students can expect to gain in very generalised terms or from a specific teaching event or session (and from what they term 'summary statements' in relation to 'fairly small pieces of learning') (Hussey and Smith, 2008). Their role when dealing with 'larger areas of knowledge' or 'assemblages of skills' is particularly limited.

In practical terms, such considerations dictate a need for lecturers to be clear about how, exactly, they propose to explain what they expect from students – especially when dealing with skills like Research which may, in fact, comprise a number of distinct components. Furthermore, different sub-sets of skills may only be relevant at different stages in the task's timeline. For example, if a learning outcome is cast in very general terms (as they generally are in most module descriptors) then guidance and assessment criteria needs to be provided to students which reduces what is required to discrete elements.

In line with good practice, if learning outcomes indicate that a skill is being assessed then assessment criteria should be provided which is then mirrored by the contents of marking schemes. This facilitates good quality feedback, and gives the student confidence that he or she knows where any shortcomings have occurred.

'Competency standards' in Law skills assessment

The limitations of learning outcomes became clearer after early EM projects. These suggested that if IL elements are to be effective in raising the quality of outputs, not only must participants be clear about what, exactly, research skills outcomes actually require, but this needs to be set out in precise 'guidance' that builds on the general content of the module's learning outcomes. The value of doing this was seen in *Immigration, Work & Homelessness: UK–Poland*

Comparisons (2008/9) – one of the first EM projects after *People, Diversity & Work*. The research for this study was undertaken by students over a period of six weeks, and ahead of a joint seminar of Staffordshire University and Rzeszów University Social Welfare Law students in December 2008. The focus of the research, and subsequent presentation of results to fellow students, was on immigration, homelessness, disability, and human rights aspects of in-work welfare support for migrant workers. The project generated a lot of valuable comparisons between the law and social conditions in Poland, Ukraine and the UK, and produced material of a high standard. However, a number of features distinguished the approach taken on this occasion when compared with the earlier *People, Diversity & Work* pilot. First, detailed guidance was provided in a briefing during a workshop that preceded work commencing on the research. Among other things, this enjoined the researchers to take a number of 'preliminary steps' before they attempted to construct a research plan and 'questions'. Second, key elements in that guidance were reinforced by clear links to assessment points in the formal marking scheme. The need for adherence to the 'guidance' was stressed, pointing out that a failure to do so could result in 'loss of marks'. In general terms, IL principles featured strongly in the guidance – particularly in guiding the project's early stages.

In particular, the guidance was informed by points adapted from ACRL Standards One and Two. Among other things, participants were advised to:

- Take advantage of the whole-group workshop discussions that preceded the project, during which the topics of immigration for work, and support from host communities, featured in class-room discussions: these provided the necessary law, policy, and advice studies 'back-drop' in which the context of the research was set – and which acted as a springboard for the researchers' development of their own particular interests, enabling them to take those interests further, and autonomously.

- Discuss potential information sources, and participants' particular interests, before allocating specific tasks which could then later inform the project's aims as a whole.
- Having identified those areas of interest, and potential areas of enquiry, formulate a realistic plan for the project as a whole, factoring in:
  - the use of different forms of enquiry, rather than *just* on-line methods (Google, law databases, etc.);
  - a viable time-line for completing the agreed tasks;
  - enquiry methods that are effective in cost-benefit terms;
  - adequate reflection/discussion time with fellow researchers.
- Build in at least two stages at which the group would meet, enabling the research plan to be re-evaluated and modified if necessary; and enabling any 'gaps' in the information to be filled, if necessary by deploying new/better search strategies.

In the event, our evaluation concluded that the provision of this guidance had made a significant difference to the quality of the students' work, and in their confidence that they were managing the project effectively. In the feedback, we as well as the students learnt a great deal about the dynamics that shape projects in this area of EBL. It also gave us, as a project team, more confidence in providing such pre-task guidance in the future – for example in advising later projects that implementing task-specific IL requirements is a responsibility that needs to be *shared* equally by all the members of a project team.

Another area in which IL competency standards have been relevant to the project's work is communications aspects of Research skills, and it is this aspect of EM work that is now considered.

Presentation, reward and 'communication' aspects

Affording researchers the opportunity to present their work, and debate their findings with other participants, is another valuable dimension. This is a theme that EM project members like Geoff Walton have been particularly interested in, for example when discussing the opportunities that online discourse and collaborative learning can provide (Walton et al., 2007a, 2007b; Walton 2008). In formal assessment terms, opportunities given to students to communicate and discuss their research also links to the need to look at better ways of *assessing* such work fairly and effectively.

As well as rewarding students for good presentation of their work (and in ways that accords with IL competency standards relating to communication), the opportunity to do this and to be seen by the peer group, potential employers, and others to have done this effectively, should now be viewed, we suggest, as an integral part of EBL options like project work (Pope and Puttick, 2010). Besides gaining 'marks' in a module, and thereby improving the student's eventual degree classification, 'reward' elements in this area may take other forms – all of which assist in encouraging adherence to IL requirements. This is certainly the experience in the USA, as seen for example in the opportunities given to Law students to contribute to Law School journals, online conferencing and workshops, and pursue subject interests in the way that research active lecturers publicise their work (Walkington and Jenkins, 2008).

In some cases, for example as part of an EM-evaluated exercise 'Public Order: History & Law' in 2010, students who produced winning presentations of their work also went on to have their good work reported and discussed in the Law School's *News Bulletin*. The students concerned (twelve, in all), reported that this was a significant 'reward' in itself, supplementing the other positive benefits associated with participation in the exercise.

Competency standards for 'communication' and the 'ethical' dimension

Several EM pilot projects since 2008 have been looking at ways in which improvements can be made to the quality of the student experience when opportunities to deploy presentation skills are designed; and when work is being assessed, as part of formative and formal assessment schemes. Among other things, we have been evaluating the role that better, more targeted pre-task guidance can play (Puttick, 2009; Pope and Puttick, 2010). In practice, we found that a lot of modules identified 'communication' as a key element in learning outcomes – but without necessarily disaggregating this from other elements in the assessment of 'Enquiry', or providing much in the way of guidance on how, exactly, communication skills featured in the assessment process. In revisiting this area, several of the EM pilots have not only addressed the 'disaggregation' point, but have also sought to provide a clearer context for designing tasks and providing pre-task guidance (Pope et al., 2010: 106). In doing so, we have been addressing QAA and ACRL IL standards on the need to consider research 'audiences' and their particular needs. The 'audience' might, for example, be other students in a workshop, a legal client, a court, or some other 'audience'. ACRL Standard Four is particularly relevant. This stipulates that the 'information literate student communicates the product or performance effectively to others', and outcomes relate, in particular, to the choice of communication medium and 'the format that best supports the purposes of the product or performance and the intended audience'. Allied to this is the requirement that the student should communicate *clearly*.

Among other things, we have been looking at how, in the United States, law schools' 'know your audience' principles help in the design and assessment of research and research-related skills. Essentially, the expectation is that that the student's research results must be written up and presented in ways that meet the needs of specified groups. Typically, these might be sophisticated corporate clients, a court, or colleagues in other professional groups involved in transactions, such as accountants or HRM professionals. In the UK legal context similar considerations are relevant, too. Accordingly, in providing formal guidance to our students we have factored this in to the design and assessment of research tasks in a variety of ways (Pope and Puttick, 2010). For example, in a task requiring students to research substantive law points dealing with arrest, detention, and questioning (and suspects' rights in the process), but which also introduced students to communication aspects of research skills, guidance was provided which explicitly asked the students to 'take account of the audience for your presentation'. The task was this:

> You are working for a Law Centre in a Midlands city where clients are often detained and taken back to the

police station, sometimes in circumstances where it is not always clear if they have been formally arrested or not. Nor are people very sure of their rights after they have been taken to the station, and then detained and questioned.

Task Prepare a short presentation (approximately 15–20 minutes) that identifies detainees' key rights in the process, including their rights on arrival at the station, time limits on detention, rights during interrogation, and the effects of breaches of the Police and Criminal Evidence Act 1984 and Codes. You should provide examples, and be ready to provide your sources. Be ready, as well, to answer the audience's queries – e.g. on 'voluntary attendance', and when a person can insist on leaving the station. You should take into account the needs of your audience, and the kind of questions they might ask you. Your audience is a campaign group concerned about the police force's abuse of powers in the area.

In the event, the exercise was completed well. As the evaluation showed, however, one significant weakness (which was fed back to participants) was that some of the presentations, and material used to support them, were not always easy to understand by an audience of lay people – some of whom had little or no empathy with the law. It was pointed out that a key part of the researcher's role, particularly in legal studies and advice work, is to produce information in a 'usable form' – and in this case that required adapting points in the presentation from complex sources like Code of Practice C and the Police and Criminal Evidence Act 1984 in a way that could be readily understood by a lay audience. Had the 'audience' been different, for example 'fellow advice workers at the Law Centre who don't know anything about police powers law', the approach taken might well have been different.

The 'ethical' dimension in 'communication'

Most lecturers and information specialists tend to regard this aspect of research work and IL as something that focuses, primarily, on issues like academic honesty, plagiarism, and compliance with the law. While this is right, in the EM pilots we started to take a rather wider view of what 'ethical requirements' encompasses. In doing so we looked to sources like ACRL Standard Four (which no doubt mirrors standards being deployed in other countries). This states that: 'The information literate student understands many of the economic, legal, and social issues surrounding the use of information and accesses and uses information *ethically and legally.*' Among the more obvious 'outcomes', as might be expected, are matters like privacy, security, respect for intellectual property, and 'netiquette', and acknowledgment of the use of information sources. However, in assessing elements like communication of research results, formal expectations can, in fact, be wider ranging.

Interestingly, when students themselves were consulted, and asked to offer suggestions on what *they* thought this area should encompass, it was suggested that based on their experience of previous occasions when students had presented their work a significant concern was the propensity to *exaggerate* – and in a worse case scenario to *distort* findings. Examples were given of presentations where statistical information was accompanied, in the same Powerpoint slide, by visual imagery aimed at shocking the audience (for example in its graphic portrayal of violence in order to heighten the impact of the statistical 'message').

Interestingly, this was also a concern articulated by lecturers when evaluating presentations in the EM-evaluated exercise 'Public Order: History & Law' already referred to.

The role of IL in level 3 assessed dissertation and 'project' work

By the end of 2008 the EM project started to trial a number of new approaches to the way our students are helped to prepare for final year/level 3 research tasks. These include dissertations or projects designed by the students themselves, and which can now be undertaken individually or in small groups.

To underline the importance being given to the assessment of skills elements in such work, the Law School has pioneered a new Use of Sources & Legal Skills module. This has been aimed at helping students on the Law School's Graduate Diploma in Law/LLB (CPE) programme, a conversion course for non-Law graduates. At Staffordshire University, students on this programme study seven core topics plus an eighth which is a dissertation or project focusing on social welfare law. The module includes a number of skills development tasks that precede commencement of work on the eighth short subject research dissertation or project which must be completed – and since 2008 completion of the module (and the assessed tasks involved) now acts as a mandatory 'gateway' before work can commence on the main dissertation or project, which is a five thousand words long task.

The first skills workshop in the new module that students must attend is led jointly led by the module leader (the author) and the school's Senior Law Subject and Learning Support Librarian (Alison Pope). It is aimed at building on research skills and literacies (including technology literacies) which, as graduates, they are already assumed to possess. In practice, however, we have found that, notwithstanding their graduate status, skills competences and IT proficiency can be *very* variable. In this regard, the EM project's evaluation of students operating on the programme bear out some of the important conclusions reached by the Independent Committee of Inquiry into the Impact on Higher Education of Students' Widespread Use of Web 2.0 Technologies (Melville, 2009), and studies that express concerns about the potential for mis-use of information, digitally created information resources, and what some of them refer to as the 'Google generation'. The main thrust of those studies suggests that a sizeable proportion of entrants to HE programmes may have developed competencies in the use of IT but do not necessarily have the range of skills identified by IL competency standards as necessary to the processes of carrying out effective searches, or evaluating and using sources effectively. Besides such considerations, there is plainly a need for graduate researchers like this to be able to manage their time effectively – something that maps on to the bigger question of trying to ensure that information is accessed and managed efficiently.

After reconnecting them to introductory-level skills development work they will have undertaken during the CPE programme's induction phase, they are reminded of the main resources and methods available to Law researchers. The importance of undertaking preliminary research in order to become familiar with the topics being researched is emphasised, as is the need to make full use of a variety of different forms of enquiry (rather than just relying on online searches and law databases). The need for accuracy, and ensuring the most up-to-date sources is also stressed. Given that participants are graduate conversion students undertaking a busy and demanding programme, the need to create a realistic and achievable timetable for completing the work was highlighted. Following the initial workshop, and in order to hone their research skills, participants undertake a number of short research tasks to give them experience of researching legislative, case-law, and journal resources as well as a short project in which they research law and policy in a topical area of law with which they are unlikely to be familiar (the topics are allocated in a 'lucky dip'). Having completed the work over the ensuing five weeks, feedback is provided.

In the next stage of the module programme, and before work commences on the eighth short subject dissertation or project itself, the participants are also expected to produce a summary of their proposed research. After providing a structured phase in which they have the opportunity to reflect on the general subject-area, sub-fields, and the potential enquiry methods and sources to be used, their 'outline' is submitted for assessment, and feedback is provided.

The module has only been in operation for a year, and a fuller and better evaluation is not proposed until 2011. However, at this stage we believe it is significant that as a result of the introduction of the new module, a much larger proportion of the GDL-LLB cohort have elected to devise their own project rather than going for the 'off-the-peg' titles in Employment Law and Social Welfare Law that provided as the main option by the eighth subject's assessment regime. What is even more promising, the marks gained by students in June 2010 for the eighth subject dissertation/project are significantly higher than the marks gained by students in recent years. It is too early to conclude that this is the result of the new module, or the effects of the pre-task 'guidance' which was also provided before work on the eighth subject commenced – and no doubt a fuller evaluation may identify other factors in play. Nevertheless, the fact that student feedback from the 2009/10 cohort suggests that most students felt that they benefited from the structured preparation for the eighth subject, and that this equipped them better to elect to devise their own project, was very encouraging.

Conclusions

Although it is still early days, the EM project's work has shown that that embedding IL requirements in the Law curriculum offers considerable potential for improving the quality of students' research, empowering them to learn independently (Hepworth and Walton, 2009: 3), and to be 'producers of knowledge' rather than just 'knowledge consumers' (Hampton-Reeves, 2010). However, this generally depends on IL requirements being assessed effectively, with a sharper focus on rewarding evidence of good practice in conducting effective search, authentication and critical evaluation, a role for assessment seen as important by the Melville Report (at para. 73). There are also wider benefits to be gained. In particular, the approaches being developed do appear to be promoting the 'higher order thinking' described by Bloom and others (Bloom et al., 1956) – i.e. the ability to comprehend, analyse, apply, synthesise and evaluate information. In the bigger picture, we also like to think that we are creating the conditions needed to promote a wider range of EBL options in the Law curriculum, and encourage more students to contribute to Law programmes' 'knowledge pool'.

References

Association of College and Research Libraries (ACRL) (2000) *Information Literacy Competency Standards for*

Higher Education, Chicago, IL: Association of College and Research Libraries, *http://skil.stanford.edu/intro/research.html* (accessed 27 October 2010).

ACRL Standards (2004) *Information Literacy Competency Standards for Higher Education* (adopted by the American Association for Higher Education in October 1999 and the Council of Independent Colleges in February 2004), *http://www.ala.org/ala/mgrps/divs/acrl/standards/informationliteracycompetency.cfm* (accessed 27 October 2010).

Bent, M. and Stockdale, E. (2009) 'Integrating Information Literacy as a Habit of Learning: Assessing the Impact of a Golden Thread of IL in the Curriculum', LILAC Conference 2009, Cardiff. *http://www.slideshare.net/nmjb/lilac-2009-information-literacy-as-a-habit-of-learning?from=share_email* (accessed 27 October 2010).

Bloom, B. S., Engelhart, D., Furst, E., Krathwohl, D. and Hill, W. (1956) *Taxonomy of Educational Objectives: the Classification of Educational Goals: Handbook 1: Cognitive Domain*, New York: David McKay Company Inc.

Bone, A. (2009) 'The twenty-first century law student', *The Law Teacher* 43(3): 222–245, *http://pdfserve.informaworld.com/682813_917190603.pdf* (accessed 16 July 2010).

Boyer Commission (1998) The Boyer Commission on Educating Undergraduates in the Research University, *Reinventing Undergraduate Education: A Blueprint for America's Research Universities* (Sponsored by Carnegie Foundation for the Advancement of Teaching, Princeton NJ), Stony Brook, NY: New York State University, *http://naples.cc.sunysb.edu/Pres/boyer.nsf* (accessed 18 July 2010).

Butterfield, F. (1990) 'First Black Elected to Head Harvard's Law Review', *New York Times*, 6 February.

Chang, H. (2005) 'Turning an undergraduate class into a professional research community', *Teaching in Higher Education* 10(3): 387–394.

Empowering People to Work (2006) *A New Deal for Welfare: Empowering People to Work*, London: Department of Work & Pensions, Cm 6730.

Enquiring Minds Project (2007–2012) 'Enquiring Minds: Strategies for the Design and Use of Enquiry Tasks that Promote the Law Teaching-Research Nexus, Cross-Disciplinary and Comparative Law Studies, and Effective Deployment and Assessment of Students' Enquiry Skills at Level 3/H Level', *http://www.staffs .ac.uk/about_us/university_departments/personnel/cpd/ rit_project.*

Hampton-Reeves, S. (2010) The 21st Century Academic: Implementing Research-Informed Teaching, *http://www .staffs.ac.uk/research/research_informed_teaching/events/* (accessed 12 January 2011).

Harrison, C., Pope, A., Puttick, K. and Walton, G. (2010) 'Enquiring Minds & Information Literacy: Infiltrating the Curriculum and Challenging the Assessment Agenda', Association of Law Teachers' 2010 Annual Conference *Legal Education: Making the Difference* (29–31 March 2010, Clare College, Cambridge).

Healey, M. and Jenkins, A. (2009) *Developing Undergraduate Research and Inquiry*, York: Higher Education Academy.

Hepworth, M. and Walton, G. (2009) *Teaching Information Literacy for Inquiry-Based Learning*, Oxford: Chandos.

Hodge, D., Pasquesi, K., Hirsh, M. and LePore, P. (2007) *From Convocation to Capstone: Developing the Student as Scholar*, Network for Academic Renewal Conference, Association of American Colleges & Universities, Long Beach California, 19–21 April 2007.

Hussey, T. and Smith, P. (2008) 'Learning outcomes: A conceptual analysis', *Teaching in Higher Education* 13(1): 107–15.

Idaho (2009) *Law Student Handbook: College of Law, Idaho University*, Moscow, ID: Idaho Faculty Publications.

Jenkins, A., Healey, M., and Zetter, R. (2007) *Linking Teaching and Research in Disciplines & Departments*, York: Higher Education Academy

Joughin, G. (2009) 'Assessment, learning and judgement in higher education: A critical review', in Joughin, G. (ed.) *Assessment, Learning and Judgement in Higher Education*, Rotterdam: Springer, Netherlands, *http://www .springerlink.com/content/j565566gjl77666m/* (accessed 27 October 2010).

Levy, P. (2009) 'Inquiry-Based Learning: A Conceptual Framework (Version 4)', Sheffield: Sheffield University Centre for Inquiry Based Learning in the Arts & Social Sciences.

Melville Report (2009) 'Higher Education in a Web 2.0 World: Report of the Independent Committee of Inquiry into the Impact on Higher Education of Students' Widespread Use of Web 2.0 Technologies' (under the chairmanship of Sir David Melville), *http://www.jisc .ac.uk/media/documents/publications/heweb20rptv1.pdf* (accessed 15 July 2010).

Pope, A. (2009) 'Integrating legal research skills into the curriculum and into life', *Legal Information Management* 9(4): 246–9.

Pope, A. and Puttick, K. (2010) 'EM & Information Literacy: Challenging the Assessment Agenda', Research Informed Teaching Conference, Staffordshire University, 14 July 2010.

Pope, A., Puttick, K. and Walton, G. (2010) 'The Enquiring Minds Project at Staffordshire University: Integrating

Information Literacy into the curriculum and assessment', *Legal Information Management* 10: 104–8.

Presidential Committee on Information Literacy: Final Report of the American Library Association's Presidential Committee on Information Literacy (1989), *http://www.ala.org/ala/mgrps/divs/acrl/publications/whitepapers/presidential.cfm* (accessed 27 October 2010).

Presidential Proclamation (2009), 'Presidential Proclamation on Information Literacy' (President Barack Obama), *http://www.febab.org.br/2009literacy_prc_rel.pdf* (27 October 2010).

Puttick, K. (2009) 'Enquiring minds: information literacy in the design, completion and assessment of student research tasks'. Seminar presentation at the Staffordshire University Information Literacy Community of Practice (SUILCoP) workshop on 29 April 2009, *http://www.staffs.ac.uk/suilcop/events/previous/29april2009.php#puttick* (accessed 12 January 2011).

Puttick, K., Hammond-Sharlot, R. and Spence, J. (2009) 'Enquiring Minds: The "Project" & Strategies for Promoting (Better) Research, Autonomy & Deployment of Skills at Level 3', Conference Paper at LILAC 2009, *Concepts of Culture in Legal Education*, 23–24 January 2009, University of Warwick, *http://www.ukcle.ac.uk/resources/learning-and-learner-support/puttick/* (accessed 12 January 2011).

QAA (2007) *Subject Benchmark Statement for Law* (QAA 199 12/07), *http://www.qaa.ac.uk/academicinfrastructure/benchmark/statements/Law07.asp* (accessed 27 October 2010).

QAA (2008) *The Framework for Higher Education Qualifications in England, Wales, Scotland & Northern Ireland* (QAA 264 08/08: Quality Assurance Agency for Higher Education).

Spronken-Smith, R., Walker, R., O'Steen, W., Matthews, H., Batchelor, J. and Angelo, T. (2008) *Reconceptualising Inquiry-Based Learning – Synthesis of Finding*, Wellington: Ako Aotearoa National Centre for Tertiary Teaching Excellence, *http://www.akoaotearoa.ac.nz/project/inquiry-based-learning/resources/books/reconceptualisinginquiry-based-learning-synthesis-fi* (accessed 19 July 2010).

Staffordshire University (2007) *Information Literacy Statement of Good Practice*.

UKCLE (2007) *Revised Law Subject Benchmark Statement: UKCLE Response*, Warwick: UK Centre for Legal Education.

Walkington, H. and Jenkins, A. (2008) 'Embedding undergraduate research publication in the student learning experience: Ten suggested strategies', *Bookes e-Journal of Learning & Teaching*, 2(3), *http://bejlt.brookes.ac.uk/article/embedding_undergraduate_research_publication_in_the_student_learning_experi/* (accessed 12 July 2010).

Walton, G. (2005) 'Assessing students is essential for success', *Library and Information Update*, 4 (1–2): 36–7.

Walton, G. and Pope, A. J. (eds) (2006) *Information Literacy: Recognising the Need*, Oxford: Chandos.

Walton, G., Barker, J., Hepworth, M. and Stephens, D. (2007a) 'Facilitating information literacy teaching and learning and exercise module by means of collaborative online and reflective learning', in Andretta, S. (ed.) *Change and Challenge: Information Literacy for the 21st Century*, Adelaide: Auslib Press.

Walton, G., Barker, J., Hepworth, M. and Stephens, D. (2007b) 'Using online collaborative learning to enhance information literacy delivery in a level 1 module: an evaluation', *Journal of Information Literacy*, 1 (1): 13–30.

Walton, G. (2008) *Using Online Collaborative Learning as a Means of Promoting Information Literacy*, Stoke-on-Trent:

Staffordshire University Centre for Professional Development.

Webber, S. and Johnston, B. (2006) 'Working towards the information literate university', in Walton, G. and Pope, A. (eds) *Information Literacy: Recognising the Need*, Oxford: Chandos.

6

Are we sharing our toys in the sandpit? Issues surrounding the design, creation, reuse and re-purposing of learning objects to support information skills teaching

Nancy Graham

Abstract: This chapter will look at a wide range of issues surrounding design and creation of information literacy reusable learning objects (IL RLOs) that are used to support information literacy teaching. Librarians, both in the UK and internationally, are creating electronic content to support the teaching of information literacy. Even though much of this content is generic and could be used by others, this content is usually kept within the creator's institution or organisation. There are some obvious benefits (time saving, building on existing good practice) and issues (finding material in the first place, copyright) to sharing and re-purposing content, so how will librarians exploit the benefits and find ways to deal with the issues?

Key words: re-usable learning objects, information literacy, online library tutorials, open educational resources, librarians.

Introduction

This chapter will look at a wide range of issues surrounding design and creation of information literacy reusable learning objects (IL RLOs) that are used to support information literacy teaching. It will also focus on how that material can be reused and re-purposed by the library community. For this chapter, the definition of RLO will include not only small chunks of learning material (e.g. a one page diagram) but also more complex material such as library tutorials.

Librarians, both in the UK and internationally, are creating electronic content to support the teaching of information literacy. There is a wide variety of learning content, from basic Word documents explaining how to use a database through to interactive quizzes designed to teach referencing. Even though much of this content is generic and could be used by others, this content is usually kept within the creator's institution or organisation.

The Good Intentions Report (McGill et al., 2008) outlines the current culture of sharing learning content and highlights strategies for successful sharing of content, including subject-based communities of practice, such as academic libraries.

There are some obvious benefits (time saving, building on existing good practice) and issues (finding material in the first place, copyright) to sharing and re-purposing content, so how will librarians exploit the benefits and find ways to deal with the issues?

After an encouraging symposium at the 2009 Librarians Information Literacy Annual Conference (LILAC), in Cardiff in March (Graham et al., 2009), it was agreed that a community of practice was needed to encourage the sharing of learning content to support information literacy teaching.

Literature review

A literature review was undertaken to get an overview of the published evidence of work being done in this area. Databases searched included Library, Information Science and Technology Abstracts (LISTA), Library and Information Science Abstracts (LISA), Applied Social Sciences Index and Abstracts (ASSIA), the Arts and Humanities Citation Index (AHCI) and individual journals.

Currently published literature indicates that there is less being done in the area of reuse and re-purposing but that the creation of RLOs is still widespread. From attendance at the Librarians Information Literacy Annual Conference (LILAC) and visiting library websites (both in the UK and abroad) there is a lot of evidence to suggest that creation of IL learning material is still a major activity in all types of libraries.

This literature review is broken down into five areas:

- Overviews/literature reviews
- Individual projects
- Pedagogy
- Future innovations and use of Web 2.0
- Reuse/re-purpose/sharing.

Overviews/literature reviews of IL RLO use

Nancy Dewald's 1999 article is a good starting point and outlines some key aspects of IL RLO design. Dewald's seven principles (noted later in both Somoza-Fernandez and Abadal (2009) and in Tancheva (2003)) lay the foundations for transferring face-to-face IL teaching to online tutorials. She concludes that tutorials should be explicitly linked to curricula and that other web developments should inform how IL RLOs are created.

Tancheva's paper of 2003 builds on this to argue for what she considers good practice in developing web-based tutorials. She argues that there are five essential elements to include in a good IL RLO: preliminary assessment, branching capabilities, making the tutorial problem-based and concept-based, that it should always be interactive and that there should be some form of assessment and feedback. Tancheva concludes that online library tutorials are still a work in progress.

Two papers published in 2009 focus on reviewing existing library tutorials. Sharon Yang looks at 372 tutorials from colleges in the United States and Canada. Her own review concludes that IL RLOs are still too static and need to include more games, quizzes, etc., in order to be more effective.

Somoza-Fernandez and Abadal (2009) looked at 180 online tutorials from academic libraries in countries across the globe. They set criteria and searched both aggregated sources and individual academic library websites. They found that there is still a tendency toward generic tutorials that do not specify user level or learning objectives and that do not include evaluation or assessment. They also note that few RLOs give any permissions information and only a handful utilise Creative Commons licences. This is particularly crucial if librarians are to share their learning material more openly. Their conclusion (a rather depressing echo of Tancheva six years earlier) is that '. . . web-based tutorials offered by academic libraries are at an early stage of development' (p. 130, Somoza-Fernandez and Abadal, 2009).

Blummer and Kritskaya's 2009 literature review concludes that there are five factors to ensure success including: knowing the purpose of the tutorial (learning outcomes/

objectives); collaborating with others (librarians, academics, learning technologists); the use of standards such as those developed by the Association of College and Research Libraries (ACRL) in the US and the Society of College, National and University Libraries (SCONUL) in the UK; to map learning outcomes, student engagement and evaluation through assessment.

Individual projects

As indicated by the reviews above there have been hundreds of individual projects aimed at creating IL RLOs. Some literature is available but much of the information on these projects is presented at conferences (LILAC, 2010) and other face to face events. Of the articles found, the following provided some useful consensus.

In describing their IL Toolkit, Bent and Brettell (2006) outline the steps used to map their RLOs on to an academic module's learning outcomes, making them truly practical for academics to embed in their curricula.

Jackson and Mogg (2008) at Cardiff University write about the creation of an Information Literacy Resource Bank (ILRB) which provides access to a range of freely available IL RLOs for both academics and other librarians. They highlight evidence of the reusability of the objects, through requests from external librarians to reuse particular RLOs. Lynwood and Flanders (2006) chart the development of IL RLOs at Birkbeck University. This project included both a subject librarian and a multimedia developer and, crucially, saw them sharing and adapting similar learning objects with Cardiff University.

The Hunsaker et al. (2009) article highlights a project in which librarians not only gathered information on existing RLOs available for reuse but also developed a suite of locally-appropriate objects, using criteria to ensure that they collated high quality content. These criteria could be used by anyone undertaking a similar task.

Smith (2007) explains how using active learning techniques and humour in developing IL RLOs helped her to engage students in IL classes. Both Matesic and Adams' (2008) article and Emily Dill's (2008) article stress that using 'clickers' and the associated RLOs do not improve retention of knowledge, but do improve student engagement with a topic.

Wales and Robertson (2008) from the Open University describe how the literature informed development of their Adobe Captivate RLOs, focusing on the use of storyboarding and self-assessment to ensure both granularity and active learning. Their article shows how starting with an overview can help with creating at a micro level.

Newton et al. (1998: 129) describe a project in public libraries to collate existing IL RLOs. However, they found that most IL RLOs are created '. . . expressly for use by academic staff and students . . .' rather than public library users. So, rather than reusing existing content they had to create their RLOs from scratch.

Bailin and Pena (2007) chart the development of a library tutorial using scripts to reproduce a structure akin to a face-to-face reference interview. Interestingly, their evaluation shows that the majority of students did not use the tutorial in this linear fashion but instead used it to find key information at point of need.

Graham and James (2007) describe the Birmingham Re-Usable Material (BRUM) project in which librarians developed IL RLOs and presented them on an open website for academics to use with minimal librarian support.

Pedagogy

Pedagogical considerations are crucial when developing IL RLOs, as this can affect take up and effectiveness of the RLO. The experience of librarians at Southampton Solent University is outlined in two articles (Browne and Dixon, 2010; Apps, 2009) both looking at their development of IL RLOs using a constructivist approach. They changed their approach from purely subject-based RLOs to also providing generic material for some topics (referencing).

Norwegian librarians (Skagen et al., 2008) describe how they used a didactic relation model as a framework to create an online IL tutorial, which focused on learning goals, learning process, learning conditions, settings and assessment to develop material.

At the 2010 LILAC conference Cathy Palmer from the University of California, Irvine (Palmer and Canaday, 2010) ran a workshop on developing an online IL tutorial which included a checklist of key factors to consider in the planning stages. She emphasises the use of a sound pedagogical structure before embarking on using technology.

Web 2.0 and beyond

A survey of librarians' use of Web 2.0 (Luo, 2009) highlights the different levels at which IL can incorporate new technologies. As well as discussing the disadvantages (technical challenges, online vandalism and students' own Web 2.0 knowledge) the author reiterates the importance of looking at pedagogy before technology to ensure that students' information skills needs are met.

Developers at the RLO Centre of Excellence in Teaching and Learning (CETL) discuss how they created and honed a multimedia learning object (MLO) for use with mobile phones. They went through several iterations of the MLO, testing with both peers and students and conclude that MLOs are appropriate for use with mobile devices as long as: 'The underlying design, or pedagogical pattern, is viewed as providing the true basis for reuse' (Bradley et al., 2009: 176). The ongoing work of the RLO CETL provides librarians with much needed development advice in terms of both reusability and help with technical challenges.

Reuse/re-purpose

Mardis and Ury (2008) discuss a small scale research project focused on getting students to rate the reusability of IL RLOs. Many of us request student feedback on how effective RLOs are but not much on what they think of the reusability of it, so this is an interesting article for those researching into student participation. IL trainers at Staffordshire University (2010) have also involved students in providing feedback in order to update their Assignment Survival Kit (Adams et al., 2008; Walton and Pope, 2010).

In their final report (Wrathall, 2009) the Study Methods and Information Literacy Exemplars (SMILE) project team outlines several barriers to re-purposing existing IL RLOs including not having a central location to look for material, time taken to re-purpose material, lack of evaluation criteria (which they then developed), and copyright issues. The findings of this project, which was part of the Joint Information Systems Committee (JISC) funded ReProduce programme of projects looking at re-purposing, will be invaluable to any librarian wishing to reuse or re-purpose existing IL RLOs.

A project team at Limerick Institute of Technology (LNSS, 2010) has also been experimenting with reuse/

re-purpose of existing IL material from other higher education institutions. They plan on expanding this project to include sharing material with librarians in other EU countries.

On a more general note on re-use, Campbell and Currier's 2005 article includes criteria to ensure that digital learning material is developed with true reusability in mind, learning from the JISC funded 5/99 projects (JISC, 2009). Nicky Whitsed (2004) also offers some introductory insight into designing learning material with maximum re-usability in mind, referencing Rachel S. Smith's (2004) practical online monograph 'Guidelines for Authors of Learning Objects'.

The need to provide evidence or 'proof' of re-use is an obvious follow-on from creating IL RLOs and Paul Betty's (2009) excellent article describes how to use Google Analytics to track use of library learning material. He advises that collaboration with IT departments on implementation and not taking the usage at face value are important to bear in mind.

Sharing

Other articles cover sharing in repositories (Satta, Chaudhry and Khoo, 2008) and frameworks from which librarians can produce learning material (Jennings and Cashman, 2008) to then be deposited in repositories. The latter, a highly practical guide to developing RLOs from the Republic of Ireland's National Digital Learning Repository (NDLR, 2010a), includes a development model, ADDIE (Analyse, Design, Develop, Implement, Evaluate) that takes the developer through a process of planning, creation and evaluation. The NDLR has also supported an information skills community of practice (ISCoP). This community, brought together online by a shared repository, aims to share expertise in face to face meetings and share material online (NDLR, 2010b).

Building on the concept of the Massachusetts Institute of Technology's Open Course Ware project (MIT, 2010) the JISC funded Open Educational Resources (OER) projects (JISC, 2010) have explored many issues surrounding sharing learning and teaching material and their individual final project reports will make crucial reading for those looking for advice on sustainable sharing.

Use of Creative Commons licensing is something that has been an inherent part of the OER projects and needs to be explored further by librarians wanting to share material. Creative Commons recently released a new web page specifically aimed at those wanting to share educational resources (Creative Commons, 2010).

There is a wide variety of locations where librarians (and other educators) can share their learning material including: national repositories (Jorum, NDLR) that host objects; international repositories, such as the Multimedia Educational Resource for Learning and Online Teaching (MERLOT) (MERLOT, 2010); International Federation of Library Associations (IFLA) that host dynamic links to material hosted elsewhere (IFLA, 2010); individual IL RLO sources such as the ILRB (Cardiff University, 2010); and individual library websites.

MERLOT is an interesting example as an organisation that has championed open sharing but via dynamic links rather than hosting material centrally. MERLOT also utilises user comment facilities and peer reviewing editorial boards for different subject areas in order to ensure material is of a high standard. An online book chapter (Iiyoshi and Kumar, 2008) explains how the system works and the benefits of the community approach.

Design of RLOs for information skills

Where to start: pedagogy vs technology

For many of us it is very natural to play around with technology to see if it will be useful for us when developing RLOs and allow the software to dictate what sort of RLOs we use. This testing and discovery needs to be encouraged in all librarians as it is the only way that innovation and good practice can flourish. The Creatively Using Learning Technology website (University of Worcester, 2010) can help librarians to decide which technologies will be useful for specific learning contexts.

However, this exploratory phase has to be followed by a focused planning stage looking at the learning context of your RLOs. Without taking pedagogy into account from the very beginning, the true purpose of your RLOs can quickly become lost in the excitement of wanting to use the latest bit of kit. Remember, your most effective RLO could be a simple Microsoft PowerPoint presentation. As Blummer and Kitskaya (2009) argue, it is crucial to collaborate with others in the development and this is a good opportunity to work with our learning technologist colleagues who have expertise in both pedagogy and technology.

Looking at existing good practice

Blummer and Kritskaya (2009) advise on first looking at existing examples of RLOs. The IL RLO Share wiki (Graham, 2010) is a good place to start looking for existing material to reuse, both in the UK and beyond. There is an A–Z listing of repositories and individual projects, all with material that is freely available for others to reuse. Licence information is included where known.

Aspects of good design for IL RLOs

The key to these design aspects are that we are creating with *reuse* in mind. We all spend time creating RLOs for our own use, but how many of us are thinking of colleagues, internal and external, when planning what our RLOs will be like. As well as other generic design advice, Table 6.1 will include design aspects to consider, making your learning material as re-usable as possible.

These guidelines are by no means thoroughly comprehensive and you may pick and choose the sections that are appropriate for your needs. However, they are a collation of expertise and advice from the literature and by adhering to them as closely as possible will ensure that you build on existing good practice.

Sharing your content

Opening up your content

The section on designing for reuse in Table 6.1 covers those aspects which you may want to consider if you want to open up your learning material for others to use. There is an international open educational resources (OER) movement aimed at encouraging and supporting open sharing of learning material. This movement includes the setting up of repositories and funding projects (Jorum, iTunesU, JISC OER, MIT Open Course Ware) to get educators sharing.

The Good Intentions report (McGill et al., 2008) outlines several successful business models for sharing, including one which is founded on the concept of a shared curriculum. Librarians are already set up to share both curriculum and content. We already have a community of practice; all we need to do is gather material together, host it and then regularly raise awareness of what is available.

Table 6.1   Design aspects

Factor to consider	What does this mean practically?	References
Planning, pedagogy, curricula	Before doing any practical planning of content you will need to consider the specific learning outcomes/objectives for your learners.	Dewald (1999)
	This may be a good time to consult your academic colleagues if your learning material needs to be subject-specific.	Blummer and Kritskaya (2009)
		Tancheva (2003)
	You could also consider using existing standards to help you develop material, such as the ACRL information literacy competency standards (ACRL, 2000) or the SCONUL seven pillars (SCONUL, 1999).	Skagen et al. (2008)
	Even if you are creating a simple one-page diagram for Boolean searching, think about who your audience is and what it is *they need* to know (remember, this can sometimes differ drastically from what *you want* to teach them!).	NDLR (2010a, b)
		Hunsaker et al. (2009)
	Include a pre-diagnostic test so that students are fully aware of how the learning outcomes will improve their knowledge/skills base.	Smith (2004)
	For maximum reusability consider:	
	▪ Making the learning outcomes generic and explicit so that they can be used by as many different audiences as possible.	
	▪ Including learning outcomes for different levels.	

Continued

Table 6.1 Design aspects (cont'd)

Factor to consider	What does this mean practically?	References
Content design	Consider the following aspects to include: ■ Using a storyboard to plan your content. ■ Interactivity – this will support active learning and the constructivist approach. ■ Branching – this appeals to different levels of learner and non-linear learners, allowing students to access information at point of need. ■ Graphic look and feel – this may be the time to consult learning technologist colleagues for instructional design tips. ■ Branding – consider the reusability if you are to cover your material with the branding from your organisation/institution. By all means include copyright statements but think about how adaptable your content will be with a logo on it. ■ Pilot – if you have the time consider piloting your RLO and test with both users and colleagues for input into future iterations.	Bradley et al. (2009) Blummer and Kritskaya (2009) Tancheva (2003)
Collaboration	Academic and learning technologist colleagues have already been mentioned but it is also important to include internal (and sometimes external) library colleagues for advice on content. You may also need to speak to academic department administrative staff about including material in departmental websites/intranets.	Blummer and Kritskaya (2009)
Subject vs. generic	This is not mentioned to a great extent in much of the IL RLO design literature but is mentioned in the reuse literature. As librarians we share a curricula and many topics are generic, sharing the same concepts regardless of subject disciplines: ■ basic information retrieval ■ evaluation of online information ■ referencing ■ Boolean logic.	Apps (2009) Browne and Dixon (2010)

	If you are developing any RLOs around these concepts, then consider making them generic or transferable so that others can edit or alter any mention of subject topic to suit their own needs. Even if you are planning on keeping your material within your organisation/institution consider how other library colleagues could utilise your learning material. Could they pick up your teaching material and with a little tweaking use them with their students? This should be a benchmark of reusability.	
Technology use	When thinking about which software or platform to use when developing and hosting your material, consider the following points, which are pertinent for usability *and* reusability: ■ Will the software you use help or hinder your students to meet the learning outcomes? ■ Can the RLO be used on more than one platform (VLE and standalone)? ■ Will the need to download any special plug-ins in order to use your RLO be a barrier to uptake? ■ Would it be possible to use a web-based platform to host/develop RLOs (blogs, wikis)? ■ Are you using ubiquitous software that 'most' people should expect to have access to? ■ Are you using free/open source software? ■ If the software that you are using is new to you, how long will it take to get to know how to use it and is this worth your time? ■ Does your choice of software ensure maximum accessibility for all users (for UK users you need to, *at the very least*, comply with the Disability Discrimination Act)? As with other points above, this may be a good time to consult with learning technology/IT colleagues for advice on software capabilities and limitations. It is important to keep up with the latest software, whether it's free or proprietary.	Yang (2009) Bradley et al. (2009) Matesic and Adams (2005) Dill (2008) Wales and Robertson (2008)

Continued

Table 6.1 Design aspects (*cont'd*)

Factor to consider	What does this mean practically?	References
Evaluation of RLO	How will you know if your RLO is effective in meeting learning outcomes? Here are some points to consider: ■ You may have already involved students in user testing. Once you have your final iteration, test again. ■ Include space/opportunity for user comments, so that you can keep on receiving feedback. ■ Conduct focus groups, surveys and collect anecdotal evidence of effectiveness. ■ You will also need to build in some sort of obsolescence check. An annual review is useful to ensure that your material is kept up to date.	Blummer and Kritskaya (2009)
Student assessment	Closely linked to ensuring effectiveness of the RLO is the inclusion of student assessment. As part of interactivity you could include multiple choice quizzes for students to track their own learning. You could also include teacher feedback on learning tasks completed. For smaller RLOs you could use something more straightforward to test knowledge acquisition, like a show of hands or using 'clickers'. These quick methods will let you know immediately if your learning outcomes have been met.	Skagen et al. (2008)
Factors for reusability design		
Metadata	If you want your RLOs to be reused by others, they will first need to find it. As part of the design you may want to consider tagging your material with meaningful metadata for easier discovery and indexing. See Appendix A for which fields are useful to include. It is particularly important to include the following information: ■ permissions/licensing ■ pedagogic information (learning outcomes, intended audience, level) ■ technical specification.	Whitsed (2004) Smith (2004) Wrathall (2009)

Granularity	By developing material as small chunks to be added together will ensure flexibility for users and reusers: ■ It will be easier to edit if you only need to change one section. ■ Users will find it easier to pick and choose the learning material they need (e.g. by picking one section of a larger library audio tour). ■ Others will find it easier to reuse and re-purpose content if it is presented at a granular level.	Campbell and Currier (2005) Hunsaker et al. (2009)
Licensing	One of the biggest reuse/re-purpose issues is potential users not knowing what they are allowed to do with material they wish to edit. Be explicit in how others are allowed to use your material. This can be added into the metadata or on web pages or other host locations. Consider using Creative Commons licences to protect your content. (See the Creative Commons for education website for guidance.) Speak to your institution's legal/copyright advisor for a clear answer on what permissions you can add to your material – in many cases your employer will own the copyright and may have a policy that you will need to adhere to.	Keller and Mossink (2008) Wrathall (2009) Smith (2004)
Sharing locations	As outlined in the sharing section of the literature review, where you choose to share your learning material will have an impact on uptake. If you house your material within your own organisation, within closed files or VLE, external (and possibly internal) take up will be minimal. However, if you consider adding your content to your institutional repository (if you have one) or website, others will have a greater chance of finding it (especially if you have added some metadata). Having shared curricula boosts the chances of real sharing and reuse amongst librarians so a library based repository or list of links would also be useful (Graham, 2010).	Wrathall (2009) McGill et al. (2008)

Continued

Table 6.1 Design aspects (cont'd)

Factor to consider	What does this mean practically?	References
Sharing locations –*continued*	There are also national learning object repositories, such as Jorum or MERLOT, to consider. The more places that you share, the greater chance there is of someone finding your material. In order to support sustainable sharing, it is important to think about the locations that you host your material and the file types and software that you use. To ensure maximum longevity for your material, think about developing RLOs in interoperable software and regularly updating versions. Keep up to date with host locations and move or copy material to several places for safe keeping.	
Tracking	Once you have opened up your learning material, either on your own website or on a repository, it will be important to track who is using your material and how. Tracking usage can be difficult as there is currently no standardised or sustainable way of doing this. However, here are a few things to consider: ■ Google Analytics is one way of tracking use, and although it has its limitations, it is worth considering adding the tracking code to your RLOs and analysing use (more information in Betty and at the Google Analytics website). ■ You could also include the opportunity for user comments; star ratings, etc., wherever you host your material, to see how others have reused. ■ Add a note requesting feedback wherever you host your material.	Betty (2009)

We do not, as a matter of course, tend to link our content to the outside world as this is not the primary purpose of why we create content. However, we must change this view and design both our material and the host environment so that it is as open as possible. Find out if your institution has a repository, and if it has, upload your material to it. If your organisation has a website, find out if you can load material to be accessed openly. There are also a number of national and international repositories where you can upload your material for others to use. JorumOpen (Jorum, 2010) in the UK and MERLOT (MERLOT, 2010) in the US are country-based websites but anyone in the world can access and download material from the sites. Other sources are listed on the IL RLO Share wiki (Graham, 2010).

The biggest issue in opening up your content will be the licensing and each organisation will have a different view of your intellectual property rights (IPR) and what you will be allowed to do with your own content. However, the JISC has encouraged those running the OER projects to use Creative Commons licences. The questionnaire at the end of Keller and Mossink's 2008 report is a very practical guide through tricky licensing decisions.

Another useful guide (with the emphasis firmly on designing content for openness) to help you open up your material is the CORRE (Creation, Openness, Reuse and Re-purpose, Evidence) framework (University of Leicester, 2010), devised as part of a JISC OER project.

Reusing/re-purposing others' material

The flip side of opening up your own content is you may also want to reuse or re-purpose material that you find created elsewhere. The ReLo logbook (see Appendix) uses a checklist approach and guides the user systematically through reusing content. This checklist should ensure that you take into account all the key factors of reuse and re-purpose including learning outcomes, technical information and, probably most importantly, licensing.

The ReLo logbook was developed as part of the ReLo project at the University of Birmingham and its aim is to explore issues in sharing IL learning material and to encourage librarians in re-purposing each other's IL RLOs. The logbook is designed to support re-purposing by providing a practical checklist to ensure those that want to re-purpose do it thoughtfully and as sustainably as possible.

Flickr now has a dedicated Creative Commons section (Yahoo! UK and Ireland, 2010) in which all images (currently standing at over 12 million) have a CC licence attached, clearly stating permission. This is a real step forward and means that users can reuse and re-purpose safe in the knowledge that they have permission.

Sharing good practice

As was obvious from the attendance and feedback from the 2009 LILAC symposium on IL RLOs (Graham et al., 2009) there is a demand from librarians to share both content and expertise. Both face-to-face events and an online presence are necessary to ensure this community of practice is pro-active in sharing. It is imperative that as librarians with a reason to share, we attend the appropriate conferences, keep up with the literature and contribute to the events and online spaces so that we capture and learn from good practice.

The LILAC is a good place to start, both to see the content that is being produced and to discuss best practice and reuse with others. The Information Literacy website (Information Literacy Group, 2010) is the starting point for the online community of librarians with an interest in information literacy and associated resources. The IL RLO Share wiki (Graham, 2010) is an informal space, which includes listings of freely available resources, the 2009 LILAC symposium findings and a discussion forum.

Conclusion

Librarians have been creating learning material in order to teach information skills to users for decades. We have, between us, an enormous amount of expertise in pedagogy and instructional design and this expertise needs to be shared to support the development of learning material. We already have communities of practice within which we can share best practice and, instead of keeping our material in silos, we now need to use these communities to embrace open sharing of our learning material and building on existing expertise in designing, reusing and re-purposing RLOs.

Appendix: Reuse logbook

(Re) Logbook
Unique Object Number Plate:

Creation details

- Object name
- Location

- Author
- Institution
- Date
- Description of intended use (level and number of students, generic/subject-specific)
- Associated learning outcomes
- Learning Design details (DDA compliant, pedagogical considerations)
- Keywords
- Reuse restrictions (CC licence terms listed)

Usage details

- How does this LO support the following: independent learning, EBL, transferable skills and competencies?
- Success rate (including student feedback) – did it achieve its objective/learning outcome?
- Notes

New 'owner' details

- Author
- Institution
- Date
- External LO/Internal LO (if external, please give details of location)
- Description of reuse (level of student, generic/subject-specific)
- Associated learning outcomes
- Keywords

- Reuse restrictions (CC licence terms listed)
- Notes

Reuse/re-purposing details
Reuse

- New audience/intended use
- How does this LO support the following: independent learning, EBL, transferable skills and competencies?
- Associated learning outcomes
- Success rate (including student feedback) – did it achieve its objective/learning outcome?
- Notes

Re-purpose

- Details of technical changes
- Time taken
- Software/hardware used
- Ease of re-purpose

  Very easy

  Fairly easy

  Fairly difficult

  Very difficult
- Further comments (why user chose object, was user searching for similar LO or was it serendipitous, was the re-purposing worth it, how well did the object work after re-purposing, would you look for other material in this way?
- Associated learning outcomes
- Success rate (including student feedback) – did it achieve its objective/learning outcome?

- How does this LO support the following: independent learning, EBL, transferable skills and competencies?

Catherine Robertson and Nancy Graham,
University of Birmingham
September 2009

References

Adams, J., Pope, A. and Walton, G. (2008) 'Using Web 2.0 to enhance the Staffordshire University Assignment Survival Kit (ASK)', in J. E. Parker and P. Godwin (eds), *Information Literacy Meets Library 2.0* (pp. 139–150). London: Facet Publishing.

Apps, K. (2009) 'Online Information Skills Tutorials: Southampton Solent University reviews its approach', *SCONUL Focus*, 46: 77–81.

Association of College and Research Libraries (ACRL) (2000) Information Literacy Competency Standards for Higher Education. Available from: *http://www.ala.org/ala/ mgrps/divs/acrl/standards/informationliteracycompetency .cfm* (accessed 5 May 2010).

Bailin, A. and Pena, A. (2007) 'Online library tutorials, narratives, and scripts', *Journal of Academic Librarianship*, 33(1): 106–17.

Bent, M. and Brettell, S. (2006) 'What's wrong with a good idea? An Information Literacy Toolkit in practice', *ALISS Quarterly*, 2(1): 27–32.

Betty, P. (2009) 'Assessing homegrown library collections: Using Google Analytics to track use of screencasts and flash-based learning objects', *Journal of Electronic Resources Librarianship*, 21(1): 75–92.

Blummer, B. A. and Kritskaya, O. (2009) 'Best practices for creating an online tutorial: A literature review', *Journal of Web Librarianship*, 3(3): 199–216.

Bradley, C., Haynes, R., Cook, J., Boyle, T., and Smith, C. (2009) 'Design and development of multimedia learning objects for mobile phones', in Ally, M. (ed.), *Mobile Learning: Transforming the Delivery of Education and Training*, Edmonton, Athabasca University Press, pp. 157–82.

Browne, S. and Dixon, H. (2010) Case study: developing INFORMe, a suite of online information skills tutorials for Southampton Institute, using a constructivist approach to learning. Available from: *http://www.solent.ac.uk/library/informe/general/general/Case%20studyalfinal.doc* (accessed 5 May 2010).

Campbell, L. M. and Currier, S. (2005) 'Evaluating 5/99 content for reusability as learning objects', *Vine*, 35(1): 85–96.

Cardiff University (2010) Information Literacy Resource Bank. Available from: *https://ilrb.cf.ac.uk/* (accessed 4 May 2010).

Creative Commons (2010) CC in Education. Available from: *http://creativecommons.org/education* (accessed 4 May 2010).

Dewald, N. (1999) 'Transporting good library instruction practices into the Web environment: an analysis of online tutorials', *The Journal of Academic Librarianship*, 25(1): 26–32.

Dill, E. (2008) 'Do clickers improve library instruction? Lock in your answers now', *Journal of Academic Librarianship*, 34(6): 527–9.

Google Inc. (2010) Google Analytics. Available from: *www.google.co.uk/analytics* (accessed 4 May 2010).

Graham, N. and James, A.-M. (2007) 'Helping to drive independent learning: the BRUM project', *ALISS Quarterly*, 2(4): 32–4.

Graham, N. (2010) IL RLO Share wiki. Available from: *http://ilrloshare.wetpaint.com* (accessed 4 May 2010).

Graham, N., Mogg, R., and Siminson, N. (2009) LILAC 2009 group discussions. Available from: *http://ilrloshare.wetpaint .com/page/LILAC+2009+group+discussions* (accessed 10 May 2010).

Hunsaker, M., Howard, F., Liu, S. H., and Davis, J. (2009) 'Digital learning objects: A local response to the California State University System Initiative', *New Library World*, 110(3–4): 151–60.

Iiyoshi, T. and Kumar, M. S. V. (2008) 'Extending the Impact of Open Educational Resources through Alignment with Pedagogical Content Knowledge and Institutional Strategy: Lessons Learnt from the MERLOT Community Experience', in Iiyoshi, T. & Kumar, M. S. V., eds., *Opening up Education: The Collective Advancement of Education through Open Technology, Open Content and Open Knowledge*, Cambridge: MIT, pp. 181–95.

Information Literacy Group (2010) Information Literacy. Available from *www.informationliteracy.org.uk* (accessed 10 May 2010).

International Federation of Library Associations (IFLA) (2010) Information Literacy International Resources Directory. Available from: *http://infolitglobal.net/directory/ en/home* (accessed 5 May 2010).

Jackson, C. and Mogg, R. (2008) 'Supporting anti-plagiarism teaching with the Information Literacy Resource Bank', *ALISS Quarterly*, 3(3): 28–30.

Jennings, D. and Cashman, D. (2008) *Developing Reusable Learning Resources (RLRs)* Dublin: National Digital Learning Repository.

Joint Information Systems Committee (JISC) (2009) 5/99 projects webpage. Available from: *http://www.jisc.ac.uk/ whatwedo/programmes/learningteaching.aspx* (accessed 5 May 2010).

Joint Information Systems Committee (JISC) (2010) Open Educational Resources projects webpage. Available from: *http://www.jisc.ac.uk/oer* (accessed 5 May 2010).

Jorum (2010) Jorum website. Available from: *www.jorum .ac.uk* (accessed 4 May 2010).

Keller, P. and Mossink, W. (2008) Reuse of material in the context of education and research. Available from: *www.surffoundation.nl/en/publicaties* (accessed 17 March 2011), 1–32. SURFfoundation.

Library Network Support Services (LNSS) (2010) Library Network Support Services. Available from: *http://www.lit .ie/lnss/index.html* (accessed 4 May 2010).

LILAC (2010) Librarians Information Literacy Annual Conference 2010. Available from: *http://www .lilacconference.com/dw/programme/index.html* (accessed 7 May 2010).

Luo, L. (2009) 'Web 2.0 integration in information literacy instruction: an overview', *Journal of Academic Librarianship*, 36(1): 32–40.

Lynwood, W. and Flanders, D. (2006) 'From Montaigne to Orwell: the development of learning objects at Birkbeck College', *ALISS Quarterly*, 2(1): 23–6.

Mardis, L. A. and Ury, C. J. (2008) 'Innovation – An LO Library: Reuse of Learning Objects', *Reference Services Review*, 36(4): 389–413.

Massachusetts Institute of Technology (MIT) (2010) MIT Open Course Ware. Available from: *http://ocw.mit.edu/ OcwWeb/web/home/home/index.htm* (accessed 5 May 2010).

Matesic, M. A. and Adams, J. M. (2008). Provocation to learn – A study in the use of personal response systems in information literacy instruction', *Partnership: The Canadian Journal of Library and Information Practice and Research*, 3(1).

McGill, L., Currier, S., Duncan, C., & Douglas, P. (2008) Good Intentions report. Available from: *http://ie-repository.jisc.ac.uk/265/1/goodintentionspublic.pdf* (accessed 5 May 2010).

MERLOT (2010) Multimedia Educational Resource for Learning and Online Teaching (MERLOT) website. Available from: *http://www.merlot.org/merlot/index.htm* (accessed 5 May 2010).

National Digital Learning Repository (NDLR) (2010a) National Digital Learning Repository web site. Available from: *http://www.ndlr.ie/* (accessed 4 May 2010).

National Digital Learning Repository (NDLR) (2010b) Information Skills Community of Practice (ISCoP) website. Available from: *http://www.ndlr.ie/iscop/* (accessed 4 May 2010).

Newton, R., McConnell, M., and Sutton, A. (1998) 'Information skills for open learning: a public library initiative', *Library Review*, 47(2): 125.

Palmer, C. and Canaday, C. (2010) Plan and produce the Information Literacy Tutorial @ Your Library! Available from: *http://www.lilacconference.com/dw/programme/parallel_sessions_detail_4.html#12* (accessed 5 May 2010).

Sattar Chaudhry, A. and Khoo, C. S. G. (2008) 'Enhancing the quality of LIS education in Asia: organizing teaching materials for sharing and reuse', *New Library World*, 109(7–8): 354–65.

Skagen, T., Torras, M. C., Kavli, S. M. L., Mikki, S., Hafstad, S., and Hunskar, I. (2008) 'Pedagogical considerations in developing an online tutorial in information literacy', *Communications in Information Literacy*, 2(2): 84–98.

Smith, F. A. (2007) Games for teaching information literacy skills. *Library Philosophy and Practice (online journal)*,

2007 (April), available from: *http://unllib.unl.edu/LPP/f-smith.pdf*.

Smith, R. S. (2004) Guidelines for authors of learning objects. Available from: *http://archive.nmc.org/guidelines/NMC% 20LO%20Guidelines.pdf* (accessed 5 May 2010).

Society of College National and University Libraries (SCONUL) (1999) Information skills in higher education. Available from: *http://www.sconul.ac.uk/groups/ information_literacy/papers/Seven_pillars2.pdf* (accessed 5 May 2010).

Somoza-Fernandez, M. and Abadal, E. (2009) 'Analysis of web-based tutorials created by academic libraries', *Journal of Academic Librarianship*, 35(2): 126–31.

Staffordshire University (2010) Assignment Survival Kit. Available from: *http://www.staffs.ac.uk/ask/* (accessed 4 May 2010).

Tancheva, K. (2003) Online tutorials for library instruction: an ongoing project under constant revision. Available from: *http://www.ala.org/ala/mgrps/divs/acrl/events/pdf/ tancheva.pdf* (accessed 17 March 2011).

University of Leicester (2010) CORRE framework. Available from: *http://www2.le.ac.uk/departments/beyond-distance-research-alliance/projects/otter/about-oers/Corre-web.pdf* (accessed 4 May 2010).

University of Worcester (2010) Creatively Using Learning Technologies. Available from: *http://www.worcester.ac .uk/ils/cult/cult.html* (accessed 4 May 2010).

Wales, T. and Robertson, P. (2008) 'Captivating Open University students with online literature search tutorials created using screen capture software', *Program: Electronic Library and Information Systems*, 42(4): 365–81.

Walton, G. and Pope, A. (2010) Having a shufti: using student focus group findings to map unchartered territory in the information literacy landscape. Paper presented at LILAC

30 March 2010. Available from *http://www.lilacconference .com/dw/programme/Presentations/Tuesday/Wogan_Suite/ Walton_Pope_ask.pdf* (accessed 27 October 2010).

Whitsed, N. (2004) 'Learning and teaching', *Health Information and Libraries Journal*, 21: 201–5.

Wrathall, K. (2009) Study Methods and Information Literacy Exemplars (SMILE) Final Report. Available from: *http://www.jisc.ac.uk/media/documents/programmes/ elearningcapital/smilefinalreport.doc* (accessed 5 May 2010).

Yahoo! UK and Ireland (2010) Flickr Creative Commons. Available from: *http://www.flickr.com/creativecommons/* (accessed 4 May 2010).

Yang, S. (2009) 'Information literacy online tutorials: an introduction to rationale and technological tools in tutorial creation', *The Electronic Library*, 27(4): 684–93.

7

Spielberg your way to information literacy: producing educational movies and videos

Gareth Johnson

Abstract: This chapter looks at how simple it has become for library staff with even the most inexpensive of equipment to create effective promotional, marketing or instructional videos. It first examines the various roles that movies can play, from complementing elements of taught sessions through to reinforcement of learning or marketing goals with external readers. As well as considering the production of bespoke video works, it also considers the trade-offs in outsourcing elements of the production process and making use of off-the-shelf movies. Tips on selling the benefits of film making and pitching film concepts to potentially sceptical stakeholders and managers are also covered.

The main part of the chapter takes the prospective producer from their original concept and pre-production planning activities, through the scripting, filming, editing, reviewing and evaluation processes. The importance of maintaining a clear narrative vision throughout the whole process is stressed as an important central theme. Guidance is included on the key team roles and responsibilities, along with scripting and plotting templates as a production aid. Additionally, a focus is placed on making maximum advantage of the visual delivery medium by utilising action, rather than relying on dialogue alone to convey information.

Consideration is given throughout to illustrating the common pitfalls and obstacles that can frustrate the would-be producer, and the easy steps that can be taken to overcome them. Short examples of film projects are used to illustrate real world examples of the how the production techniques can be applied. Particular attention is drawn to the time and staffing resource requirements to successfully complete a filming project.

A selection of advice on suitable equipment and software, a glossary of specialised terms and a range of suggested further readings and exemplar viewings are provided at the end of the chapter.

Key words: video, production, library, edutainment, planning, multimedia.

Introduction

The advent and availability of inexpensive but impressive video cameras and powerful yet accessible suites of editing software in recent years has placed the ability to produce movies in the hands of any educator. The question has shifted from 'Should I be making films as part of my training?' to 'Why aren't I making films?' If the answer to the second question is lack of experience, uncertainty about the process and the practical steps; then welcome potential Spielberg.

However, just because you are able to produce a film does not necessarily mean it will be an effective information literacy delivery method. In this chapter we will examine the process and forethought needed to produce video outputs that will compliment effective teaching. We will explore the process from initial concept to final screening, using readily understandable underpinnings of film theory and production; guiding you through the creation of your own first videos. For those advanced producers who have already dabbled in the celluloid arts hopefully the guidance will help refine your techniques.

While in a single chapter there is a limit to what can be covered, hopefully through following these guidelines, and with appetites whetted, you will soon be producing satisfying educational videos.

Using videos

Videos can serve a number of purposes within all kinds of information literacy or staff training sessions. We will be primarily looking at them as a complementary component of taught classes, although viewed in isolation they can still act as valuable training objects. The ways in which videos can be brought into play successfully are detailed in Table 7.1.

Reflect back on recent classes you have led. Chances are one or more of the uses shown in Table 7.1 should fit the bill and should go a way towards answering key educational needs within your own teaching. Even if you are somewhat sceptical about the use of visual media in this way, try it and evaluate your audience's reaction; you may be pleasantly surprised.

Attention and length

A slight caveat, as with all educational approaches videos will not connect with every audience member. However, for other participants the same might be true for long demonstrations or hands-on sessions or workbooks. As a further weapon in your educational arsenal, videos will allow you to pitch your teaching to a broader range of learning preferences, delivering improved retention of training outcomes.

Table 7.1 The seven video roles

Relaxation	Introducing a session with a video provides an ice-breaker for audiences expecting to hear a *dull library* talk. This will counter preconceptions and warmed up they will be more receptive to your subsequent teaching.
Reinforce	Illustrate concepts that you will talk about during the session. By exploring them from two differing perspectives you will connect with a wider portion of your audience.
Respite	Using a film to break up a lecture allows the trainer to take a moment, gather their thoughts and to reflect on any student questions or concerns that have arisen.
Refocus	Similarly a shift of focus has been shown to aid audience attention. Changing format from speaker to screen and then back again will refresh attention to a considerable degree; enhancing impact and retention.
Re-usable	Once created it will be possible to reuse videos repeatedly. As you become skilled in producing films you may find creating even a small library of them, without sell-by-dates to their content, will enable their regular reuse.
Remote	Videos can serve as vodcasts, mounted on your website and accessed by learners at their leisure. Especially beneficial for any students studying outside their native language or wishing to revisit key elements.

Throughout this chapter the focus is on short videos, of around five minutes duration. Why no longer? Again, attention span is key here. The longer a non-interactive video continues, the greater the risk of attention drop-off. As you will see in the 'Concept' section both brevity and impact of your core message are linked.

Bespoke vs reusing

While we are concerned with the production of custom videos there is no reason why you should not make use of the vast collection of materials produced by other librarians and educationalists. Sites such as YouTube and educational sites such as Jorum Open and institutional repositories are rich sources of films for easy reuse. Explore them, seek colleagues' recommendations or see the Videography for a few initial suggestions. Even if you want to make customised videos but feel you lack the time or resources to create them yourself, this does not rule out bespoke creation. See, the sections on 'Filming' and 'Editing' for more on how to outsource elements of production.

Pre-production

Before we look at outlining concepts, it is important to familiarise yourself with an overview of the film-making process (see Table 7.2). This pre-production phase usually takes minutes, although it may take longer the first time. The question to answer here is 'Am I prepared to devote time and effort to make a video?' Assuming the answer is *yes* then yourself, and a small team, should be able to take the first practical steps into the production process.

The process of producing a short educational movie is in many regards not dissimilar to that for longer movies. As with all good formulas it is important to start at the beginning and work through each phase sequentially, resisting the temptation to jump ahead. You will find the phases interlock in a complementary progression and your final product will consequently be more polished and professional.

Table 7.2 Production phases

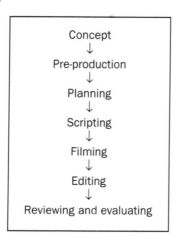

Concept
↓
Pre-production
↓
Planning
↓
Scripting
↓
Filming
↓
Editing
↓
Reviewing and evaluating

Too many would-be library movie moguls jump directly to filming, and then wonder why their editing steps are hellish, their narrative garbled or audience reviews so negative. By working through this process your outputs will be superior, with as little time wasted as possible.

Time commitment

One of the most common questions a new film-maker, or their manager, has is 'How long will this take?' Moving from initial idea to final product will take a non-trivial portion of time, especially initially. With experience some steps, such as scripting, will become faster exercises. Others, such as editing, may actually take longer as you bring to bear more of the tools and special effects that your software allows. Since each film-maker will take a variable period of time to accomplish them let's illustrate this with an example:

Example 1: Good book hunting

James, a first time movie maker, intends to make a three-minute video illustrating a student performing a poor catalogue search for books, followed by another performing a superior search in support of an essay. Each will be filmed performing a couple of searches along with reaction shots respective to their relative successes. Finally, the video is bookended by James talking to camera, highlighting the lessons learned.

There are maybe a dozen separate shots in this film, three actors to organise, one of whom is doubling as producer and director, along with a camera operator. For James to go from start to finish would likely take the time shown in Table 7.3. Nearly 12 hours might seem a lot of time, although it is less than two working days. Some of the commitment can be split across other members of the team so that one person will not carry the whole burden. However, these are sequential rather than parallel steps, and some stages (editing and reviewing) can often involve more than one person in the process, so the team's **total** commitment may exceed 12 hours.

It might be possible to reduce the time James spends on each of these steps, although there is one likely outcome from

Table 7.3 Time commitment

Production stage	Anticipated commitment
Planning	1 hour
Concept	30 minutes
Scripting	2 hours
Filming	2–3 hours
Editing	2 hours
Reviewing and evaluating	2 hours

this skimping. The final product will be less than satisfactory and he may need to re-shoot, re-write or re-edit in order to save the video. James might be able to revive the project from what he has already shot, but would probably end up investing yet more time on it. Haste, makes a waste of his time.

Convincing your managers

While you might be keen to use video, given the required time commitments you will need to obtain senior or line management buy in. As with any new development it is important to be able to stress the benefits, not solely to your teaching practice but to the organisation's goals and activities (as shown in Table 7.4). Hopefully, you will get to make your pitch face to face. Be prepared to make a simple business case keeping in mind the points shown in Table 7.4.

Table 7.4   Pitching to management

Be proactive
- Present an outline plan, including time and personnel requirements
- Stress future teaching time savings
- Indicate value added to library services

Sell your concept
- Highlight educational benefits offered
- Demonstrate how it answers student demands
- Indicate service marketing opportunities

Stay positive
- Even in the face of lacklustre responses
- Keep them onside for future endeavours

Accept knock-backs
- Try again as another opportunity emerges

It may well be that you might want to go ahead and make a video in your own time. Even without management's initial blessings this kind of *guerrilla librarianship* can deliver dividends. Now you can demonstrate real production experience, a strong awareness of actual time commitment and perhaps a favourable audience response as a demonstration of feasibility.

Concept

Every film starts with an idea. Every great film starts with a concise concept. Knowing what you want to communicate is essential in ensuring your video actually has a clear message that your audience can take away. The very best educational films have this message embedded in every moment.

There is a temptation to cram videos full of information, which is the complete converse of what your audience will be able to digest. Video is a non-interrogative medium with a limited engagement span, thus message clarity is very important. Many library-produced videos have generalised or vague core concepts and the muddy results are neither engaging nor particularly effective education. Take Caroline's idea:

> **Example 2: Caroline's confused pitch**
> Our video will be about how important it is for students to think about searching lots of different resources, how to access ebooks and the new mobile phone application that the systems team has written. Oh, and it will also explain which referencing style is the most practical one for students.

Good luck getting all that across succinctly in just five minutes! Chances are the resultant video from Caroline's pitch would be muddled, rushed and unsatisfying for her audience. Your core message must ring out from every scene. There is simply too much information in a idea like Caroline's to convey in a short time-frame. Thankfully there is a simple tool that can help.

The pitch

In Hollywood they believe in the *25 words or less* movie pitch; that is any good film can be boiled down to a short concept (see Table 7.5). This effective tool helps to ensure that your idea is a solid one and can be communicated within the brevity of a video. It will also help sell your proposal to key stakeholders such as management. Let us illustrate how this approach works with some real movies.

While these potted concepts do not give the full details, they do give you the distilled essence of these films. Enshrining this kind of clarity in your production will aid in shaping the script by helping identify what is truly relevant in your visual narrative and provide a benchmark for reviewers to evaluate against. Table 7.6 shows some library examples.

Table 7.5   Film concepts

Concept	Film
All of reality is a computer game, but someone has the cheat codes.	*The Matrix*
Biography of a rise and fall of a small time hood, and the lives he touches.	*Goodfellas*
Classic fantasy tale of noble heroes and heroines against evil overlords and their fortress of terror; in space!	*Star Wars*
Respected man and only possible suspect tries to prove he did not murder his wife as he flees unstoppable and dogged pursuit.	*The Fugitive*

Table 7.6	Library concepts

Dressing appropriately for the job means that customers will treat staff with respect.

Boolean operators are powerful tools, and can save students time and effort to find articles.

Using the library catalogue to renew books will save you money, but only you have the power to do it!

Now think of what you want to communicate in a film. Write it down, *in 25 words or less*. If it takes more than 25 words, chances are you are trying to cram too much in. Better to split these ideas across multiple videos.

Now you are clear on what your audience should take away from watching, it is time to start planning the details.

Planning

Fail to plan? Then plan to fail. It's a maxim that applies to video making as much as other endeavours in life. Now you have committed to making a film it is essential to first gather your team, set a production schedule and set a semblance of a project plan in place. This helps ensure that you will deliver a product to the satisfaction of yourselves and your stakeholders.

Roles and responsibilities

Educational video making works well as a team process from bouncing ideas off each other to assisting in the overall production process (see Table 7.7). Like any project it will work more smoothly where people accept clearly defined

Table 7.7	Production roles
Role	**Responsibility**
Producer	Oversees and drives entire film making process. Troubleshoots problems where necessary. Coordinates support for other roles.
Director	Organises film shoot. Directs cast and camera operator. Sorts set, props and shooting locations.
Script writer	Plots, writes and revises script. On-hand to advise on scripting issues during shoot.
Camera operator	Films video. Assists director during shoot.
Editor	Splices filmed segments together in scripted sequence. Edits audio and visual effects. Works with producer to ensure final product is as desired.
Cast	Appear on screen and enact your video.
Production assistants	Multitasking team members working where the producer applies them.
Investors	Management and other stakeholders keep a close eye on the time invested.

roles, ensuring activities are completed in a timely and successful manner.

The producer is the most crucial role, driving forward the whole process and overseeing the work of others. Commonly in small teams this role is merged with that of the director. It is possible for one person to embody all of these roles, although this will increase the pressure upon them. As with all projects, a small team will ease the producer's burden, allowing the producer to take a more high-level overall quality control viewpoint. For those unwilling to take on a named role, assume they have taken on the task of production assistants: willing helpers to all of the other key production staff.

With roles agreed and plans in place it is time for the producer to move the team into the next phase, script writing.

Scripting

Think about your favourite film. What is it that engages you, the audience member, in its narrative? Is it the characters, plot, genre or dramatic performances? Chances are, while the answer will be different for each reader, all of your chosen works will have one thing in common – they hooked you from the start, drawing you in. The counterpoint to the hook is the sting – the final moment or line of a movie that drives a point home or reinforces what you were trying to communicate. Therefore it is the opening and closing lines of dialogue that you must focus the most attention on getting just right.

You don't need to know a lot about screen writing, though it might help a little. Just remember to always write with your intended audience in mind. Carefully consider brevity, clarity, punch and message; as well as terminology and language. Where possible try and use naturalistic spoken phraseology and syntax, rather than formal language; although you should minimise slang.

Scripting layout

Laying out a script (see Table 7.8) may be a little different to anything you have written previously. You may also be astonished by how few words (perhaps 200) you can have your actors speak on screen in a three-minute script. Visuals

Table 7.8   Script layout

[Title]

[Opening credits/title]

INT/EXT   [Location] [Day/Night]

[SCENE] *Details of set/scene layout*
[SHOT] *Instructions for camera & director*
[SFX] *Music or visual effects*

[SPEAKER]
Spoken words. (*emphasis*)

[Transition] *Cut to next scene*

[End credits]

[© Notice]

-End-

and action will have impact on your audience beyond the spoken narrative which supports a brevity of spoken word.

The following is an example of a simple screen writing format, that should be readily comprehensible to your team. This layout format will mean one script page equates to approximately one minute of screen time.

Let us illustrate this with a script extract (see Table 7.9) to give you an idea of how this might look on the page.

You do not need to follow this style exactly and you will likely develop your own house style, but it should help in laying out your earliest scripts. It also illustrates how much more than simple dialogue makes up a script, since actions, sets and camera directions all play a part. Let us explore how to plan out a good script.

Table 7.9 Extract: Librarians dress for success

INT   Different library. DAY

[**SCENE**] *Ruined landscape and dead animals everywhere – burning flames/smoke if possible tracking across the scene.*

[**SHOT**] *WIDE tracking from R->L, then cut to close ups of dead animals*

[**SFX**] *Clanging sad/haunting tune*

NARRATOR
(mournful)

The librarians of Mountsorrel Community Library didn't think the dress code was important. Too late they learned that their patrons no longer respected them, or the library code.

[**SHOT**] *Close up on Library Code of Practice – burned and tattered*

NARRATOR
(continued)

Chaos was inevitable. Do you want to know more?

[**ON SCREEN TEXT**] *Do you want to know more? (Green lurid font)*

[**Transition**] *Fade through*

INT   Another library (2) with busy workers. DAY

[**SFX**] *Shift to more upbeat main theme music*

NARRATOR
(encouraging)

Dressing correctly demonstrates to our customers the respect in which we hold them.

Plotting

Put simply, plot is the sequence of events that will occur in your video and will be used to guide the dialogue and actions performed by the cast. How you plan out your plot is up to you. A list of scenes is easy enough, or if you are artistic you might prefer to storyboard them as a series of illustrations. Alternatively you can use the following template approach (see Table 7.10). Planning out each scene and establishing resource requirements for the shoot can also save the director and camera operator time later.

Large *post-it* notes are ideal for recording this sort of detail. These can be arranged to help plan out the ·plot sequence visually, and should you want to re-order the events of your video they can be easily rearranged. A plot outline for one of James' Example 1 scenes might look like the one shown in Table 7.11.

Table 7.10   Plotting template

Scene [X]	
Activity	Cast
Location	Resources

Table 7.11   Example scene

Scene 3	
Activity	Cast
Searches catalogue with random key words and guesses, with poor results.	Tim – poor searcher, slovenly dressed
Location	Resources
Floor 1 catalogue terminals	None – other than actors and crew.

With each scene plotted in this way James can easily plan out the half-dozen or so that make up his video's narrative. However you prefer to approach it, once you are happy with the event sequence it is time to write the dialogue.

Dialogue

While it may be the visual cues and actions on screen that carry your narrative forward, it is dialogue that will punctuate the situations and give them context. Always write the dialogue before you decide on the actions or camera work, otherwise you may find it hard to make it flow naturally. Aside from the hook and sting the flow of dialogue is important to maintain your audience's attention.

The easiest construction to aid this flow is the question and answer technique between two characters, mirroring many real world conversations. In practice this might look like this:

> **Example 3: Q&A**
> **HUGH**
> How does the catalogue help me?
>
> **MAY**
> It lists all the books the library has, and it's easy to use too.
>
> **HUGH**
> Really? I had a real problem last time I tried to use it.
>
> **MAY**
> Don't worry. I'll show you how you can save time and get better results too.

In this way you can see how this example video would continue into a demonstration of good searching techniques.

Questions and answers mirror the audience's thoughts which will help their engagement with your message.

Pacing

For education videos speech needs to be delivered at a steady pace, a little slower than normal conversation. This will limit the number of words you can use in a script. Don't worry about this when you write the initial draft, but when you come to revise it try focusing on brevity and impact. A more staccato pattern, such as in Example 3 works better than long expository passages. Aim ideally for between 150–200 words in total.

Edutainment

A touch of light educational comedy (or *edutainment*) can improve a video's impact significantly. Conversely an utterly straight-laced approach will diminish the audience's attention span and engagement with your topic. Humour offers in many respects as powerful a communication tool as does rhetoric or repetition within an information literacy setting. More importantly within a video it offers three key advantages for your message: engaging the audience's interest, making messages memorable and subjects more digestible. In this way humour will deliver serious audience engagement and recall dividends.

Action

However powerful your dialogue is, a video script needs to show more than just a pair of heads talking to camera. One of the major advantages of video is that you can take your audience to locations, times, and circumstances beyond that which they would be able to experience within a lecture hall. It also needs to include any actions, locations and special effects you anticipate using. The maxim *show don't tell* is key here; it takes more dialogue to *describe* how short loans can be borrowed than to simply *show* it in action. With lecture slides you do not put every word up on screen to be read, because you are talking about the topic as well. In the same way a video will be able to show how to accomplish something without a speaker having to explain it all in words.

Visual shorthand or cliché can be a useful tool here. For James it could be an effective shorthand to have his poor and good searchers dressed slovenly and smartly respectively along with a note in the script for the former to slouch and their counterpart to sit neatly. A large amount of information will now have been communicated to the audience about their respective approaches without a word being uttered.

Video is a medium that is predicated on movement. Static shots of people standing and talking are visual poison to an audience. Show people entering a room, reacting to their situations and other speakers and carrying out the activities you are demonstrating. It will save on your dialogue budget and convey your message effectively. Otherwise you may as well forget the video and simply lecture to your audience.

Even if you feel you cannot engage with a humorous approach do make the most of the dynamic video medium. At the very least try and avoid the mundane talking head to camera paradigm and you will find that your audience will respond positively.

Polishing

By now your script should be full of engaging dialogue and well thought out sequential actions which all convey your core message. The most effective way to discover if your dialogue works is to have it read aloud by someone unconnected with your project. Does it flow? Are there moments that lack clarity? Did your attention wander? Take these perceptions away and revise your script to tighten up the dialogue. Rehearse it with your cast and make any final minor modifications.

Once done it is time to take your narrative and capture it on camera.

Filming

Shooting a video short is not brain surgery, although a steady hand or a camera tripod are a must. Let's examine some key shooting elements.

Location, location, location

You may well expect to shoot most of your videos in library-related locations. If you have in mind something a bit different be prepared to get filming permission. Public places can limit the times at which you can film without interference from passersby, although having a production assistant keeping onlookers back can be invaluable. If your script calls for a more unusual setting, then it will be up to the producer and director to come to a realistic compromise if it is unavailable locally.

The first time you use a location, shoot some test footage and then view it. Does the POV (point of view) of the audience take in too much or too little of the set? How well lit does it appear? Is it difficult to make out your cast against the background? How does the dialogue sound? With these thoughts in mind the director can then make the final decisions about the locations used and the set-up.

Sets and set-up

Many of your sets will need little dressing or set-up, for example filming scenes set at an issuing desk, although you will need to allow room for actors to enter and leave the frame of your shot.

It can be easier to substitute a mock-up location than use a real one. Seminar and meeting rooms can be easily redressed with desks, lecterns and other props to imitate other areas with the advantage that you will not be interrupted mid-scene by a passing customer. The relative privacy can help coax less confident members of your cast into better performances. You also should not have to worry about keeping the noise down so much either.

Wherever possible avoid busy backgrounds. Library shelves may be visual shorthand for the library, but they can be a distraction if the focus of that scene is on the speaker. Simple cloth or wall backdrops ensure the viewer's focus is on your cast's situation, and not trying to read the titles of books behind them.

Shooting footage

Good camera work comes from operator experience, as much as good direction. Make sure you frame the speakers centrally, keep the shots steady and remember the maxim: shoot once, shoot twice, shoot thrice. Chances are at least some takes will be of inferior quality. Re-shoots can be problematic in terms of getting your cast back together or even accessing your filming location again. Through capturing multiple takes, the editor will be able to splice the movie together from a choice selection of shots.

Lighting

Illuminating a set well is key since most camcorders will struggle with even the best office lighting. Without good lighting camera auto-focus will struggle and your final product will look gloomy and unappetising. Obtaining a free-standing spotlight will help enhance visual quality and multiple spotlights can help eliminate shadows behind your subjects giving a more professional on-screen look. Be wary of directly lighting reflective surfaces as glare may ruin the shot.

Strong back-lighting, like a window, can wipe out any clear impression of your cast so be cautious filming near them. Exterior shooting introduces additional lighting complexities that there is not room to cover here. However, for most interior shoots it is sufficient to light locations to minimise shadows, illuminate the focus of attention and ensure the cast can be clearly differentiated from the background.

Cast

In an ideal world your cast would be word perfect, have memorised your script and have a background in amateur dramatics. In reality you may well have to make do with whomever of your colleagues are available. They must be able to speak clearly and audibly, prepared to repeat actions and lines; and crucially prepared to listen and respond to the director's instructions.

Be prepared to be a patient but firm director as you uncover the divas in your midst. Working with peers can be difficult if you have not defined responsibilities at the outset. Persuade rather than order, but remember it is the director's goal to deliver the shoot as required from the script and so the whole production team should be prepared to back them up. If you make sure your cast know what you expect from them, fewer tantrums, a more professional work ethic and a smoother shoot will result.

Outsourcing or Do-It-Yourself?

You may have a choice between filming yourself or making use of organisational audiovisual assets, though there are pros and cons in either case. Outsourcing means you can draw on superior equipment and experience, likely ending up with a more polished final product. On the downside you will need to slot filming and editing sessions around their timetables. It is also possible that they will not have quite the same creative vision which in a worst case scenario might necessitate re-filming portions yourself.

Keeping the whole process in-house means you will retain a much stronger creative control of the final product. It might not look quite as polished but you can be sure few of your audience will notice. It also allows you to be more adaptable to your cast's availability and to any last minute script revisions. Drawbacks include a need for initial outlay on equipment, and the time to become familiar with it to film and edit the video. The choice is something you need to carefully consider in pre-production.

Whatever your approach, once all the key scenes have been captured it is time to edit them into your final video.

Editing

Editing takes time, care and attention to detail but it is a rewarding role to produce the video from the raw shooting footage. If someone else is editing your shoot then there is no need for you to learn the software packages; although you will need to regularly view their rough cuts to ensure that the visual narrative matches your aspirations. Don't be afraid to ask them to recut it; many a potentially good educational movie can be ruined by third parties editing the shoot to match their vision. Nothing is worse than suddenly discovering the day before your premier that the video needs a complete re-edit. If you edit yourself then you will need to become familiar with the software. Attend training, read the manual, find a good website or get someone who is experienced to take you through the basics.

If you have never edited a film together before, then it is best to start small and short, since more complex scripts make for longer, and more frustrating, editing processes. For each minute of final screen time it will probably take initially around an hour of editing time to produce a reasonably polished product, although speed comes with experience. Adding visual or audio effects, multiple shot angles and even cutting between speakers all increases process complexity and editing time. Let us consider an example:

Example 4: Hunting for searching success

A 90 second video involving 20 lines of dialogue between two speakers discussing the importance of well constructed search strategies set to a royalty free soundtrack. Each speaker is shot separately in close up, along with a wide angle establishing shot.

In this short video the editor will need to make a number of cuts, working with the director to ensure everything looks okay before making the final version. As a rough estimate there are at least 42 visual cuts needed here, on screen titles, credits and any audio adjustments to ensure that speakers can be heard. Only once these are done can the final cut be produced.

Splicing

Step one of any edit is to take the raw footage and arrange it in sequence of the scripted scenes. Here the plot outline and script can be valuable references. Glance through the footage to ensure that at least one take from each scene is of usable quality. If not let the director know as soon as possible that they will need to reshoot.

Selecting

The next step is to select which of the multiple takes you will use in the final film. Once you have cut out the unused takes you will have the very first rough cut. Do not worry about exact timings or silence between scenes as you will refine these later. Screen this rough cut for the director and team to give them an idea of the final product. If some scenes need to be re-shot then this is a decision best taken sooner rather than later.

Fine edit

Once the team are broadly satisfied the editor will refine the rough cut and will trim footage around the dialogue, remove silence and irrelevant moments and ensure a strong and engaging visual narrative. While high action drama may cut the viewer's POV every three seconds, shots of 20–30 seconds are quite acceptable in an educational video, although the editor may introduce additional cuts for timing and flow if judged appropriate. You might wish to cut a scene up into several shots, perhaps inter-cutting a speaker with reaction shots of someone listening. This is a more advanced technique, but looks excellent on screen.

An almost imperceptible pause of a second is needed between the end of each speaker's line and any response; otherwise the audience will find it hard to follow the conversation's thread. Where speakers are on screen at the same time and there is no gap, it is possible to slow the footage down or insert an interstitial shot to provide the necessary pause for the audience to process the speech.

Where a speaker's line has been poorly recorded or delivered, but the visual is strong, it is possible to overdub replacement dialogue. This works well in distanced shots as matching mouth movements in close up is hard. This is one of the ways in which an editor can rescue a video from minor shooting flaws.

SFX

Most training videos do not call for extensive special effects. However, you may wish to strengthen your on-screen presentation through the addition of scene transitions, video effects, captions, subtitling, music or sound effects. These can enhance the viewer's engagement if used well. They will detract from your message if overused; like too many PowerPoint animations. Use sparingly for maximum effect, remembering that each one will add complexity and time to the editing process.

Still images with voice-over can be used to occasionally illustrate points, but overuse will make your video look more like a narrated slide-show. Using text captions over your scenes to highlight points, complementing the cast's actions on screen, is a better approach.

Final cut

Once your edits for time and quality are made, credits and captions positioned and any special effects added it is time to output the final video. Produce this in two sized formats: a compact web-ready version for swift downloading and a larger high quality version. This higher quality version will be the one used in face-to-face lectures and archived for long-term storage; and the one you will present to your stakeholders and students for review.

Reviewing and evaluating

Before you go live with the video in a taught class it is worth showing the final cut to a small assembled audience. If time permits you might have been able to do this during the editing process, but if not this is the final opportunity for the team and stakeholders to provide constructive criticism. Oral feedback is useful but a questionnaire (see Table 7.12) can help in recording detailed comments.

Be prepared for criticism as much as praise. At this late stage, if the reaction is entirely negative it is more effective to start the production process again rather than waste hours attempting to re-edit what you have already shot into a passable product. Where there are minor comments on timing or audibility of dialogue or clarity of message, do go back and make minor revisions.

Table 7.12   Screening review questionnaire

In no more than 10 words – what impact did the video make on you?
What were the strongest features of the video?
What elements of the video could have been improved?
What message was the video trying to convey?

With these made it is time to celebrate your endeavours with the other team members. However, it is not the end of the process because now you must deploy the video in the role for which it was created: within an information literacy session.

Evaluating

As you premiere your video to a live classroom audience, take a moment to reflect back on how much you will have achieved by this point. Remember not all of your audiences will love your video so be prepared for some critical reactions. Learn from their reactions to your screening as well as their comments afterwards. Observe them as they watch the movie. Which bits resonate with them? Where do they smile? Where do they react? Where do they appear not to be watching? All of these insights will become invaluable guidance in producing your *next* video project!

Next steps

Hopefully your next step will be to start planning work on creating your own films. You may well be lucky enough to have access to filming equipment and expertise through your audiovisual departments. You might not, or may just decide it is more practical to have your own in-house filming equipment.

Cameras

Read some of the popular electronics review magazines, such as *Which?* and *What Digital Camera*, before trying to identify what is suitable. A few hundred pounds will buy a camcorder sufficient for your filming needs, and even a 'Flip Video Camcorder' can produce reasonable quality results. Born-digital (hard-drive or flash) is an easier format to work with since there is less physical media (discs, tape, etc.) lying around and you never have the problem of forgetting to load the camera and then losing a session's shooting. It is also simple to transfer camera footage onto computers or network drives.

Preferably obtain a camcorder with an optical as well as digital zoom and make sure it has a name brand lens (like *Zeiss*) as your results will be significantly sharper. You can invest in other add-ons like microphones if you like and while not essential it can be worth future-proofing your purchase by making sure there are compatible peripherals available.

There are a lot of places to buy cameras and filming equipment from and online retailers probably offer the broadest selection and range of prices, alongside helpful user reviews. You might even be able to take advantage of organisational deals with local firms.

Software

Editing software is relatively inexpensive and may be already available locally. The Corel VideoStudio packages are excellent, but Adobe Premier, Microsoft Moviemaker or iMovie might well suit your needs just as well. They all offer user friendly interfaces allowing for easy editing, and graduated discovery of more advanced functionality. You can practically go from installation to editing your first video within minutes.

Final thoughts

Hopefully this chapter has offered a few words of guidance for those of you looking to create your own educational, promotional or otherwise illuminating videos. You will probably have your own ideas about where you want to explore next. It is only a starting point and there will be much to learn through hands-on experience. Experiment as you become more confident with your equipment, cast and locations, and soon you will be producing quality and high impact information literacy-enhancing videos.

Golden rules

Some final tips to remember when producing your own films:

- Sell your idea to obtain management buy-in.
- Commit sufficient time to all stages of production.
- Keep the concept and message in mind throughout production.
- Get someone to read scripts out loud to identify dialogue problems.
- Do not let your background detract or distract from your intended focal point.

- Keep it light, keep it bright, keep it clear – get some spotlights.
- Shoot multiple takes to avoid lengthy re-shoots.
- Screen rough cuts as soon as possible for comment.
- Produce web-ready and high archival quality final versions.
- Do not be afraid to experiment.

Glossary

Establishing shot – wide-angled shot used to establish the location and characters present.

Final cut – final master version of your video.

Hook – opening line or visual/audio cue that grabs the viewer's attention.

POV – short for *Point of View*, the viewer's perspective as framed by the film-maker's camera.

Rough cut – unfinished video assembled in scene order without exact timings or effects. Reviewed to establish if shot footage is adequate to the task.

Shoot – the process of filming your video.

Shooting script – final version of the script including camera directions, set details and any special effects required.

Sting – closing line or visual/audio cue that underscores a video's message.

Visual narrative – the message the video conveys in a structured and understandable sequence.

Vodcast – the use of video as a downloadable, rewatchable information resource.

Suggested further reading

Costello, John (2006) *Writing a Screenplay*, 2nd edn, Pocket Essentials.

Cresswell, Julia (2000) *The Penguin Dictionary of Clichés*, London: Penguin Group.

Frensham, Raymond G. (1996) *Screenwriting*, London: Hodder Headline Plc.

Johnson, G. J. (2009) Weaselling your way into your student's hearts, CILIP Umbrella, University of Hartforshire, online at: *http://www.slideshare.net/GazJJohnson/weaseling-your-way-into-your-students-hearts-1735226* (accessed 13/7/09).

Johnson, G. J. (2009) The Weasel That Roared: Creating and using effective promotional educational videos for libraries and information services. University of Staffordshire workshop, Online at: *http://tinyurl.com/o9kf3g*.

Johnson, G. J. (2008) The Weasel Dialogues. UC&R/CoFHE Joint Conference, Liverpool Hope. Online at: *http://www.slideshare.net/GazJJohnson/the-weasel-dialogues* (accessed 8/5/10).

Johnson, G. J. (2010) Puppetry For Information Literacy Videos?! AOSEC Winter Workshop, Portsmouth, online at: *http://www.slideshare.net/GazJJohnson/puppetry-for-information-literacy-videos* (accessed 8/5/10).

Muchnick, A. (2004) When Pancakes Go Bad: Optical Delusions with Adobe Photoshop, Course Technology PTR.

Novelly, Maria C. (1985) *Theatre Games for Young Performers*, Meriweather Publishing Ltd, Colorado Springs.

Wikipedia (2009) Comedy, online at: *http://en.wikipedia.org/wiki/Comedy* (accessed 27/5/09).

Videography

Better Library Inductions for New Readers & Students, online at: *http://www.youtube.com/watch?v=nYRQ4KLlyMw* (accessed 24/5/10).

Boolean Logic & Database Searching, online at: *http://www.youtube.com/watch?v=enPSOq1_QmY* (accessed 24/5/10).

Common Craft, online at: *http://www.commoncraft.com/* (accessed 24/5/10).

Explaining Twitter Simply, online at: *http://www.youtube.com/watch?v=G4__htJ-IdU* (accessed 24/5/10).

Handling difficult customers, online at: *http://www.youtube.com/watch?v=z3Jud4b9ik0* (accessed 24/5/10).

How to Evaluate Websites

☐ Part 1: Reliability & Relevance, online at: *http://www.youtube.com/watch?v=lrXNCj9n6e4* (accessed 24/5/10)

☐ Part 2: Currency & Purpose, online at: *http://www.youtube.com/watch?v=PYV3ZmThuIs* (accessed 24/5/10)

☐ Part 3: Accuracy, Evidence & Presentation, online at: *http://www.youtube.com/watch?v=ta1RMXVOig0* (accessed 24/5/10).

Learning objects: Movies and demonstrations, online at: *http://ilrb.cf.ac.uk/bank_type/demos.html* (accessed 24/5/10).

Librarians vs UFOs, online at: *http://www.youtube.com/watch?v=kdWUxV1F054* (accessed 24/5/10).

Librarians Dress to Impress: appropriate attire in the library, online at: *http://www.youtube.com/watch?v=otCRqwHvEYk* (accessed 24/5/10).

Professor Weasel goes on a Mandate, online at: *http://www.youtube.com/watch?v=MBdM_0pfyQ8* (accessed 24/5/10).

Understanding Academic Copyright, online at: *http://www.youtube.com/watch?v=7giW7efQggo* (accessed 24/5/10).

University of Liverpool Library's Videos, online at: *http://tinyurl.com/24wmxok* (accessed 24/5/10).

Part 3
Obesity, overload and opportunity

8

Information literacy and noöpolitics

Andrew Whitworth

Abstract: This chapter extends a resource-based analysis of politics, or 'geopolitics', into the sphere of information, producing a perspective that has been called 'noöpolitics'. Control over information's production, accessibility, dissemination and even meaning are conduits for the transmission of cultural hegemony, and noöpolitics also sheds light on how we can be excluded from informational spaces within organisations, and how our working lives and social relationships can be managed through information. These all give rise to competing notions of value. As information literacy is fundamentally about assigning value to information sources, the IL educator must be aware of noöpolitics. The question of what information literacy is for can be analysed as a political question. Contradictions and conflicts may arise between different possible answers to the question. These may give rise to political issues, which could prevent the politics of IL being manifested.

Key words: informational resources, noöpolitics, values, exclusion, hegemony, information literacy.

When one watches some tired hack on the platform mechanically repeating the familiar phrases – *bestial atrocities, iron heel, bloodstained tyranny, free peoples of the world, stand shoulder to shoulder* – one often has a curious feeling that one is not watching a live human being but some kind of dummy. . . . The appropriate noises are coming out of his larynx, but his brain is not involved as it would be if he were choosing his words for himself. If the speech he is making is one that he is accustomed to make over and over again, he may be almost unconscious of what he is saying, as one is when one utters the responses in church. And this reduced state of consciousness, if not indispensable, is at any rate favourable to political conformity.

George Orwell, *Politics and the English Language* (1957, pp. 152–153)

Introduction

This chapter continues a debate I first engaged with in a chapter published in the collection, *Change and Challenge* (Whitworth 2007) and then with my book, *Information Obesity* (Whitworth 2009a). It will summarise ideas I developed in these earlier publications, but not revisit them in depth: interested readers should turn to one of these other works for the necessary detail.

Here, my intention is to take a more explicitly political stance on the question: what is information literacy (IL) for? And if there are different answers to this question – which I will suggest is the case – how might contradictions and conflicts between these different views give rise to political issues? In consequence, how might politics prevent the benefits of IL being manifested? And how can IL educators meet these political challenges?

I begin this task by reviewing the idea of 'information obesity' and the environmental model of information, as these are essential foundations for the later discussion. Viewing information as an environmental resource is a metaphor, but like all metaphors, it provides a tool for seeing the world in particular ways. I therefore develop the model by considering how a resource-based analysis of politics – or *geopolitics* – can be effectively reworked around the environmental model of information to provide a perspective that I call *noöpolitics*. I want then to suggest that IL education, whether practitioners are aware of this or not, is one route through which noöpolitical issues are contested, resolved and then embedded into the informational environment and the technical and social tools which we use to interact with that environment. These tools include IL. Like all educational activities, IL therefore has unavoidable political implications. Awareness of noöpolitics should therefore become part of the development of IL educators.

The theories which underpin this discussion are relatively complex, and space is limited here. The chapter is also a contribution to a book that is not about political theory but is directed at IL educators, therefore, I have omitted any in-depth discussion of these ideas. My argument is ultimately founded in critical theories such as Habermas's notion of colonisation (1984/7) and Gramsci's description of hegemony (1971). For detail see Whitworth (2009a, part 3).

Information abundance and information obesity

It has proven difficult to assess the impact of the huge increases in the quantity of information available to the average person without resorting to metaphor. Information is essentially intangible, but has real effects on the world. Perhaps as a consequence, almost all the terms used to describe its impact make analogies with physical effects. *Information overload* is one example (Toffler 1970). Here, the image being evoked is of a system, or perhaps a vehicle or beast of burden, suffering under a greater load than it can carry comfortably. The impression is that this is a dangerous situation. Fuses may blow, axles or backs break. Either way the ongoing health of the system, vehicle or beast is threatened. Thus, the term 'information overload' brings to mind potentially dramatic and dangerous consequences of having access to a large quantity of information. At the very least, we will suffer a loss in quality of engagement with information, and require new tools and strategies to deal with overload: an argument first made effectively by Bush (1945).

Another metaphor is that of *data smog* (Shenk 1997). As with information overload, the damaging effects are acknowledged, but here their impact is more insidious. Smog may be invisible, but it remains a pollutant which can gradually overwhelm our defences. We may not realise we are in an unhealthy environment.

Information overload and data smog are both negative metaphors. Put simply, the claim is that there is too much information and its effects are damaging. Such a view may seem natural to us as it has come to dominate the literature, but this is, in itself, a sign of the impact of a metaphor and the way it can affect how we see things. As Morgan says (1999: 4):

> metaphors imply *a way of thinking* and *a way of seeing* that pervade how we understand our world generally. . . . The metaphor frames our understanding. . . in a distinctive yet partial way. . . . In highlighting certain interpretations it tends to force others into a background role.

Contrast these negative metaphors with a more positive phrase, 'information abundance'. This is rather less frequently used, though see Gandel et al. (2004), and Tennant and Heilmeier (1992). Abundance itself is not really a metaphor, but a synonym for 'available in large quantities'; nevertheless, there is an analogy being drawn, with information likened to a natural resource. From an abundant resource one can take as much as one needs, without damaging others' ability to make the most of the resource themselves (cf. Cleveland 1982). In addition, the ease of information production in the modern world means that all of us can contribute to this abundance. Hence, the information commons (Hess and Ostrom 2007) is fertile, ever-evolving and richly diverse.

Yet even here there are concerns about the true impact of this fertility. Gandel et al.'s article (2004) still suggests that abundance is a potential problem rather than a benefit. Quantity is not a substitute for quality (Burns 1991: 54, cited in Gandel et al. 2004); or, rather, it is because of sheer quantity that information of quality is obscured. Abundance obscures information of *relevance* (Ackoff 1967, cited in Gandel et al. 2004). Over-production of information is also considered problematic by writers such as Keen (2007), who denounces what he calls the 'cult of the amateur', and Thompson (2008) who similarly blames the ease of production, as well as the decline in traditional sources of authority and ignorance of the principles of scientific method for the rise in what he calls 'counterknowledge'. The problem for these authors, and also for Shenk (1997), is a lack of *gatekeeping*: abundance is a symptom of the decline in checks and balances on who can publish, and what can be published. Rather than seeing this abundance as a fertile, rich and diverse environment, they view it as a chaotic jumble, without signifiers of quality and ultimately, a block on the development of knowledge. The abundance of information can be seen as polluting rather than resourcing, and the information commons damaged by overuse (Hess and Ostrom 2007) rather than sustained.

What must be established is the specific problem that these negative metaphors are highlighting. This is what I attempted to do with the metaphor *information obesity*. This is intended to evoke a situation in which resources are being consumed, but not used in a productive way to sustain individuals, communities, organisations and societies. Information is not being turned into knowledge and then fed back into the environment to be drawn on later. In more technical terms, information obesity is a block on what Goodwin (2009, cited in Luckin 2010: 11) calls 'cooperative semiosis':

> a continuous transformation process through which signs that are secreted into the environment by people are built upon by others to produce sign operations that create a new environment. Thus action and meaning are built through a social process.

It is this ongoing, continuous and *autonomous* transformation of their own informational resources that is blocked when individuals, communities and organisations suffer from information obesity. However, this is not caused only by information abundance. As with physical obesity, there are causes at all levels of society, which essentially amount to a failure to *manage* the abundant resource. The individual, inattentive to what they are consuming and/or unaware of the potentially damaging effects of their indiscriminate consumption, may be seen as blameworthy; countering information obesity at this level may include the raising of awareness and exercises to enhance one's mental 'fitness'. There are also structural causes: the power of the information industries which have a financial interest in increasing consumption, and reducing critical attention by consumers to what is on offer. These industries also seek to reduce costs, with a concomitant reduction of quality. Finally, there are community-level causes of obesity which are often overlooked (see Levine 2007); with information obesity these include a neglect of local information resources (such as archives, libraries, museums), the decline in social capital (Putnam 2000), and the increasing tendency for community-level association to be regulated and/or replaced by state or corporate intervention, a process that Habermas (1984/7) has called *colonisation*.

From geopolitics to noöpolitics

Politics is the study of how decisions are made. It is therefore concerned with how values are assigned to different options and what, indeed, value consists of in particular contexts. Not all decisions are made consciously, and the study of politics must therefore also concern itself with how structures of various kinds – physical structures, organisations, belief systems and so on – affect the way we act, and even the way we think.

The non-living spheres of the Earth, collectively known as the *geosphere*, and the biosphere, or sphere of life, are among the fundamental bases for politics. Duverger places 'physical structures' first in his discussion of the field (1971). This is geopolitics (or sometimes, biopolitics). An excellent example of such an analysis comes at the start of Reischauer and Fairbanks' history of Japan (1958: 451–6). Starting with the simple geographical fact of those islands' physical isolation, 115 miles (184 km) from the Asian continent, and also attending to factors such as Japanese terrain, climate and supply of natural resources, Reischauer and Fairbanks build hypotheses about the development of Japanese culture, economy and, ultimately, history. They do so with respect to both the differences between that nation and other peoples, and also between different regions of the country.

Geopolitical factors are not all-important, of course, but because they work at such a fundamental environmental level, their effects can be far-reaching, and cumulative. A simple study of any map will show the tendency of urban areas to cluster around good harbours, important river crossings and other key points of passage. Even where advances in technology (for example, the rise in air travel) cause some geopolitical factors to lose significance over time, extant cities remain important. Environmental feedback loops develop, with a city pulling in investment and cultural resources: transport and communications infrastructure come to centre on it. Inequalities between regions may therefore emerge.

Here we start to see the crossover between geopolitical concerns, rooted in the geosphere and biosphere, and the sphere of information, communication and thought, termed the *noösphere* (Vernadsky 1945):

> Much of what we see in the world around us is the result of interactions of the noösphere with other parts of the environment. This is clearly true of constructed, urban landscapes, in which different types of information interact with natural environments to produce cities and towns. . . . But even a rural landscape will have been shaped by the knowledge required to farm and manage it, and a wilderness may only be such because it is protected by human legal constructions which 'fence' it off from development. Information is as much embedded into, say, a railway viaduct as into a page of the London *Financial Times*. Indeed, considering why railways were built, it is, at least in part, the same kind of information. (Whitworth 2009a: 5–6)

All the spheres of the Earth are interconnected, and it was my argument in part 1 of *Information Obesity* (particularly Whitworth 2009a: 20–2), drawing also on the notion of the information commons developed by Hess and Ostrom (2007), that this means we must see concepts such as environmental health, diversity, and sustainability as applying just as much to the informational sphere as the physical ones. A *noöpolitical* analysis of history, and present politics, is therefore just as valid as geopolitical explanations, and can productively draw on the metaphors already introduced, such as information abundance and its opposite, information scarcity. As Gandel et al. (2004, n.p.) say:

> The history of human learning can perhaps best be described in terms of a lack of abundance, or scarcity. Before the invention of moveable type, literacy and learning were placed in the service of the secular or ecclesiastical ruling elites. Sacred and secular texts were copied by hand and stored in imperial palaces or monastic scriptoria for protection from both the elements and prying eyes. The diffusion of knowledge in an era of such scarcity was necessarily slow and highly controlled. Access to learning and knowledge was mediated by privilege and social standing; literacy was limited and rationed both because of the prevailing technologies (e.g., the hand copying and illuminating of manuscripts) and because of the desire to enforce social control. . . . Until recently, the scarcity of information and of the means to manage it has been a defining character of human history. Political and social orders have rested on a foundation of scarcity, and our management systems have been configured largely to ration, conserve, and optimize the use of scarce resources.

Noöpolitics is interested in where control over informational resources is asserted. The environmental model of information shows that what were once commonly-held resources can be enclosed, fenced off behind legal barriers such as copyright, patents, or Official Secrets Acts, which block the legal exchange of information (see Kranich 2007). Information can be exploited for profit: for example, advertising targeted on consumers depending on what a supermarket 'loyalty' card records about their spending habits. Surveillance records not just our physical movements through a space but our navigation of the WWW, e-mails sent and received, contacts on Facebook and so on. In certain cases (see below), information is used as a weapon of war.

One reason why 'abundance' can be considered a more positive metaphor than overload or smog – and a more desirable state than scarcity – is that potentially, abundance poses a challenge to controlling and exclusionary practices. If censorship, for instance, blocks access to a particular website, there are likely to be ways to sidestep the blockage and access the information anyway. The more diversity there is in the information environment, the more options are available to searchers. Yet just because a resource is abundant does not mean it spreads itself evenly throughout available space, nor that access to the resource will be free:

> In many ways, the markets for knowledge and learning are evolving like those for food. From a planetary perspective, we have the capacity to produce enough food to sustain human life in a reasonable fashion. The problems of nutrition and world hunger relate more to issues of distribution, global politics and economics, and education. (Gandel et al. 2004, n.p.)

We should remember the interconnections of the spheres. Noöpolitical power depends in part upon geopolitical power. Control of physical resources, economic resources, can (though does not always) equate to control of informational resources, and vice versa.

The term 'noöpolitics' is not mine, but it has been little used in the literature. At the time of writing, a book edited by Hauptmann et al. (2010) was in press, but no copies were available for consultation. Lazzarato (2004) uses the term to denote power relations that work on the memory and manipulate attention, and this idea is developed further in Terranova's paper (2007), which is the main prior discussion of noöpolitics that I want to use here.

Terranova explains how control over information's production, access, dissemination and even meaning are all conduits for the transmission of cultural *hegenomy* (Gramsci 1971). For Gramsci, hegemony is 'manufactured' consent to power and inequality. It does not constitute repression: indeed, a regime that has to resort to repression to retain its status has lost its hegemony. Hegemony denotes not just control, in a Marxian sense, of the economic structures of society, but its cultural and social structures as well; through such a process, crises such as economic difficulties or wars can be deflected, and prevented by the ruling elite from becoming political crises (Adamson 1980: 11). In these latter senses, cultural hegemony is (Terranova 2007: 125):

> the process by which, in Stuart Hall's early formulation, a temporary alliance of dominant groups or historical bloc, 'strives and to a degree succeeds in *framing* all competing definitions of reality *within their range*, bringing all alternatives within their horizon of thought' (Hall 1977: 333; see also Hall 1996a).

Terranova's prime example of the noöpolitical construction of hegemony is the production and reproduction of a distorted and deliberately alienating image of Islam by US and other 'Western' news agencies. She discusses this with reference to Edward Said's (1978) work on 'orientalism'. Hegemonic utterances – in this case the 'threat' posed by Islam to the Western 'way of life' – are presented as discursive 'truths' by confronting the viewer with images of Arabs and other Moslems that are then associated with 'feelings of anger, fear, hostility and resentment in the majority of the American public' (Terranova 2007: 133). Terms like 'terrorism' are presented without attempts to define them properly: instead, the common mode of argument is to repeat the association, or accusation, rather than providing any justification for it (ibid., via Massumi 2005: 10). Through such hegemonic discourse, the public is persuaded to accept the diffusion of military and corporate objectives into everyday public opinion (see also Arquilla and Ronfeldt 1997: 6). Toffler and Toffler (1997) note a *deep coalition* of interests here which wield cultural hegemony to help manufacture consent to their own goals and means. (For another view of these issues, with particular emphasis on how children are targeted by these messages, see the film *Beyond Good and Evil* (Challenging Media 2006).)

Representations like these '*mediate* the apprehension of the world' (Terranova 2007: 127). It is not the content of these messages that mediates, but the means by which they are constantly produced and reproduced. 24-hour news channels allow a constant bombardment. Hollywood movies are also culpable, including fantasy and other unrelated subjects which nevertheless constantly project an image of 'the Other' as dehumanised villains inevitably overcome by 'necessary' violence. All in all, according to Terranova (2007: 130), there exist:

new techniques of power (public relations, advertising, communication management, infotainment) to which corresponds another mode of conflict – a regime of information warfare. These techniques of power and regimes of warfare express an important mutation in the means by which the effect of cultural hegemony is accomplished.

This kind of disinformation is directed at multiple targets. In this case, the effects are directed both to 'Western' publics, persuading them to back the objectives of the deep coalition. But they also destabilise Moslems too, closing up available discursive spaces: degrading 'adversaries' capacity for *understanding* their own circumstances, and their capacity to make any effective use of whatever *correct understandings* they might achieve' (Terranova 2007: 132, via Rothrock 1997).

This kind of political action can be just as damaging at the micro-scale as the macro-. Noöpolitics in the everyday sheds light on how we can be excluded from informational spaces in organisations, how our working lives, social relationships and so on can be managed through information and its manipulation. In a hegemonic discourse, there is (Terranova 2007: 127): 'a kind of unrepresentability of the subaltern, who cannot speak within the discourse that constitutes her as such (Spivak 1988).' The very structures and content of language can be used to exclude. The ability to enter particular discourses may be limited to those who have mastered certain jargon, or can put across an argument in particular ways. The legal profession is perhaps the most obvious example of such gatekeeping, but it can happen in more informal ways as well, being part of the socialisation practices which happen in almost all organisations and their subcultures (e.g. Turner 1971). Connell (1980) discussed how media presentations of events such as industrial action used language in subtle ways to define the debate despite claims of impartiality. For example, audiences will hear that 'hopes are high of a return to work' whereas there will be 'fears that the strike will continue'. Whose hopes? Whose fears?

These are linguistic 'rules', even genres (Bakhtin 1986) which are pushed at us subtly, but continually. And yet none of this is undertaken through overt censorship, nor on absolute restrictions on who can publish. Indeed, it can sit quite comfortably alongside the great opening-up of communications media. These have 'made it possible for "anyone in fact to say anything at all" while at the same time sifting all statements "either towards the dominant mainstream or out to the margins"' (Said 1997: 392). As already noted, the implication is that increased quantity of information, and increased access to media, lead ultimately to a deterioration in quality. The essential search for *relevant* information – harder and harder in a state of abundance – has led to the increasing application of (expensive) technologies such as data mining, surveillance, pattern-matching algorithms and so on. The technical ability to store, analyse, filter, process and apply information is thereby a foundation of hegemonic power. Control over these technologies, asserted either by their physical possession or by laws which restrict access and availability, is the noöpolitical equivalent of the medieval fortress which controlled the access points into and out of a strategic region, or the seagoing vessels which could monopolise trade and force the opening of unfriendly ports in the 18th and 19th centuries.

Competing forms of value

Politics should matter to the IL educator because information literacy is largely concerned with judgements about value

(Whitworth 2009a: 11–23; 2009b). In standard IL definitions, such as that of the ACRL (2000), the emphasis is on an individual student's subjective valuations of the information that they find. The information literate student is one who determines the extent of the information needed, conducts a search and then evaluates its result. Yet there are other forms of value which must come into play and which are addressed by the ACRL guidelines indirectly, if at all. Objective and intersubjective values are also important. These domains of value are what move us away from the sort of subjective judgements we make as very young and self-oriented children, and into higher stages of intellectual development (see Kitchener and King 1981) where we can acknowledge that there are truths which, in different ways, have been *validated* by others. This validation can take place using the rules of scientific method (including social science); it may also be embedded in a moral or legal code. Validity claims stand behind every utterance or representation, and it is a prerequisite of fair and effective communication that these claims are open to scrutiny and accounted for by the other parties in the communicative exchange (Habermas 1984/7). It is characteristic of the kind of disinformation referred to in the previous section that this precept is at least potentially violated by such communication.

Objective, subjective and intersubjective value therefore work together to form the complex structure of existing knowledge – what Habermas calls the *lifeworld* (1987) – against which we must assess the validity of found information (Whitworth 2009b). Without subjective value, individuals would not be able to critically investigate, within specific contexts, the information, values, beliefs and so on that are 'pushed' at them by organisations and communities. The result would be 'groupthink', defined by Janis (1972: 9) as a situation where '[group] members' strivings for unanimity override their motivation to realistically appraise alternative courses of action'. This not only leads to bad decision making, but stifles creativity; indeed, without subjective value creativity would be impossible. Without objective value, we may come to accept found information, or sometimes entire belief systems, that are widely believed to be valuable but which have no scientific validity. Thompson (2008) calls this *counterknowledge* and includes within this umbrella term contemporary myths such as creationism and conspiracy theories. Finally, without intersubjective values such as laws and morals, we risk *relativism* – the poisoner seeking information on how to manufacture deadly gas, and doing so in accordance with good technical IL practice, would otherwise be seen as legitimate. We must note that economic value is also intersubjective, and there are times when it is appropriate to evaluate information against economic criteria; a way of working or thinking that requires more resources than are available in a company, family or environment is not a sustainable one, and should not be pursued.

In short, though subjective value remains important, intersubjective and objective values are those which have been developed over time precisely to overcome its deficiencies. Scientific method, for instance, is a structure of validation processes intended to ensure that what counts as 'science' is based on more than subjective hunches on the part of individual thinkers. Laws, morals and consensual agreements exist to prevent a 'might makes right' approach to resolving differences of opinion.

As a theoretical model, it is acceptable to see the three forms of value as interdependent, which I have visualised in the following diagram (first used in Whitworth 2009b); relating the forms of value to other works including Egan's

(1990) models of literacy and Bruce et al.'s (2007) six frames of information literacy (Figure 8.1).

However, the discussion of noöpolitics now allows us to see ways that in practice, values are in competition with each other, and this can distort the information that is available. Subjective value is deficient as the sole basis for judgements partly because of the existence of various *cognitive biases* which affect how we absorb information from the world (see Whitworth 2009a: 143–6; Blaug 2007). We seek patterns, and are reluctant to admit we are wrong; thus we may not even notice information that challenges our existing beliefs – at best, we can be easily persuaded to ignore or misinterpret the information. We overestimate our powers of prediction and while we will take the credit for our successes, we shift the blame for failure onto others. These are all natural tendencies in our minds, and should not necessarily be seen negatively: cognitive biases like this help us join the world, and overcome what might otherwise be insurmountable ego-blocks against taking any decisive action at all. But they can also prevent us from learning (Blaug 2007).

At an intersubjective level, these cognitive biases can be exploited within organisations and communities. These

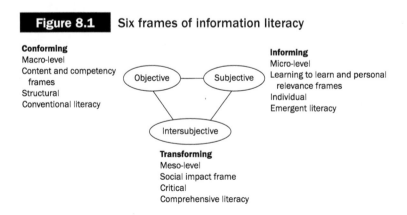

Figure 8.1   Six frames of information literacy

Conforming
Macro-level
Content and competency frames
Structural
Conventional literacy

Objective — Subjective

Informing
Micro-level
Learning to learn and personal relevance frames
Individual
Emergent literacy

Intersubjective

Transforming
Meso-level
Social impact frame
Critical
Comprehensive literacy

collectives can 'push' ways of thinking at individuals. Though this oversimplifies the process somewhat, this largely takes place through *reification*, another cognitive bias:

> Reification (a term best developed by Lukacs 1971) describes the 'tendency of socially authored structures to appear as real, as external to and independent of, individuals' (Blaug 2007: 32) ... These ... become embedded into the sociotechnical systems which we use to organise activity. Scripts and schema are products of prior knowledge and are *stored*, thus favouring certain activities, ways of thinking, and filtering decisions. Even an information literate actor is not free to determine for themselves the grounds on which they are filtering information, particularly not as much of this may take place before they start conscious cognitive work. But these schema are not necessarily the products of the *actors'* prior knowledge and experience. Within organisations, they are as likely to have been designed by others. (Whitworth 2009a: 146)

Reification shifts the intersubjective or subjective to the objective, giving something the status of 'truth' when in fact it is just a 'socially authored structure'. Schema, or ways of thinking, are designed and imposed, and individuals subjected to them are obliged to restrict their own judgements in order that they conform to the schema. For example, employees in an organisation may not pass on information they have gathered which could be in conflict with operational objectives, vision statements or things they otherwise believe the management want to hear. Eventually, they may even stop 'seeing' the information altogether. The members of the organisation see the world differently depending on what side of the power divide they are on (Blaug 2007: 39–40).

Failures of learning like these have arguably caused some major institutional collapses of recent years, such as those of Barings Bank and Enron. More generally, pushed cognitive schema can lead to the creativity and self-reflective practices of many employees being disregarded (cf. Robins and Webster 1987: 184). In terms developed by Henry Mintzberg (1989) this represents a deskilling of the professional core and an increased use of the technostructure, being that part of the organisation mandated to plan and control the work of others.

We should also note that procedural rules can be technostructural, and can serve to direct attention towards particular types of information and away from others. In education, assessment criteria fulfil this role. Though there is, almost certainly, no *political* motivation for the manipulation of students' information searching in this way, it is difficult to argue that assessment criteria are not consciously designed to direct students' attention towards particular information and away from others. The argument that this is done for students' benefit, to help them pass a course and meet instrumental objectives, is beside the point. Whatever the motivation, the result is that students are not free to filter information on purely subjective grounds, as the ACRL (2000) imply.

Thus, noöpolitics becomes manifested in the design of organisations: which are, largely, information-processing systems. It is through such manipulation of cognitive schema that people become excluded from informational spaces. It is because of these subtle organisational processes that we must note the argument from Massumi (2005: 2, via Terranova 2007: 134): 'that it is too simplistic to see a clear, linear cause-and-effect here, and a conscious and behaviorist manipulation of people's minds by media'. Stokes (1991) makes the point that not all hegemonic messages are ignorantly absorbed by 'subordinate' groups – that, often, it is in fact precisely those in privileged positions to whom the messages are directed. Subordinates, on the other hand, ignore, subvert or parody these kinds of communication.

In addition, we cannot simply say that cognitive schema are damaging. As with the example of student assessment criteria, there may be times when it helps to direct attention. The political question here is not the existence of cognitive schema but the way they have been constructed, and whether they become reified, or instead remain open to continuous review and scrutiny. As with hierarchy, there are times when it helps to give over control of our activity to others: what we must do is remain *vigilant* (Blaug 1999) over its effects, and learn to see what these structures are often designed to conceal. This is where the politically-aware IL educator can make a difference.

A politically aware information literacy education?

As Bruce et al. (2007) have described, there are several ways of conceiving of IL, each with its own means of justifying, teaching and assessing IL. Not all are oriented towards overcoming cognitive biases, or challenging the colonisation of the lifeworld, the enclosure of informational resources, the deterioration in quality and inequalities in access and power over information. Education is as much a political battleground as other significant shapers of public opinion and activity, such as law and the media. In recent decades, a dominant current in educational practice has been 'instrumental progressivism', which 'arguably forms the basis for educational policy across much of the world'

(Whitworth 2009a: 128). In Robins and Webster (1987: 204–5) it is linked:

> directly to the requirements of the corporate sector and its influence over educational policy. The objective is 'education for flexibility', and 'contracts in which students assume responsibility for their own development', but this is not intended to empower learners to act autonomously in public community life.

The standard model of IL education, epitomised by the ACRL definitions, contains no requirement within it for learners to challenge, or even be aware of, the cognitive schema that are 'pushed' at them by hegemonic interests. Nor are measures of competency, interested only in how effectively students retrieve information, sensitive to context. These basic IL competencies are an essential foundation for the construction of knowledge, and thus informational resources, that is true; but they must be applied through engaging in active work with information that, ultimately, must have *social impact* (cf. Bruce et al. 2007: 41) if it is to work towards the sustenance of informational resources and thus, combat information obesity.

> Deprived or disadvantaged communities can be empowered, from within, or with expert, communicatively-rational help, to improve their informational skills and resources (Warschauer 1999: Chapters 4–6), and do so with the intention of transforming their environments, even in the face of opposition and perhaps oppression from vested interests. These learning processes are happening all over the world, usually beneath the radar: hence

their power. Remember that physical obesity, and poor health generally, is more likely to affect lower-income and other disadvantaged groups; general environmental quality is also lower in these communities (e.g. higher pollution, less aesthetic value). Applying this judgement to these communities' information resources is, as this book has tried to show throughout, not just a transfer of a metaphor. It is a real contribution to the lack of control that many people have over their own lives. Information obesity is thus politically disempowering. To reverse its effects requires educational work across a wide spectrum of settings, from the formalised classroom, to the technological development process, the workplace, the local community, the family, and the social movement. (Whitworth 2009a: 193)

Gramsci's notion of hegemony was not absolute. Within it he recognised that its opposite was not repressed out of existence: that *counterhegemonic* practices could be knowingly and actively engaged in. Later, Habermas's related notion of colonisation was similarly juxtaposed with *decolonisation*. The strength of both ideas comes about because these oppositional forces are not abstract, idealistic states or thought experiments, like a fictional Utopia, but activities which can be engaged with in everyday situations, where any political act (the assignation of value, the formation of opinion, the making of a decision) is taking place. Attempts to reach a consensus rather than impose a viewpoint; opening up resources for public use that were previously inaccessible (perhaps by a change in a law or procedure, perhaps by scholarly work, translation, or tagging); empowering individuals or communities to undertake research work aimed at solving a problem they face (cf. Levine 2007; Whitworth 2009a: 195–8); all these are the sort of work engaged in by what Gramsci called 'organic intellectuals'. For Gramsci, the whole of society is a school, with the 'intellectuals' including not only scholars but 'anyone whose social functions is to serve as a transmitter of ideas within civil society' (Adamson 1980: 142–3). Institutions that encourage the maturation of organic intellectuals must be developed as part of a transformative process that 'allows "every citizen to govern" or at least, places him or her "in a general condition to achieve this [capacity]"' (Adamson 1980: 144, via Gramsci 1971: 40).

This kind of educational work does not simply designate some representations as 'bad' and seek to replace them with 'good' ones – for such a view is just relativist. Instead, intersubjective values are developed by showing 'how all representations are constructed, for what purposes, by whom and with what components' (Said, 1994: 280, cited in Terranova, 2007: 127). Ultimately, information literacy requires not just the ability to retrieve information but to critique it, scrutinise it, as essential aspects of the filtering process; because of cognitive bias this critique should be conducted not against subjective value alone but also against objective and intersubjective criteria. It requires a sense of the *scientific validity* and the *public value* of the information, as well as its content, and how well it meets subjective needs.

'Public value' is a term which has recently risen in stature in political discourse. Moore's 1995 book, *Creating Public Value*, is the usual citation, and was a work oriented towards managers of public institutions. This is a useful perspective, and one echoed by writers such as Senn Breivik and Gee (2006), which emphasise the role of the library here. I have not really mentioned these institutions at all in this chapter, which is not to dismiss their historic role and usefulness in these endeavours. Libraries are essential resources for a community, however defined; both in their existence as repositories, and as contact points with trained information professionals. But they cannot act as the drivers of transformation. Librarians are specialists in the retrieval of information, but not its creation (Whitworth 2009a: 102).

Counterhegemonic and decolonising activity must come from the bottom up. It takes place wherever communities and individuals, otherwise kept apart, come together to reach some kind of understanding, communicate across boundaries and engage in shared activity without resorting to hierarchy. This is not to say all such work is effective in bringing about change. Yet one of the strengths of a noöpolitical analysis is that it shows not only what issues must be addressed, but the challenges which will be faced. Hegemony works partly by keeping communities and publics polarised, whether through creating clearly-defined roles in organisational structures, or using stereotypes, language and disinformation to do so in culture and the media: as with the discussion of 'orientalism' already referred to. This fragmentation is enhanced by information overload (Shenk 1997) and:

> 'the conditions for a colonisation of the lifeworld are met' (Habermas 1987: 355), as diffused 'local cultures' cannot be sufficiently co-ordinated. Lacking, then, any intersubjective ways of valuing and filtering information, and of then turning this information into knowledge and other resources which will be useful to them in the future, these local cultures – individuals and communities – are half-encouraged, half-forced to adopt merely a passive role with respect to the information flowing around their activity systems, and as a result, become obese on it . . . (Whitworth 2009a: 132).

Examples of practice which engage with this kind of critical, emancipatory work exist, though they are rarely called 'IL education'. Critical media literacy or media studies, dismissed as it always will be by those with vested interests in the broadcast media who (rightly) see it as one of the few challenges to their hegemony, makes only one appearance in Beetham et al.'s (2009) list of exemplars of UK IL education, but it is there, as is the ACME site at *http://www .acmecoalition.org/* (accessed 26 May 2010). Warschauer (1999: 189) describes an example of 'Cyber service learning', where students' literacy (including, but not limited to, information literacy) work was devoted to producing material relevant to the relatively deprived and ethnically diverse community which was located around the University of Hawaii. This work was not just an example of student activism but was connected specifically to 'structured opportunities intentionally designed to promote student learning and development' (Jacoby 1996: 5), and thus accreditable by the formal institution. Bruce (2008) has studied what he calls the process of 'community inquiry' as manifested in the Paseo Boricua district of Chicago, an underprivileged immigrant neighbourhood. His work is motivated by the same assumptions that drive all these and other examples of emancipatory education:

> First, there is the assumption people can both understand the world and act through some sort of collective process. Second, this community inquiry is needed for social progress, because individual thought and action is too often dormant, scattered, or even counter-productive. Third, the process of community inquiry is itself integral to social progress, in fact is part of what social progress means. Finally, community inquiry is fundamental to moral action and development. (Bruce 2008: 5)

Conclusion

It is a shame to end this discussion with such a cursory review of practice in this area, but the aim of this article was merely to raise awareness of the possibilities. As Blaug (1999) says, hierarchism – a hegemonic belief system – works effectively to direct our awareness away from ongoing activity like this. Instead we are persuaded to believe that work like this is difficult or even impossible, and/or undesirable. It is exactly the process of 'learning how to see' decolonising, counterhegemonic work that is the important thing. I hope this chapter has at least started its readers on such a path. As I have said before:

> Information is a resource, and could be managed in ways that not only keep it abundant, but retain its quality, accessibility and the possibility that from it, knowledge may emerge in users, and be communicated and shared. That said, neglect could lead to the pollution or deterioriation of this resource. Do we have the capacity to train our minds and adjust our systems to cope with this latest, ICT-generated boost to the noösphere's dynamism and abundance? Or will we and our systems overload and shut down? In this question lies the move from information obesity to a healthier, more sustainable diet of information. (Whitworth 2009a: 50–1)

References

Ackoff, R. (1967) Management Misinformation Systems, *Management Sciences*, 14(4): B147.

ACRL (Association of College and Research Libraries) (2000) *Information Literacy Competency Standards for*

Higher Education. Available at *http://www.ala.org/ala/ mgrps/divs/acrl/standards/informationliteracycompetency .cfm* (last accessed 26 May 2010).

Adamson, W. (1980) *Hegemony and Revolution: A Study of Antonio Gramsci's Political and Cultural Theory*, Berkeley, CA: University of California Press.

Arquilla, J. and D. Ronfeldt (1997) 'A new epoch – and spectrum – of conflict', in J. Arquilla and D. Ronfeldt (eds), *In Athena's Camp: Preparing for Conflict in the Information Age*. Santa Monica, CA: RAND Corporation.

Bakhtin, M. (1986) *Speech Genres and Other Essays*. Austin, TX: University of Texas Press.

Beetham, H., L. McGill and A. Littlejohn (2009) *Thriving in the 21st Century: Learning Literacies for the Digital Age*, Glasgow: The Caledonian Academy. Available at *www.academy.gcal.ac.uk/llida/outputs.html* (accessed 10 April 2010).

Blaug, R. (1999) The Tyranny of the Visible: Problems in the Evaluation of Anti-Institutional Radicalism, *Organization*, 6(1): 33–56.

Blaug, R. (2007) Cognition in a Hierarchy, *Contemporary Political Theory*, 6(1): 24–44.

Bruce, C., S. Edwards and M. Lupton (2007) 'Six frames for information literacy education: a conceptual framework for interpreting the relationships between theory and practice', in S. Andretta (ed.), *Change and Challenge: Information Literacy for the 21st Century*. Adelaide: Auslib, 37–58.

Bruce, B. C. (2008) 'From Hull House to Paseo Boricua: the theory and practice of community inquiry', in B. Dicher and A. Luduşan (eds), *Philosophy of Pragmatism (II): Salient Inquiries*, Cluj-Napoca, Romania: Editura Fundaiei pentru Studii Europene (European Studies Foundation Publishing House). Available at *https://www.ideals .illinois.edu/handle/2142/13166* (accessed 26 May 2010).

Burns, C. (1991) 'Three Mile Island: the information meltdown', in F. Horton Jr. and D. Lewis (eds), *Great Information Disasters: Twelve Prime Examples of How Information Mismanagement Led to Human Misery, Political Misfortune, and Business Failure*. London: Aslib, 54.

Bush, V. (1945) As We May Think, *Atlantic Monthly*, July: available at *http://www.theatlantic.com/doc/194507/bush* (accessed 26 May 2010).

Challenging Media (2006) *Beyond Good and Evil*, available at *http://www.youtube.com/watch?v=CggjBd7o-PM)* (accessed 26 May 2010).

Cleveland, H. (1982) Information as a Resource, *The Futurist*, 16(6): 34–9.

Connell, I. (1980) 'Television news and the social contract', in S. Hall (ed.), *Culture, Media, Language*. London: Hutchinson, pp: 139–56.

Duverger, M. (1971) *The Study of Politics*. New York: Crowell.

Egan, K. (1990) *Romantic Understanding: The Development of Rationality and Imagination, Ages 8–15*. London: Routledge.

Gandel, P., R. Katz and S. Metros (2004) The 'Weariness of the Flesh': Reflections on the Life of the Mind in an Era of Abundance, *EDUCAUSE Review*, 39(2): 40–51.

Goodwin, C. (2009) *Calibrating bodies and cognition through interactive practice in a meaningful environment*. Keynote speech, Computer Supported Collaborative Learning Conference 2009, Rhodes, Greece.

Gramsci, A. (1971) *Selections from the Prison Notebooks of Antonio Gramsci*. London: Lawrence & Wishart.

Habermas, J. (1984) *The Theory of Communicative Action Volume 1: Reason and the Rationalisation of Society*. London: Heinemann.

Habermas, J. (1987) *The Theory of Communicative Action Volume 2: Lifeworld and System – A Critique of Functionalist Reason.* Cambridge: Polity.

Hall, S. (1977) 'Culture, media and the ideological effect', in J. Curran, M. Gurevitch and J. Woollacott (eds), *Mass Communication and Society.* London: Arnold.

Hall, S. (1996) 'The relevance of Gramsci for the study of race and ethnicity', in D. Morley and K.-H. Chen (eds), *Stuart Hall: Critical Dialogues in Cultural Studies.* London and New York: Routledge.

Hauptmann, D., W. Niedich and A.-K. Mustafa (eds) (2010) *Cognitive Architecture: From Bio-politics to Noo-politics,* forthcoming publication.

Hess, C. and E. Ostrom (eds) (2007) *Understanding Knowledge as a Commons: From Theory to Practice.* Cambridge, MA: MIT Press.

Jacoby, B. (1996) *Service Learning in Higher Education.* San Francisco, CA: Jossey-Bass.

Janis, I. (1972) *Victims of Groupthink.* Boston, MA: Houghton Mifflin.

Keen, A. (2007) *The Cult of the Amateur: How Today's Internet is Killing our Culture and Assaulting our Economy.* London: Nicholas Brearley.

Kitchener, K. and P. King (1981) Reflective Judgement: Concepts of Justification and their Relationship to Age and Education, *Journal of Applied Developmental Psychology,* 2(2): 89–116.

Kranich, N. (2007) 'Countering enclosure: reclaiming the knowledge commons', in C. Hess and E. Ostrom (eds), *Understanding Knowledge as a Commons: From Theory to Practice.* Cambridge, MA: MIT Press, pp. 85–122.

Lazzarato, M. (2004) *La politica dell'evento.* Cosenza: Rubbettino.

Levine, P. (2007) 'Collective action, civic engagement and the knowledge commons', in C. Hess and E. Ostrom (eds.), *Understanding Knowledge as a Commons: From Theory to Practice*. Cambridge, MA: MIT Press, pp. 247–76.

Lukacs, G. (1971) *History and Class Consciousness*. London: Merlin.

Luckin, R. (2010) *Redesigning Learning Contexts: Technology-rich, Learner-centred Ecologies*. London: Routledge.

Massumi, Brian (2005) 'The Future Birth of the Affective Fact', in *Conference Proceedings: Genealogies of Biopolitics*. Available at *http://browse.reticular.info/text/collected/massumi.pdf* (accessed 26 May 2010).

Mintzberg, H. (1989) *Mintzberg on Management*. London: Collier Macmillan.

Moore, M. (1995) *Creating Public Value: Strategic Management in Government*. Cambridge, MA: Harvard University Press.

Morgan, G. (1999) *Images of Organization*, 2nd edn. London: Sage.

Orwell, G. (1957) 'Politics and the English language', in *Inside the Whale and Other Essays*. London: Penguin, pp. 143–57.

Putnam, R. D. (2000) *Bowling Alone: The Collapse and Revival of American Community*. New York: Simon & Schuster.

Reischauer, E. and J. Fairbanks (1958) *East Asia: The Great Tradition*. Boston, MA: Houghton Mifflin.

Robins, K. and F. Webster (1987) *The Technical Fix: Education, Computers and Industry*. Basingstoke, UK: Macmillan.

Rothrock, J. (1997) 'Information warfare: Time for some constructive skepticism?', in J. Arquilla and D. Ronfeldt (eds), *In Athena's Camp: Preparing for Conflict in the Information Age*. Santa Monica, CA: RAND Corporation.

Said, E. (1978) *Orientalism: Western Conceptions of the Orient*. Harmondsworth: Penguin.

Said, E. (1994) *Culture and Imperialism*. London: Vintage.

Said, E. (1997) *Covering Islam: How the Media and the Experts Determine How We See the Rest of the World*. London: Vintage.

Senn Breivik, P. and E. G. Gee (2006) *Higher Education in the Internet Age: Libraries Creating a Strategic Edge*. Westport, CT: Praeger.

Shenk, D. (1997) *Data Smog: Surviving the Information Glut*. New York: Harper Collins.

Spivak, G. (1988) 'Can the subaltern speak?', in C. Nelson and L. Grossberg (eds), *Marxism and the Interpretation of Culture*. Basingstoke: Macmillan Education.

Stokes, S. (1991) Hegemony, Consciousness, and Political Change in Peru, *Politics & Society*, 19(3): 265–90.

Tennant, H. and G. Heilmeier (1992) 'Knowledge and equality: Harnessing the tides of information abundance', in D. Leebaert (ed.), *Technology 2001: The Future of Computing and Communications*. Cambridge, MA: MIT Press.

Terranova, T. (2007) Futurepublic: On Information Warfare, Bio-racism and Hegemony as Noopolitics, *Theory, Culture & Society*, 24(3): 125–45.

Thompson, D. (2008) *Counterknowledge*. London: Atlantic.

Toffler, A. (1970) *Future Shock*. London: Bodley Head.

Toffler, A. and H. Toffler (1997) 'Introduction', in J. Arquilla and D. Ronfeldt (eds), *In Athena's Camp: Preparing for Conflict in the Information Age*. Santa Monica, CA: RAND Corporation.

Turner, B. (1971) *Exploring the Industrial Subculture*. London: Macmillan.

Vernadsky, V. (1945) The Biosphere and the Noösphere, *American Scientist*, 33: 1–12.

Warschauer, M. (1999) *Electronic Literacies: Language, Culture and Power in Online Education*. Mahwah, NJ: Lawrence Erlbaum.

Whitworth, A. (2007) 'Communicative competence in the information age: towards a critical theory of information literacy education', in Andretta, S. (ed.), *Change and Challenge: Information Literacy for the 21st Century*. Adelaide, Australia: Auslib, pp. 85–113.

Whitworth, A. (2009a) *Information Obesity*. Oxford: Chandos.

Whitworth, A. (2009b) Teaching in the Relational Frame: The Media and Information Literacy Course at Manchester, *Journal of Information Literacy*, 3(2): 25–38.

9

Contemporary technologies' influence on learning as a social practice

Ben Scoble

Abstract: Over the centuries, media communications technology innovation and development have had profound impacts on the societies that have embraced them. In the last 20 years the Internet has provided us with the latest example of how such developments can change the fundamental ways in which people communicate, learn and undertake the process of knowledge construction. Traditional learning experiences that involve accessing information from formal institutions are now being challenged by the new 'social' media and Internet-based information sources that are more informal in nature and autonomous. These new forms of communication media and information have transformed knowledge construction and learning, with many tempted into including any unsanctioned content that is produced for the Internet and the World Wide Web (WWW). A significant area of interest for those involved in information literacy is the influence of these new informal sources of information and how they challenge traditional and more formal approaches to learning. As a cultural shift, this new form of social learning is reminiscent of the growth and popularity of coffeehouses in the 17th and 18th centuries. Through understanding how the coffeehouse altered and challenged learning, knowledge construction and society, we will hopefully understand how contemporary technologies may influence contemporary learning, knowledge construction and the current societies that embrace them. One significant outcome from this exploration is the new relationship our society now has with data, information and where it comes from. Ultimately, the challenge for educators will be to redesign contemporary pedagogies to acknowledge and incorporate the new social web and contemporary forms of knowledge construction into appropriate learning experiences. Without such an examination of contemporary technology we may be unable to maintain and manage the future quality of data, information and knowledge that is the foundation of our knowledge-based economy and modern society.

Key words: knowledge, construction, social media, technology, society.

Contemporary technology

Contemporary technologies, in particular those connected to the Internet, have had a profound impact on the lives of people living in the late 20th and early 21st centuries. Although this comes across as a trite or even clichéd statement, words cannot aptly reflect the radical nature to which these Internet technologies have changed and are continuing to change the societies that have embraced them. These technologies have been inculcated in many of the paradigm shifts that have happened to some of the most important areas of how we engage in our lives today. In 1999, Douglas Adams observed that 'the Internet is so new we still don't really understand what it is. We mistake it for a type of publishing or broadcasting, because that's what we're used to.' Adams writes further that 'the biggest problem is that we are still the first generation of users, and for all that we may have invented the net, we still don't really get it'. Adams' observations clearly illustrate that the Internet was and is such a new technology that defining what it was for and how it is to be used is both conceptually challenging and will require an on-going re-appraisal.

We often use the terms 'Internet' and 'World Wide Web' (WWW) interchangeably and without much distinction, but they are not the same and understanding this key difference explains how the Internet is influencing learning as a social practice. The Internet is essentially a global network of interconnected computers, whereas the WWW or Web is an application of services that run on and take advantage of its attributes. Therefore, the WWW is more than just access to a repository of content and a collection of resources that are linked together by hypertext, hyperlinks and web addresses (URLs). In 2007, Kevin Kelly explained that through such Internet technology, in just 5,000 days, an environment had been created which allowed global access to almost unlimited information and data (Kelly, 2007). What is even more remarkable is that through the development of these communications networks, the whole world now has access to a knowledge 'machine' that is always on, non-proprietary and has an enormous storage capacity. In addition to this, the environment is evolving to become more open, as its content can now be added to or modified by anyone that participates or engages with it.

In respect to education, Anderson (2008: 54) states that 'the greatest affordance of the Web for education use is the profound and multifaceted increase in communication and interaction capability'. This is revolutionary for knowledge construction and learning as data, information and related services was either not free or was difficult to access due to various barriers to entry before the Internet became ubiquitous. As Anderson (2008) clearly identifies, users now have Internet-based services that allow them to easily connect with other users and undertake activities that facilitate and support the free exchange of ideas and new content. What is crucial to appreciate here is that the WWW is becoming a 'social web', epitomised as the free exchange of ideas through being facilitated by and conducted within an online, social and participatory environment.

In everyday terms, our experience of the Internet at the end of the first decade of the 21st century is very different from what was experienced at the end of the 20th century. Fundamentally, the Internet is no longer just a computer-based phenomenon and has extended its reach to include many mobile and other new devices that can also access web services on the Internet. What we have experienced and are continuing to experience is the Internet going through a paradigm shift, from being a passive publishing technology that is read-only (Web 1.0) to one which has read-write capabilities (Web 2.0) for users. As this chapter will hopefully explore further, the Internet can now offer attributes and features (affordances) that go beyond merely distributing content to learners. The WWW is now an active and participatory environment that has the possibility to fully support and enhance the learning process in ways only imagined or never considered before its inception.

What makes the Internet such a radical and disruptive technology for education?

Looking at the history of the Internet through the prism of education, the first important and radical event was the use of the Internet in its original form as Web 1.0, the read-only web. Much like old publication technologies, Web 1.0 largely presented information to users who passively read or listened to what was being displayed. In addition, Web 1.0 also allowed document files to be electronically distributed, allowing users to save their own copy. This was invaluable to education as it allowed information to be distributed widely to any number of users, cheaply and easily. Related to this period, it is also important to recognise the development and adoption of e-mail as the communication tool of choice, which was equally invaluable as it also allowed information to be distributed widely, cheaply and easily. E-mail can be seen as the first major Internet technology that facilitated learning activities that were collaborative and social in their dimension. E-mail was radical as it was a tool that supported offline relationships, allowing the easy movement of text and later documents between e-mail users. However, cultivating purely online virtual learning communities was still challenging using Web 1.0. Unless you had an online presence, such as a web page that publicised your e-mail address, it was often a lot easier to contact a website's author (web master) than it was to contact a fellow anonymous user or casual browsers of the same website.

The crucial disruptive and radical moment in the development of the WWW was its transformation from read-only Web 1.0 to the read-write web, Web 2.0. This is a paradigm shift, as websites can now allow users to both contribute to them as well as consuming the information they contain. Essentially, users can now either passively browse websites anonymously or create an online profile to both access and contribute to them. Critically, Web 2.0 websites are now more than just a publication tool and can offer services that invite user input or are unique services in their own right. Many Web 2.0 services do not focus on producing any original content at all but rely on hosting user-generated content. These new user generated sites are typified as social networking sites or media hosting services that only exist to allow users to post videos, share photos, write collaborative wikis or blogs and engage in online discussions. With regard to the individual users' experience, this new Web 2.0 environment allows users to create their own virtual environments, buy and consume services and engage in totally new interactive participatory experiences online. It is important to note that defining Web 2.0 is an inexact science as it is 'not a single coherent entity, but a wide variety of different technologies and these technologies offer different affordances' (Armstrong and Franklin, 2008: 12).

Whether Web 2.0 will radically change education can only be validated in hindsight. By analysing the impacts and effects of Web 2.0 technology on society (e.g. commerce, entertainment, communications and politics) one cannot see any reason to doubt that something radical and disruptive will be happening to education. Armstrong and Franklin (2008: 5) outline that Web 2.0 will be increasingly important to education because:

- It is an active set of technologies in which the learner contributes, rather than passively consuming content (as with television).

- Its affordances are a good match for social and constructivist pedagogies as Web 2.0 is inherently social and is concerned with the co-creation and use of knowledge.

- The barriers to use are low. There are plenty of technologies which teachers and learners can use at no cost (apart from time) and which require little training or equipment to use.

- It is a natural extension of the way that many people are already using the web rather than a completely new departure.

Social learning is nothing new

In order to deconstruct and understand how the WWW, in particular Web 2.0 (Social Web), is influencing learning as a social practice, one must acknowledge that learning from social encounters is nothing new. Even before the Internet, people have always been exploiting social activities, professional individuals, friendship groups, peers networks and family connections in order to develop knowledge, further an understanding of the world and seek answers to some basic questions.

In formal education, social learning, as exemplified through the pedagogic perspective of 'Social Constructivism', is seen as learning through actively constructing new ideas by building and testing hypotheses individually or through collaborative activities and/or dialogue (JISC, 2009: 11). Beyond formal experiences, there is a strong history of self-motivated informal learning environments that demonstrate and reflect these principles of social learning. New online social networking tools and many Web 2.0 services can be seen as a modern reinterpretation and an evolution of traditional (offline) informal face to face environments, activities and relationships. The development and prolific use of web-based services and tools (such as social networking, search engines, blogs and wikis) exemplify that people are supplementing or even replacing traditional forms of knowledge construction with new augmented tools. However, as described earlier, users of this new social web can now engage in a process of knowledge construction online that increasingly involves anonymous individuals that are not known to the user.

Any historians reading this chapter will understand that we have seen this all before, as the new social web draws parallels to the development of other social spaces that have been popular throughout history. Examples of such social spaces are public houses, coffeehouses, tea rooms, union meetings, town hall meetings and public libraries. In some cases, these were originally created for one purpose, such as a commercial enterprise, but then quickly developed into an environment that had affordances that could support and facilitate discussion, conversation, discourse and innovation. Some social spaces were more radical than others, but many shared the characteristic of being an environment that facilitated learning and knowledge construction.

Standage (2003: 48) asks the question, 'Where do you go when you want to know the latest business news, follow commodity prices, keep up with political gossip, find out what others think of a new book, or stay abreast of latest scientific and technological developments?' In a modern context, the obvious answer is log on to the Internet and use a search engine, but in the 17th and 18th centuries it was through a visit to one of the many thousands of coffeehouses that were created. The popularity of coffeehouses stand out as the most radical of popular social spaces used for learning and knowledge construction. Coffeehouses had a number of key attributes that parallel the Internet and the modern phenomenon of social networking online. First, coffeehouses were sober commercial places and therefore allowed sober discourse and debate of the ideas and themes of the day. Second, the barrier to entry (cost of participation) was low and within the budget of most people. And lastly, the space itself was socially democratic, insofar as it flattened traditional hierarchical social structures and imposed its own new rules of social conduct and activity that broke from traditional norms.

Seventeenth-century coffeehouse enthusiast and fellow of the Royal Society John Houghton gives a telling account of the impact of coffeehouses in the following assessment:

> Coffee-houses make all sorts of people sociable, the rich and the poor meet together, as also do the learned and unlearned. It improves arts, merchandize, and all other knowledge; for here an inquisitive man, that aims at good learning, may get more in an evening than he shall by books in a month: he may find out such coffee-houses, where men frequent, who are studious in such matters as his enquiry tends to, and he may in short space gain the pith and marrow of the others reading and studies. I have heard a worthy friend of mine . . . who was of good learning . . . say, that he did think, that coffeehouses had improved useful knowledge, as much as [the universities] have, and spake in no way of slight to them neither. (Cowan, 2005: 99)

Coffeehouses quickly became popular and were distinct environments with attributes and activities that lead them to being commonly referred to as 'Penny Universities'. Critically, these social spaces were new informal learning environments that could challenge formal institutions. As Cowan (2005) makes clear, these 'Penny Universities' were emphatically not university institutions and the activities they encouraged were radically different from any university tutorial, both in their organisation and participation.

Much like the debate today of the value of the Internet and informal online learning environments over formal institutions, coffeehouses were not without their critics, both in support and attack. Royal Society scientist and diarist Robert Hooke was another enthusiast and saw them as serious places of work (Cowan, 2005: 105). However, many did not share Hooke's zeal and a 1661 tract complained that:

> since coffeehouse conversation proceeded with 'neither moderators, nor rules' it was like 'a school . . . without

a master'. 'Education is . . . [in the coffeehouse] taught without discipline. Learning (if it be possible) is here insinuated without method.' (Cowan, 2005: 100)

As with many Web 2.0 services on the Internet today (social networking sites, blogs and wikis), many could not see the intellectual value in engaging in the current fashion. Commentators at the time complained that the new style of conversation in public coffeehouses was found to be 'fluently romantick nonsense, unintelligible gibberish, florishing lyes and nonsense' (Cowan, 2005: 93). Beyond a view that coffeehouses were just trivial, many were concerned that patronage of these coffeehouses could be dangerous, erroneous and that unintelligent conversations could undermine formal institutions. In 1663 the vice chancellor of Cambridge University mandated that coffeehouse keepers 'suffer no scholars of this University, under the degree of Masters of Arts, to drinke coffee, chocolate, sherbett, or tea . . . except their tutors be with them' (Cowan, 2005: 93).

Despite concerns about the coffeehouses' threat to society and formal learning environments, they remained very popular for two centuries. Coffeehouses were a radical and innovative construction and resulted in either supporting or giving rise to the creation of now familiar and important institutions in British society. One example is seen through the development of the insurance company Lloyds of London. Lloyds of London demonstrates that coffeehouses evolved into specialist environments, reflecting the clientele that frequented them. In the case of Lloyds coffeehouse, the Lloyds insurance institution developed from people being attracted to Lloyds coffeehouse as it held auctions of ships, sold insurance and published a financial paper. Coffeehouses in the 17th and 18th century can be viewed in very similar ways to how the Internet is used today. Melton (2001: 226) describes them as functionally similar to the Internet as you could use them to 'find jobs, conduct business, exchange information, or celebrate important events of their lives'. These coffeehouses reflected the spirit of the age (the Zeitgeist) and these new social spaces were 'born in an age of revolution, restoration, and bitter party rivalries' (Melton, 2001: 241). Equally, as the Internet re-adjusts the relationship between institutions and its citizens, the 'coffeehouse provided public space at a time when political action and debate had begun to spill beyond the institutions that had traditionally contained them' (Melton, 2001: 241).

The potential for technologies to become a new and dominant force in social communication and learning is exemplified by the way in which the coffeehouse network developed and radically altered people's behaviour. Coffeehouses did not just operate in isolation and became interconnected and self referential. Newspapers, gazettes, pamphlets and information 'feeds' were produced from within the coffeehouse network and were about the activities going on within them. For example, early popular newspapers included the *Post Boy*, the *Daily Courant* and the *Event Post* (Inwood, 2004). One of the most famous publication names was set up in a response to the coffeehouse phenomenon, *The Tatler* in 1709 by Richard Steele. It could be argued that these types of publications were the RSS feed or blog aggregators of the 17th and 18th centuries. These publications were the output of thoughts and ideas from the leading thinkers of the day and helped shape public opinion, in the contemporary world we would conceptually know this as the Blogosphere.

This aggregation of information for publication is described in detail in the following Tatler entry (12/04/1709):

> All accounts of gallantry, pleasure, and entertainment, shall be under the article of White's Chocolate-house;

> poetry, under that of Will's Coffee-house; learning, under the title of Grecian; foreign and domestic news, you will have from St. James's Coffee-house; and what else I shall on any other subject offer, shall be dated from my own apartment. (Aitken, 2004)

The development of news media was a radical change to the ordinary person, as cheap daily printed news had not been very common before. The result of all this new mass media was the development of the daily newspaper culture, giving rise to better informed individuals that could form an opinion about current affairs.

> All Englishmen are great newsmongers. Workmen habitually begin the day by going to coffee-rooms in order to read the latest news. I have often seen shoeblacks and other persons of that class club together to purchase a farthing paper. (Shoemaker, 2007: 18)

Analysing why coffeehouses were so radical to 17th and 18th century societies affords us a useful insight into how the Internet is affecting changes to our contemporary society. Essentially, one can see that the coffeehouse phenomenon was born out of a synergism that occurred between printing technology, mass literacy, mass media, popular culture and political change. The technology of the printing press evolved to make printed material cheaper, more accessible and lead to improved literacy rates in the 17th and 18th centuries (Wheale, 1999: 90–91). This happened at the same time as coffee and chocolate becoming a popular and affordable beverage, available at numerous coffeehouses. The subsequent evolution of the coffeehouse to 'Penny Universities' allowed the free exchange of ideas that had the potential to form new formal institutions, such as Lloyds.

Through this timeline of development, the coffeehouse itself can be identified as an important 'soft technology' that influenced important economic and socio-political change. Zhouying (2005) describes these types of soft technologies as important elements in either innovation or industrial, societal and economic revolutions as they are 'both the tool and the content of technological innovation' (p. 139) that act 'as the process technology for technology transfer, technology commercialization and industrialization' (p. 139). What seems to be crucial is that 'soft technology can be seen as a servant of the transfer, and even industrialization, of other technologies' (p. 139). In simple terms, the act of people congregating together, enjoying a sober pleasure and engaging in the simple act of the free exchange of ideas and news brought forth some radical innovations. With this in mind it is apparent that the Internet can be seen in a similar light, as this new technology is facilitating communication, dialogue and information exchange that is altering the ways in which people are living their lives, socialising, conducting business and engaging in knowledge construction.

The Internet as the modern wireless 'Penny University'

As Standage (2003) identified, coffee fuelled the information exchange of the 17th and 18th centuries and contemporary coffeehouses have continued this tradition through the phenomenon of the Cyber Cafe of the mid-1990s. However, unlike the coffeehouses of the 17th century, Cyber Cafes were quickly superseded by Internet connections at home and at work. Crucially, Cyber Cafes have moved from offering pay as you go, fixed line and site specific Internet connections to now offering a free wireless connection through hosting Wi-Fi hotspots. This is not a unique situation as many other popular high street restaurant chains have copied this service by also offering Wi-Fi hotspots to attract customers. Fundamentally, contemporary communications technology is increasingly 'wireless' as in addition to Wi-Fi hotspots, web-enabled devices, such as mobile phones, use the wireless mobile telephone network to connect to the Internet. Through the development and addition of wireless communications technologies to the fixed-line network, users now have access to the Internet anytime and anywhere. This situation is revolutionary in respect to the process of knowledge construction and social learning, as it has the potential of creating a generation or a group of people that is always online in any context. Ostensibly, through having your access to information un-restricted by any barrier, one can consider information and the Internet as a new utility. Much like the traditional utilities, the Internet is something that can be connected to and a valuable product drawn from it, an important utility for the knowledge society and the knowledge economy.

In the 2006 JISC report into the 'Learner Experience of e-Learning' (LEX), students' use and attitudes towards contemporary technology in education were investigated. Their findings reflect this developing theme of information being considered as a utility. In addition, the report found that contemporary technology and the Internet played an increasingly important part in the knowledge construction process of students, both informally and formally. Fundamentally, many students considered that it was an essential part of their lives, exemplified in the following statements:

> I'm addicted, it's the first thing I turn on in the morning before I even wake up and actually it's very, very bad. I think in the future people can't cope without their

laptops. My main use of it is I guess social networking. It would be My Space and Messenger and e-mail things like that and then secondary would be information gathering in terms of like I said, my home page is the technology website and current affairs, news. I have alerts coming into me so I get information and then I use search engines for academic purposes (Emma, undergraduate business student). (JISC, 2006: 13)

I'll usually like read [the newspaper] on-line and I never realised that I'm actually learning in a way, know what I mean, because . . . you're learning about, like, the economy and like, what's happening day to day and, like, politics and stuff and it never came to me that I was actually learning something when you're reading the paper, know what I mean, but you are, so it was . . . 'Oh I'm learning and I'm not aware of it' [laughs] (Lynsey, first year undergraduate student). (JISC, 2006: 9)

I tend to be a bit of a networker in general so I would go and ask people for help, like I've got a lot of friends who would be doing computer science degrees, things like that, they would help me out, or looking up things . . . you can use the Internet to self-teach, you can get . . . tutorials and things (Emma, undergraduate business student). (JISC, 2006: 11)

The LEX report supports Efimova's (2004) examination of a contemporary student's knowledge construction in the 21st century. Efimova highlights that contemporary students are becoming modern knowledge workers engaged in the activities of 'finding, interpreting and connecting pieces of information, articulating ideas, engaging in conversations that lead to elaborating ideas and developing relations with others, keeping track of personal notes, conversations and contacts' (p. 11).

Efimova identifies that the activities that a knowledge worker undertakes can be mapped across the three dimensions of 'Ideas', 'Individuals', and 'Communities & Networks'. These three dimensions relate to either formal relationships, such as through a university, or informal relationships, such as friendship or peer groups. It is apparent that with the development of the Internet, students as knowledge workers, can now support, extend or supplant their traditional offline information sources by accessing a wider network of information sources online (such as wikis, blogs, forums and search engines). An interesting characteristic of these online information sources is that they reflect 'The Wisdom of the Crowds', which represents the principle that the many are wiser than the few. Essentially, the user of the information has no relationship to the originators of the information and must therefore decide to trust the information being supplied. This trust judgement relies on new trust indices, such as brand name or previous experience of the service. Hulme (2009: 5) reports that 71 per cent of young people questioned stated that when looking for help and advice it is best to find as "many opinions as possible. As a decision framework, Hulme (2009: 24) outlines some decision criteria that young people, the so called 'Digital Natives' (Prensky, 2001), may use:

- professional reputation;
- offline reputation (including having professional staff with resources to gather definitive and credible information);
- previous personal experience with the site;
- proof of neutral affiliation (.gov for government site; edu for education; .org for non-profits);
- tone of the writing (neutral versus opinionated);
- elements of style (use of quotes, pictures, by-lines, newspaper layout).

Dron and Anderson (2009) offer some valuable dimensions to understanding this online process of information gathering in their investigation of new 'Collectives', 'Networks' and 'Groups' mediated with social software. They postulate that the Internet environment allows students to blend their online information sources with traditional information sources from offline relationships.

Groups

Dron and Anderson (2009) see 'Groups' as formally organised associations. In a learning context these are 'educational communities or classes, typically having a well-defined membership, a clear focus, a hierarchical composition and a distinct border between activities of the group and those of the larger community'. (Dron and Anderson 2009, n.p.)

Networks

Unlike 'Groups', Dron and Anderson (2009) see 'Networks' as less formal communities that can be joined on an ad hoc basis. Essentially, these 'Networks' reflect the 'relationships between people and the groups of which they are a part, going well beyond the formal groupings formerly found in online formal educational communities. Being part of a network is often a weaker, less readily classifiable relationship than membership of a group.' (Dron and Anderson 2009, n.p.)

Collectives

Dron and Anderson (2009) see 'Collectives' as informal connections to the Internet and epitomised by the terms the 'Wisdom of the Crowds' or the 'Hive Mind'.

'Collectives are characterised by software-mediated aggregation: they are not about connections, but instead are formed by grouping people and their largely independent activities into sets.' Contemporary technologies typically associated with 'Collectives' are tag clouds (e.g. Folksonomies), search engines (e.g Google PageRank), recommendation systems (e.g. Ebay and Amazon) and reputation/ratings systems (e.g. YouTube). Dron and Anderson (2009) identify that the Internet uses such technology and software in an attempt to 'combine the implicit or explicit behaviours and opinions of the many to offer an emergent structure which is not determined by a single designer and which cannot easily be predicted in advance'. Essentially, the information contained within the Internet is being constantly reviewed by the 'Collective' to ascertain its value and is continually being graded, ranked and having additional value added to it. This process allows users to discover resources, information, opinions or sources that the 'Collective' determines to be the most relevant at that particular moment in time. (Dron and Anderson 2009, n.p.)

The phenomena that Dron and Anderson (2009) outline are supported by the following key findings of the Life Support Report (Hulme, 2009: 6).

- Young people believe the Internet provides both more and better sources of information than was previously readily available.

- The Internet plays a key role in the full process of advice gathering, exploration and action and is consistently rated alongside family (in certain specific incidences it can take precedence) and friends as a source of advice in stressful situations.

- Some 82 per cent of young people surveyed said they had used the Internet to look for advice and information for themselves.

- The significance of the Internet as the single first-advice source is illustrated by it its ranking in the top three sources across all issues. When one takes search, online forums and online help-sites together the Internet is first source for a quarter of the sample in the case of each issue.

- Up to 71 per cent of young people cross-check any advice they receive online with advice from other sources.

- The Internet plays a greater role than merely providing information. It is seen as an opportunity to learn from/ engage with others in similar situations and as a direct source of expert support.

- As many as 84 per cent of 16–24s said 'the Internet brings communities of similar people closer together'.

Hulme (2009: 32) offers us some insight into the complicated picture we find when trying to understand how young people seek to have questions answered. For example, the report finds that 47 per cent would turn to friends in the first instance to seek advice about relationship issues, while only 4 per cent would seek professional advice. When it comes to health concerns, 27 per cent would seek professional advice, with only 8 per cent asking friends first.

An interesting phenomenon that Hulme (2009) outlines is that a participatory Internet has allowed people, particularly the young, to be more interactive in the way they learn and that they see online conversation and chat as learning opportunities. Hulme (2009) identifies that 'there are those who directly solicit information, those who dispense and those who learn by watching peer-to-peer conversations with individuals probably adopting differing behaviours as appropriate to changing circumstances' (Hulme, 2009: 39). A valuable consequence of casually browsing and engaging in social network sites, bulletin boards and chat is that they are opportunities for 'incidental' learning. Foley (2004: 5) describes incidental learning as learning that occurs while people perform other activities, and that this type of learning activity is 'often unplanned, is often tacit, and may be constructive or destructive'. Foley also identifies that learning can be varied as 'the content of learning may be technical (about how to do a particular task); or it may be social, cultural and political (about how people relate to each other in a particular situation, about what their actual core values are, or about who has power and how they use it)' (2004: 5).

What is clear is that the Internet encourages learning through evoking a spirit of altruism or as a response to being merely participatory or interactive. This can almost be seen as the 'holy grail' to educators; is the Internet an environment that surreptitiously encourages people to engage in learning?

Knowing stuff: what we now do with information

One of the most interesting emergent features of the Web 2.0 era is that all users are now potentially 'Prosumers', meaning that they have the role of both consumers, producers and co-producers in the Internet. What this dual role has allowed is a cultural shift on the consumption and production of data, content, information and knowledge in the 21st century. Essentially, web users can either passively consume (e.g. lurking or browsing), create something new for the WWW (e.g. blogs and wikis) or be active consumers by being creative and 'remixing' third party outputs into new forms. In addition to this, the separation of content from design is a useful attribute of Web 2.0 as it allows users to re-purpose materials into new contexts through easy to use web tools and simple HTML. For example, online video hosting services offer embedding capabilities that allows the re-purposing of videos from one location into multiple web pages and new contexts (personal blogs, collaborative wikis and learning network sites). Hulme (2009: 18) fundamentally sees this as revolutionary for contemporary students as 'the availability and their use of the new tools gives [sic] this group a range and depth of conversation not available to previous generations'.

The findings of the Life Support Report (Hulme, 2009) demonstrate that the Internet is a potentially important technology that could support the higher order skills of critical thinking, analysis and synthesis of ideas. This type of cognitive technology joins the list of other technologies that have improved the learning process by removing some mundane or routine tasks, for example word processors, spreadsheets and presentation tools. Crucially for educators, Anderson (2008: 16) highlights that in order to promote higher-order thinking on the Web, 'online learning must create challenging activities that enable learners to link new information to old; acquire meaningful knowledge; and use their metacognitive abilities; hence, it is the instructional strategy, not the technology, that influences the quality of learning'.

The cult of the amateur and the rise of the informal learner and expert

Many commentators have identified the 'Prosumer' as being a disruptive phenomenon, having both a positive and negative impact on our modern world and our ability to construct knowledge. Popular critic of this phenomenon, Andrew Keen, released a book in 2006 entitled *The Cult of the Amateur: How Blogs, Wikis, Social Networking, and the Digital World are Assaulting our Economy, Culture and*

Values (Newsnight, 2007). Keen asserts that if we are all amateurs then there are no experts, leading to a world in which culture, economy and values are degraded. In regard to education, learning and knowledge construction, Keen makes an important point about the threats to our understanding of the world. Keen identifies that if the line between fact and fiction is blurred by uninformed and anonymous sources online, our ability to construct valid and reliable knowledge is undermined. This tension was recently exemplified through the 'ClimateGate' scandal that involved the Climate Research Unit (CRU) at the University of East Anglia and the United Nations International Panel on Climate Change (IPCC) (Hulme and Ravetz, 2009). This event demonstrated that the Internet is now a politically influencing force in which citizen commentators, amateur or 'informal' scholars are challenging formal and world leading institutions. Benny Peiser (McKie & Peiser, 2010) commentated that this situation occurred, in part, because 'the emergence of a powerful counter-culture on the blogosphere is no longer reliant on mainstream media. It is driven by new technologies and fed by independent bloggers and researchers who increasingly publish their research and investigations on interactive and autonomous media platforms.' This event highlights an increasing and popular trend opined within the Internet and society in general over the last few years, a trend centred on increasing institutional openness and transparency. Much of this comes as a result of the change in attitudes towards the 'Freedom of Information', whistle-blowing and the willingness to disclosure once restricted information on the Internet (e.g. WikiLeaks, ClimateGate e-mails and 'MPs' Expenses'). Trust in governments and public institutions has been challenged and they have reacted by making many of their data sources and formal documentation publicly available.

As a response to this new era of openness, the Internet is seen as an important influence in increasing links between 'Professionals' and 'Amateurs' (Pro-Am), allowing participants to learn from each other and advance their discipline. These 'Pro-Am' collaborations are obviously nothing new, but the ways in which the relationship is conducted and supported is radically new, and both parties can now take advantage of the following:

- share the same data sources;
- use similar tools that were once too expensive or difficult to use; and
- communicate much more easily with each other through new media tools.

Lombardi (2007: 5) sees the new affordances of the Internet as being crucial in opening up learners to authentic environments that are encouraging formal and informal learning activities with online communities of practice:

> In disciplines from ornithology to social history, students are becoming legitimate peripheral participants in virtual communities of practice, collecting data either first-hand or through remotely located smart sensors. In other cases, students use data collected by researchers (such as virtual sky data accessible through the National Science Digital Library Project) to conduct their own investigations. They are practicing higher-order analysis on real data sets while contributing to the common knowledge base.

Lombardi (2007: 2) sees these authentic learning experiences as very important as 'learners are able to gain a deeper sense of a discipline as a special "culture" shaped by specific ways of seeing and interpreting the world'. It is this access to the formal and informal world of the 'expert' that makes authentic learning a valuable learning experience for a learner. Lombardi (2007: 2) describes this as the learner being exposed to the 'subtle, interpersonal, and unwritten knowledge that members in a community of practice use (often unconsciously) on a daily basis'. This position within a community of practice fundamentally requires the learner to focus on being a subject specialist in addition to learning about the content of the subject. Formal and informal 'Pro-Am' collaborations are now a prolific feature of the Internet. Simple examples can be seen in the form of feedback and comments features on websites that allows a dialogue between a user and an institution or an expert. More complex examples are evident where formal projects invite users to sign up and take part in a formal project. Such projects can ask users to be a participant with their input adding to a growing pool of data. In other instances, the user may be asked to become an informal researcher that analyses data or running project related software that can be download from the project website, for example see The Perception Lab Project (*http:// monty.st-and.ac.uk/*).

At the core of this new 'Pro-Am' phenomenon is the principle of open and free data. This principle has led to the development of open data organisations such as the 'Open Knowledge Foundation'. Iconic figures such as Tim Berners-Lee and Tim O'Reilly have been advocates of the principles of open access to data and many governments have responded through the development of websites such as *http://data.gov .uk/* and *http://data.gov*.

In this era of easy access to highly valuable machine readable datasets, there have been some innovative, creative and useful examples of what people are doing with them. One example is seen after the Haiti earthquake of 2010. In a response to a lack of up-to-date maps for the region, a call for help went out across the Internet using social networking services, for example the following link was posted on Twitter *http:// wiki.openstreetmap.org/wiki/WikiProject_Haiti#GeoEye*. The rescue services were then able to collaborate with the global users of the 'OpenStreetMap' community to produce a current map of the main earthquake areas. Using the 'OpenStreetMap' platform and the most recent digital aerial photographs, volunteers re-drew and added useful data to the map of areas like Port-au-Prince to help aid volunteers on the ground move about the city and locate refugee centres. This was all possible as rescue services were able to access these maps via their mobile devices, all the more important in an area with very poor communications infrastructure.

Pedagogy 2.0? Opportunities and threats of contemporary social learning

Anderson (2008: 100) envisages that the Internet has the potential to change educational systems as 'technologies are a catalyst of change, resulting in the need for educators and institutions to adapt and/or transform'. This assertion is also reflected by George Siemens who, in 2003, made the following statement:

> Society is changing. Learners needs are changing. The course, as a model for learning, is being challenged by communities and networks, which are better able to attend to the varied characteristics of the learning process by using multiple approaches, orchestrated within a learning ecology.

Taken together, Anderson and Siemen are making the case that education and the learning process (praxis) needs to be re-appraised in light of an environment that is increasingly participatory and involves a wider learning environment that includes the WWW. Crucially, this contemporary learning environment is augmented by new technology and now involves external communities populated by experts, amateurs and other various 'grey' sources of information, data and knowledge. On a basic level, one could see this as a challenge to traditional learning environments to include new external sources of information, data and knowledge. However, it is clear that this is not just a content issue and that it is increasingly appropriate to see that contemporary technologies offer a valid alternative to traditional approaches through which the learning is achieved. For example, it is now possible to completely by-pass traditionally formal education systems and instead access quality sources through informal networks and groups. Obviously, this approach is a niche exercise and requires self-direction, self-discovery, self-motivation, peer learning and communities of practice. However, this situation does question the role of formal institutions in knowledge construction and is a challenging situation for traditional pedagogies used in education institutions. What this situation allows us to appreciate is that contemporary learning now involves the 'Social Web' which is giving rise to a 'learning ecology' that is best represented and possibly best served by adopting the Constructivist and Situative approaches to pedagogy. It is uncertain whether these pedagogic perspectives become the dominant or most favoured approaches to adopt. However, Goodfellow (2008: 32) sees 'Constructivist' and 'Situative' as 'ecological' perspectives and the 'ecological perspective leans towards more social and anthropological framings, such as those that inform thinking about learning in "situated", "community", and "networked" learning'.

Developing this further, Franklin (2008: 97) sees contemporary technology as offering something new to pedagogy and that 'the pedagogical foundation for using Web 2.0 in the classroom is related to both changes in students (content creators, digital media enthusiasts) and changes in learning theories conceptualized as a bottom-up, collaborative, participatory process, as in student-centred, constructivism and active learning theories, coincides with the fundamental principles of Web 2.0: community, creativity, participation, and reflexivity'. In addition, Mayes and de Freitas (2004: 10) state that approaches that are participatory, conversational and involve the wider community require that 'effort is made to make the learning activity authentic to the social context in which the skills or knowledge are normally embedded'. This identifies that making education applied and less abstract may be an important trend to consider as well.

Information literacy

In respect to opportunities and threats to education, it is clear that in order to adopt approaches that include information technology we must see information literacy as a key skill for students and educators. Without information literacy as a key skill, many users will be at a disadvantage. Many of the issues currently attributed to the use of technology in education relate to users not being;

- effective knowledge workers;
- aware of their changing role from media consumers to co-producers;
- aware that continued participation with learning will depend on their existing technical skills and how they develop them.

Participation in this new 'social web' occurs in an age of content 'abundance'. Anderson (2008) states that 'every abundance creates a new scarcity' and within the context of education this can be seen as a reference to validity and reliability. Content, data and information is now freely available, therefore the skill to make sound academic judgements on abundant content are of paramount importance. In addition to this, Anderson (2008) sees that as facilitators of the learning process educators need now to operate and create learning experiences which have the following conditions in mind:

- an abundance of information can create a scarcity of context;

- an abundance of choice can create a scarcity of advice;

- an abundance of content can create a scarcity of time;

- an abundance of people competing for your attention can create a scarcity of reputational ways to choose among them.

As an opportunity for education, Lombardi (2007: 3) sees that information literate students which are immersed in new approaches to learning, namely authentic learning activities, have the potential to cultivate the kinds of 'portable skills' that newcomers to any discipline have the most difficulty acquiring on their own:

- the judgement to distinguish reliable from unreliable information;

- the patience to follow longer arguments;

- the synthetic ability to recognise relevant patterns in unfamiliar contexts;

- the flexibility to work across disciplinary and cultural boundaries to generate innovative solutions.

In a recent *Nature* article, Xiong Zhenqin, an ecologist at Nanjing Agricultural University stated that 'research without Google would be like life without electricity' (Qiu, 2010: 1012), indicating that the inclusion of the Internet in education is without compromise. Without a concerted effort to tackle the challenges of information literacy and to appropriately frame learning and knowledge construction in partnership with the Internet, we run the risk of creating insurmountable challenges for the future. At worst we are in danger of creating and fostering cultural cul-de-sacs that ultimately damage knowledge construction and education. Researchers have argued that the Internet encourages the homophily in social learning networks and that by 'interacting only with others who are like ourselves, anything that we experience as a result of our position gets reinforced' (McPherson et al., 2001: 415). This is a troubling issue as 'if there is education there is also miseducation. Educators like to distinguish between propaganda and education, seeing the one as closed, manipulative and oppressive, and the other as open, democratic and emancipatory' (Foley, 2004: 5). What is most concerning here is the difficulty of distinguishing between valid, accurate and factual information on the Internet with mis-information, errors and the distortion of truth. As seen with other forms of media, the Internet does contain propaganda and has the potential to distort and in some instances is distorting education. Why this is occurring is manifold. However, Tim Berners-Lee has highlighted that the issue of validity and reliability is of key concern, stating that 'on the web, the thinking of cults can spread very rapidly and suddenly a cult which was 12 people who had some deep personal issues suddenly find a formula which is very believable' (Swaine, 2008). The blogosphere has the potential to therefore circumvent unbiased and multi-sourced mainstream information sources and therefore could be a key tool for propagandists. Foley (2004: 6) identifies that once established, sources of misinformation could be difficult to counteract as 'propaganda works on simplification: it appeals to fear, hatred, anger and envy'. As former British Prime Minister James Callaghan said, 'A lie can make its way around the world before the truth has the chance to put its boots on' (Newsnight, 2007). However, in the case of the WWW, the lie can now persist through repetition and many experts have personal experience of coming across the phenomenon of 'Zombie Facts', as no matter how many times you shoot down the lie they always have a habit of coming back to life on the Internet.

Conclusions

As with the social and cultural shift that happened with the period of the coffeehouse, the Internet has brought about a paradigm shift to the way our society operates, thinks and organises itself. The recent development of the 'Social Web' is the current disruptive phase of the WWW phenomenon and is likely to see learning as a social practice having a greater influence on everyday communications networks, information gathering and knowledge construction. In this new phase, finding and accessing information is no longer a problem but trusting it and so constructing reliable and valid knowledge with it is of mandatory concern.

As a concluding thought or twist, the Internet may ultimately succumb to commercial or authoritarian forces that will try to impose control over it. Greater regulation and quality control may not be in the original spirit of the WWW, but if activities continue to have a negative impact on our everyday lives and the knowledge economy on which we all thrive, the more the likelihood that the Internet will be controlled. What this future control looks like is open to debate, but it is not impossible to think that 'soft technologies' like quality kite-marks, paywalls and copyright legislation will be enacted to control it. These may seem draconian but as with all 'Tragedy of the Commons' issues it is never wise to poison the well on which you draw your water.

References

Adams, D. (1999). *How to Stop Worrying and Learn to Love the Internet* [Online]. Available from: *http://www .douglasadams.com/dna/19990901-00-a.html* (accessed 14 May 2010).

Aitken, G. (2004) *The Tatler*, Volume 1, 1899 [Online]. Available from: *http://www.gutenberg.org/etext/13645* (accessed 14 May 2010).

Anderson, C. (2008) *http://www.longtail.com/the_long_tail/2008/04/seth-godin-asks.html* (accessed 29 April 2008).

Anderson, T. (ed.) (2008) *The Theory and Practice of Online Learning*. (Second edition). Edmonton, AB, CAN: Athabasca University Press.

Armstrong, J. & Franklin, T. (2008). *A review of current and developing international practice in the use of social networking (Web 2.0) in higher education.* [Online]. Available from: *http://franklin-consulting.co.uk/ LinkedDocuments/the%20use%20of%20social%20 networking%20in%20HE.pdf* (accessed 14 May 2010).

Cowan, B. W. (2005). *Social Life of Coffee: The Emergence of the British Coffeehouse.* New Haven, CT, USA: Yale University Press.

Dron, J. & Anderson, T. (2009) Lost in social space: Information retrieval issues in Web 1.5. *Journal of Digital Information* [Online] Vol 10, No 2. Available from: *http://*

journals.tdl.org/jodi/article/viewArticle/443/280 (accessed 14 May 2010).

Efimova, L. (2004). Discovering the iceberg of knowledge work: A weblog case. [Online]. Available from: *https://doc.telin.nl/dscgi/ds.py/Get/File-34786* (accessed 14 May 2010).

Foley, G. (2004) *Dimensions of Adult Learning*. Berkshire, GB: McGraw-Hill Education.

Franklin, T. (2008) A review of current and developing international practice in the use of social networking (Web 2.0) in higher education [Online] *http://franklin-consulting.co.uk/LinkedDocuments/the%20use%20of%20social%20networking%20in%20HE.pdf* (accessed 14 May 2010).

Goodfellow, R. (2008) *Challenging e-Learning in the University: A Literacies Perspective*. Buckingham: Open University Press.

Hulme, M. (2009) YouthNet Report: Life Support – Young people's needs in a digital age [Online] *http://www.youthnet.org/content/1/c6/06/00/73/Life%20Support%20%20Young%20people%27s%20needs%20in%20a%20digital%20age.pdf* (accessed 14 May 2010).

Hulme, M. & Ravetz, J. (2009). 'Show Your Working': What 'ClimateGate' means [Online]. Available from: *http://news.bbc.co.uk/1/hi/8388485.stm* (accessed 14 May 2010).

Inwood, S. (2004). Coffee Shop Society in 17th Century London. [Online]. Available from: *http://www.gresham.ac.uk/event.asp?EventId=253&PageId=108* (accessed 14 May 2010).

JISC (2006). LEX: The Learner Experience of e-Learning Final Project Report [Online]. Available from: *http://www.jisc.ac.uk/uploaded_documents/LEX%20Final%20Report_August06.pdf* (accessed 14 May 2010).

JISC (2009). *Effective Practice in a Digital Age: A guide to technology-enhanced learning and teaching.* [Online].

Available from: *http://www.jisc.ac.uk/media/documents/ publications/effectivepracticedigitalage.pdf* (accessed 14 May 2010).

Kelly, K. (2007). *Kevin Kelly on the next 5,000 days of the web.* [Online]. Available from: *http://www.ted.com/talks/ kevin_kelly_on_the_next_5_000_days_of_the_web.html* (accessed 14 May 2010).

Lombardi, M. (2007). Authentic Learning for the 21st Century: An Overview. [Online]. Available from: *http:// net.educause.edu/ir/library/pdf/ELI3009.pdf* (accessed 14 May 2010).

Mayes, T. & de Freitas, S. (2004) JISC e-Learning Models Desk Study Stage 2: Review of e-learning theories, frameworks and models. [Online]. Available from: *http:// www.jisc.ac.uk/uploaded_documents/Stage%202%20 Learning%20Models%20%28Version%201%29.pdf* (accessed 14 May 2010).

McKie, R. & Peiser, B. (2010). Robin McKie v Benny Peiser. *The Observer.* 7th February. Available from: *http://www .guardian.co.uk/commentisfree/2010/feb/07/robin-mckie -benny-peiser-climate* (accessed 01 April 2010).

McPherson, M., Smith-Lovin, L. & Cook, J. M. (2001) Birds of a feather: Homophily in Social Networks. *Annu. Rev. Sociol.* 27: 415–44. [Online] Available from: http:// arjournals.annualreviews.org/doi/pdf/10.1146/annurev .soc.27.1.415 (accessed 31 March 2010).

Melton, J. (2001). *Rise of the Public in Enlightenment Europe.* Port Chester, NY, USA: Cambridge University Press.

Newsnight Book Club (2007). The Cult of the Amateur by Andrew Keen. The BBC. [Online] 5 June 2007. Available from: *http://www.bbc.co.uk/blogs/newsnight/2007/06/the_ cult_of_the_amateur_by_andrew_keen.html* (accessed 14 May 2010).

Prensky, M. (2001). Digital Natives, Digital Immigrants [Online]. Available from: *http://www.marcprensky.com/writing/Prensky%20-%20Digital%20Natives,%20Digital%20Immigrants%20-%20Part1.pdf* (accessed 14 May 2010).

Qui, J. (2010). A Land Without Google? *Nature*, 465 (2): 1012–13.

Shoemaker, R. (2007) *London Mob: Violence and Disorder in Eighteenth-Century England.* London: Continuum International Publishing.

Siemens, G. (2003). Learning Ecology, Communities, and Networks: Extending the classroom. [Online]. Available from: *http://elearnspace.org/Articles/learning_communities.htm* (accessed 14 May 2010).

Standage, T. (2003). The Internet in a cup. *The Economist*, 369 (8355): 48–50.

Swaine, J. (2008). Internet is fostering disinformation, says web's creator. *The Telegraph*, 15 September. Available from: *http://www.telegraph.co.uk/technology/3358458/Internet-is-fostering-disinformation-says-webs-creator.html* (accessed 10 May 2010).

Wheale, N. (1999) *Writing and Society: Literacy Print and Politics in Britain (1590–1660).* Florence, KY, USA: Routledge.

Zhouying, J. (2005). *Global Technological Change: From Hard to Soft Technology.* Bristol: Intellect Books.

10

Understanding the information literacy competencies of UK Higher Education students

Jillian R. Griffiths and Bob Glass

Abstract: There has been some interesting debate regarding the assessment of students' information literacy skills. Key questions have arisen such as: what standards and criteria should we use to assess students, what are we actually trying to measure, what type of test is the most appropriate, what do the results mean, how do we measure improvements and what are the effects of intervention.

Our research project, funded by the LearnHigher Centre for Excellence in Teaching & Learning, decided to address the above questions via the use of psychometric tests. An online information literacy audit, the ILT (Wise et al., 2005), was used to assess the information literacy skills of a cohort of undergradute students in the Department of Information & Communications at Manchester Metropolitan University from 2008 to 2010. Based on the ACRL standards the ILT measures four of the five information literacy competencies.

Our specific research aims were to ascertain if the testing methods were appropriate to UK students, identify areas for information literacy improvement raised in the test scores, identify practitioner intervention strategies and find out whether they could make a difference to students' information literacy levels.

Test results (presented and discussed in detail in the chapter) indicated that students struggled with (predictable) areas of Information Literacy, and that (a) identification and intervention in this area is useful to students and information literacy helpers (whoever they are); (b) intervention needs to be ongoing – not only in Year 1; (c) even up to their final year students continue to struggle with the same particular activities; and (d) a variety of approaches to support may be needed to help students develop their skills.

Following completion of the testing, discussions have taken place with the CILIP CSG for information literacy regarding the creation of a UK information literacy question bank.

Key words: information literacy, online, audits, tests, undergraduate, higher education, UK.

Introduction

There has been some interesting debate recently regarding the assessment of students' information literacy skills. A number of key questions have arisen such as: what standards and criteria should we use to assess students, what are we actually trying to measure, what type of test is the most appropriate, what do the results mean, how do we measure improvements and what are the effects of intervention? Is a 'one test fits all' solution practical? While a number of information literacy audits or tests exist, it was decided that this research would use one of the most widely trialled information literacy tests, the online 'Information Literacy Test' (ILT) from Steven Wise, Lynne Cameron and their team at the Institute for Computer Based Assessment, James Madison University, Virginia, USA (Wise et al., 2005).

This chapter details a longitudinal assessment of an undergraduate cohort at the Department of Information & Communications, Manchester Metropolitan University, undertaken in the context of the LearnHigher CETL (Information Literacy Learning Area) research activities.

The research aims were to:

(a) ascertain if the testing method was appropriate to UK undergraduate students;

(b) identify areas for information literacy improvement;

(c) identify practitioner intervention strategies and whether they could make a difference to students' information literacy.

The work undertaken was longitudinal in nature and was repeated with the same group of students as they progressed from year 1 to year 2 to year 3 of their undergraduate programmes. The initial testing took place during January and February 2007 and was repeated in 2008 and 2009. The test was taken by students from the Common Undergraduate Programme of the Department of Information & Communications. The test measures performance in four of the five information literacy competencies identified in US formulated ACRL standards (ACRL, 2000). Analysis of the results of this first set of test results has been undertaken using SPSS and this chapter will present findings and recommendations for future work.

The results indicated that there were indeed significant areas of weakness in students' ability measured against four of the five ACRL competency standards and, while intervention by practitioners improved student performance, it was found that ongoing support was required to ensure continued progress. The following sections will discuss this work in greater detail.

Background and context

In recent years there has been a growing recognition of the importance of information literacy. Two high profile examples of such recognition are the Executive Order establishing a California ICT Digital Literacy Leadership Council and an ICT Digital Advisory Committee posted by US California Governor Arnold Schwarzenneger (May 2009) and the Presidential Proclamation on the National Information Literacy Awareness Month, issued in October 2009 (*http://www.whitehouse.gov/the_press_office/ presidential-proclamation-national-information-literacy- awareness-month/*).

The concept of 'information literacy' was first introduced in 1974 by Paul Zurkowski, president of the US Information Industry Association, in a proposal submitted to the National Commission on Libraries and Information Science (NCLIS). He recommended that a national programme be established to achieve universal information literacy within the next decade. According to Zurkowski: 'People trained in the application of information resources to their work can be called information literates. They have learned techniques and skills for utilizing the wide range of information tools as well as primary sources in moulding information solutions to their problems' (Behrens, 1994; Bruce, 1997). In this definition Zurkowski suggested that information resources are applied in a work situation; techniques and skills are needed for using information tools and primary sources; and information is used in problem solving (Behrens, 1994: 310).

During recent years discussions about the terms information literacy and information skills, and the nature of the concepts have intensified in the UK. There are different approaches which are demonstrated by the use of differing terms such as 'information literacy' and 'information skills' and many definitions have been suggested by several organisations, institutions and authors (Virkus, 2003). Researchers of the UK's Joint Information Systems Committee (JISC) funded 'The Big Blue' project, led by the Manchester Metropolitan University, and the University of Leeds found that in many instances both terms are used to describe what is essentially the same concept: 'information literacy' and 'information skills' can be described as synonyms (The Big Blue, 2002). Stubbings and Brine (2003) also note that at Loughborough University the phrases 'information literacy' and 'information skills' are both used to convey the same meaning. The *Glossary of Information Terms* at the British Open University (OU) Library site seems to support the same approach giving the following definition of information literacy: 'a skill that involves being able to use information successfully, including finding information, searching using various tools (e.g., Internet, databases) and being able to critically evaluate the results' (OU, 2003; Virkus, 2003).

Hepworth (2000a, 2000b) highlights two main approaches to information literacy that are evident: (1) attempts to identify discrete skills and attitudes that can be learnt and measured, for example Doyle (1992), the Information Literacy Competency Standards for Higher Education (ACRL, 2000) and the SCONUL approach (SCONUL, 1999); (2) emphasis on the information literate mindset associated with how an individual experiences and makes sense of his/her world, for example the work of Bruce (1997) illustrates this approach and is described as the behavioural, constructivist and relational approaches to information literacy (Virkus, 2003).

In the UK two critical definitions have been presented, by SCONUL and by CILIP. The broadly-based definition of information skills in higher education of the Society of

College, National and University Libraries (SCONUL) Information Skills Task Force (now the SCONUL Advisory Committee on information literacy (Alvestrand, 2003)) reflects the twin dimensions of the 'competent information user' at the base level and the 'information-literate person'. For the latter level of information skills, the term 'information literacy' is used. Therefore, both information skills and information technology (IT) skills are seen as essential parts of the wider concept of information literacy. For the development of the information-literate person SCONUL proposes seven sets of skills. The outline model of information skills generated in the briefing paper has become known as the *Seven Pillars Model*. The pillars show an iterative process whereby information users progress through competency to expertise by practising the skills (SCONUL, 1999; Bainton, 2001).

In 2003 the Information Literacy Executive met to agree a definition of information literacy for use by CILIP (the Chartered Institute of Library and Information Professionals) members. The definition was approved by the CILIP Council in December 2004 as CILIP's definition on information literacy:

> Information literacy is knowing when and why you need information, where to find it, and how to evaluate, use and communicate it in an ethical manner.

Further, this definition details a set of skills (or competencies) which are required for an individual to be information literate. These are that they have an understanding of:

- a need for information
- the resources available
- how to find information

- the need to evaluate results
- how to work with or exploit results
- ethics and responsibility of use
- how to communicate or share your findings
- how to manage your findings.

The CILIP Community Services Group (CSG) sub-group for information literacy acts as advocates and facilitators for the development of information literacy awareness and education within the UK and beyond through committee work, the LILAC conference (*http://lilacconference .com*) and their website (*http://www.informationliteracy .org.uk/*).

While there have been numerous national initiatives to address information literacy it remains a key challenge as to how we measure or assess an individual's level of information literacy, and any progress that may be made to improvement of an individual's information literacy skills. The research presented here used the US ILT test and identified that specific areas for concern could be highlighted and thus targeted for intervention and that levels of information literacy varied across the three year longitudinal study, at the same time recognising that the American bias in the style of the questions and their focus might influence the understanding and subsequent performance of UK students taking the test.

The ILT is an online psychometric test comprising some sixty-five multiple-choice questions, of which sixty are scored, assessing a range of information literacy Competences. Design and validation of the test was created by psychologist Steven Wise and question content was created by Lynne Cameron, each heading up a team of associated contributors (Wise and Yang, 2003; Wise et al., 2005).

Information literacy Testing at MMU – context

A successful consortium bid to create a 'One Stop Shop' for resources for learner development in HE resulted in the creation of the LearnHigher Centre for Excellence in Teaching and Learning (CETL) in January 2005 (*www .learnhigher.ac.uk*). LearnHigher received funding as one of 74 Centres for Excellence in Teaching and Learning created by HEFCE as part of their learning and teaching enhancement strategy (*http://www.hefce.ac.uk/learning/ tinits/cetl/*).

Led by Liverpool Hope University, LearnHigher was the largest collaborative CETL with partners from 16 institutions. Each partner committed to improving student learning by providing resources to support learning development and, through practice-led research, to evaluate the effective use of those resources. LearnHigher aimed to create a network of expertise seeking to enhance professional practice and student learning, and to build capacity both within the network and across the wider sector.

LearnHigher members sought to identify, map and label the key issues and topics of learner development. Agreement on what the 'learning areas' should be, how they should be supported and what outcomes were expected was considered critical from the outset of the project. The learning areas below were chosen in the light of relevance to the project aims, expertise of the individuals and institutions taking part and consortium discussion. Most of the HEIs involved in the LearnHigher CETL were allocated one learning area; a small number had two. Manchester Metropolitan University is working in the learning area for information literacy (Glass, 2006, 2007a, b). There were initially 19 learning areas in all:

- Academic Writing
- Assessment
- Critical Thinking and Reflection
- Doing Research
- Group Work
- Independent Learning
- Information Literacy
- Listening and Interpersonal Skills
- Learning for All
- Mobile Learning
- Note Making
- Numeracy Maths and Statistics
- Oral Communication
- Personal Development Planning
- Reading
- Referencing
- Report Writing
- Time Management
- Business and Commercial Awareness.

The information literacy learning area at MMU, led by Bob Glass, was administered via a team made up of academics, library practitioners, learning support advisers and research associates. Through this team a large number of activities and resources were created and uploaded to the Information Literacy Learning Area of the LearnHigher Website (*http://learnhigher.ac.uk/Staff/Information-literacy.html*).

A requirement of the project brief was that each learning area should contribute evidence of their research activities and disseminate the outcomes. As part of the research contribution to the Information Literacy Research Area it was decided to run an information literacy audit for all year 1 students in the Department of Information & Communications, MMU, in late 2006. This project was also supported by a small grant from the Learning & Teaching Group in the Humanities, Law and Social Sciences faculty, plus the department of Information & Communications. Additionally it was decided to include around 20 students from another department in the faculty in order to generate comparative data.

The Information Literacy Test that we used was the ACRL-based (ACRL, 2000), James Madison University (JMU), 'Online Information Literacy Test' (ILT). There were a number of reasons for this including the nature of the test, the similarities in the standards and the availability of a 'product' that was ready to use. Most of the testing took place during December 2006 and February 2007. Seventy-five students in the common undergraduate programme of the department of Information & Communications and twenty from the Economics department in the same faculty were tested. The psychometric test (which is charged for on a per student basis) is based on 65 multiple choice questions. Sixty of the questions are static, five are used as 'practice' questions for development purposes and are varied as required by the test developers. It takes between 60 and 75 minutes for students to complete the test, depending on the speed of the student taking the test. The test measures performance in four of the five information literacy competencies identified in US-formulated ACRL standards (ACRL, 2000); written abilities cannot really be addressed by this kind of test. Students receive their score immediately at the end of the test, and tutors are provided with an extensive range of statistics relating to the student performance, question scores and overall test results. The data file is provided in Access, Excel, SPSS or other formats. We undertook our analysis using SPSS as this was the most convenient format to use at MMU. Previous results have been presented by Glass and Griffiths (2008, 2009, 2010).

Research methods

Longitudinal testing was undertaken with a cohort of undergraduate students over the three-year period of their academic life at MMU. The number of students participating were:

- Year 1 = 62
- Year 2 = 28
- Year 3 = 45

In year 1, students undertook the test within computer teaching labs within the Department of Information & Communications during one-hour 'seminar' sessions (allowing for 'over run' time if necessary). The sessions were formal, supervised and run as part of a year 1 compulsory unit ('Information Literacies for the Digital Age'), facilitated by Bob Glass and Chris Dawson, both departmental tutors.

In year 2, participation was semi-voluntary and unsupervised. Fewer students took part than in year 1 and those that did were those for library and information-related degree routes.

In year 3 the tests were administered, once again, in one-hour seminars as part of a compulsory unit and supervised by a tutor. Participation increased, although an element of test fatigue was noted.

The ACRL standards assess information literacy competencies using five measures. However, one of the standards (Standard 4: the student is able to use information effectively to accomplish a specific purpose – i.e. writing an essay), cannot be measured using a multiple-choice item format and was excluded from these assessments. Therefore the four standards assessed via the ILT are:

- Standard 1: defines and articulates the nature and extent of the information needed.

- Standard 2: accesses needed information effectively and efficiently.

- Standard 3: evaluates information and its sources critically and incorporates selected information into his or her knowledge base and value system.

- Standard 5: understands many of the ethical, legal and socio-economic issues surrounding information and information technology.

Results

Two performance level standards have been defined by the ACRL ILT creators, these are Proficient and Advanced. A score of 65–89 per cent (39–53 out of 60) is required for a student to be assessed as Proficient, and a score of 90 per cent+ (54+ out of 60) for a student to be assessed as Advanced.

A Proficient student will be able to:

- describe how libraries are organised;

- define major library services;

- choose appropriate types of reference source for a particular information need/identify common types of citations;

- employ basic database search strategies;

- locate a variety of sources in a library or online;

- discriminate between scholarly and popular publications;
- legally and ethically use information.

An Advanced student is able to attain the criteria for Proficient and will be able to:

- modify and improve database search strategies;
- employ sophisticated database search strategies;
- interpret information in a variety of sources;
- evaluate information in terms of purpose, authority and reliability;
- understand ethical, legal and socioeconomic issues relating to information access and use.

The mean score of students across the three years of study are shown below, demonstrating some improvement in the information literacy of the students over the period of research (see Fig. 10.1).

The mean score of students in each year of study fell just short of the score required to be Proficient, with a peak score of 64.29 noted in year 2. From field observations it was

Figure 10.1 Mean final scores for all students (%)

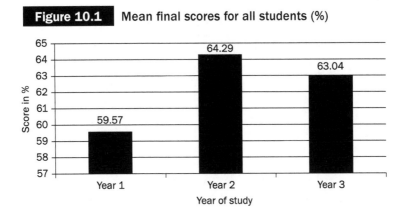

noted that the participating sample was the most focused and committed of the students and therefore the overall score was biased towards the more capable students. By year 3 a broader spread of participants were again recruited. However, overall improvement was observed from years 1 to 3.

The following sections will provide detail on student performance across each objective.

Overall results across the ACRL objectives

Results across these four standards show that the majority of students (see Fig. 10.2):

- were able to answer questions concerning defining and articulating the nature and extent of the information needed correctly: ACRL1 (range 69 per cent–74 per cent of students scoring correctly);

- were less able to answer questions concerning accessing needed information effectively and efficiently correctly: ACRL2 (range of 49 per cent–53 per cent of students scoring correctly);

- were able to answer questions concerning evaluating information and its sources critically and being able to incorporate selected information into his or her knowledge base and value system correctly: ACRL3 (range of 61 per cent–65 per cent of students scoring correctly);

- were able to answer questions concerning understanding many of the ethical, legal and socio-economic issues surrounding information and information technology correctly: ACRL5 (65 per cent –73 per cent of students scoring correctly).

From these results it would seem that the majority of students have little or no difficulty identifying the information

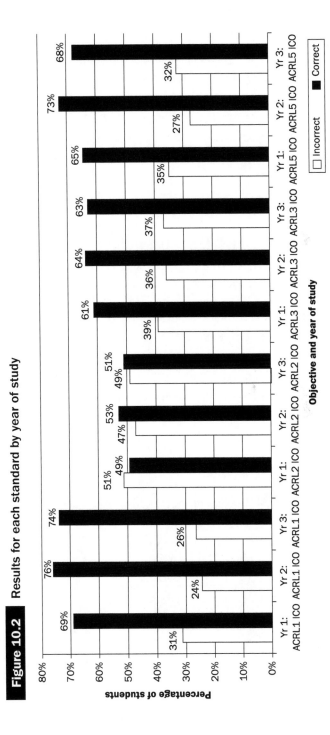

Figure 10.2 Results for each standard by year of study

they need, are able to evaluate the information and sources and incorporate the information into their knowledge and understand some of the legal and ethical issues surrounding use of information. However, some areas are causing difficulties and the results of these tests show that students in year 3 are scoring slightly lower across each standard, these will be presented in detail below.

Results for ACRL standard 1 – define and articulate the nature and extent of the information needed

Two thirds of students encountered little difficulty in defining and articulating the nature and extent of the information they needed, and an improvement was apparent from years 1 to 3. However, there was a slight drop between years 2 and 3. Detailed analysis identified that year 3 students struggled to identify correctly where and what primary sources are (44 per cent incorrect).

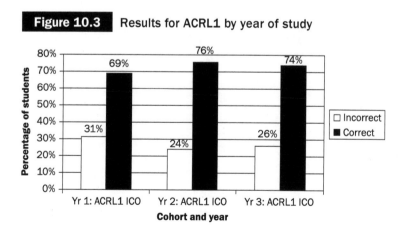

Figure 10.3 Results for ACRL1 by year of study

Results for ACRL standard 2 – accesses needed information effectively and efficiently

Some students also appear to struggle with how they go about accessing that information (see Fig. 10.4). There skills are core to our profession, critical in information literacy and an area where the library can, and does, provide excellent training; and this training can be further directed and targeted by understanding the results of this test.

In year 3 the following areas caused particular difficulties:

- Boolean strategy choice (93 per cent incorrect);

- understanding types of reference, 5 (91 per cent incorrect);

- locating journal articles (89 per cent incorrect);

- locating chapter in an edited book (76 per cent incorrect);

- phrase searching (73 per cent incorrect);

- understanding types of references, 3 (71 per cent incorrect);

- getting pdf/full-text of an article (71 per cent incorrect);

- narrowing a search (68 per cent incorrect);

- expanding strategy to get other similar items (68 per cent incorrect).

Figure 10.4 Results for ACRL2 by year of study

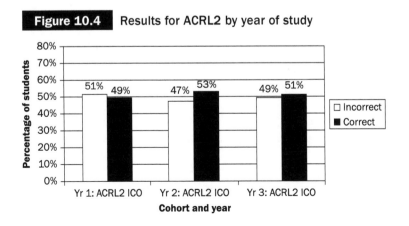

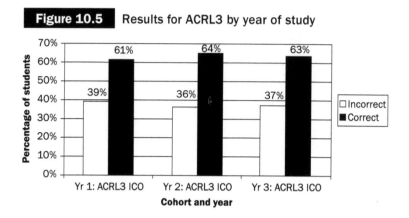

Figure 10.5 Results for ACRL3 by year of study

Results for ACRL standard 3 – evaluates information and its sources critically and incorporates selected information into his or her knowledge base and value system

In year 3 students struggled with:

- understanding census tables (63 per cent incorrect);
- understanding the conclusions of a website (69 per cent incorrect);
- understanding journal references (63 per cent incorrect);
- understanding government websites (53 per cent incorrect).

Results for ACRL standard 5 – understands many of the ethical, legal and socio-economic issues surrounding information and information technology

Students in year 3 particularly struggled with:

- understanding citation guidelines (71 per cent incorrect);
- understanding copyright law (59 per cent incorrect);
- understanding asking permission to use images (56 per cent incorrect).

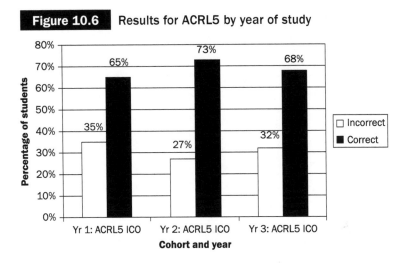

Figure 10.6 Results for ACRL5 by year of study

Conclusions and recommendations
===

Conclusions and recommendations

This longitudinal study of undergraduate students across the three years of their study has identified that students struggle with (predictable) areas of information literacy, and that:

- Identification and intervention in these areas is useful to students and information literacy helpers (whoever they are).

- Intervention needs to be ongoing – not only in year 1.

- Even up to their final year students continue to struggle with the same particular activities.

- A variety of approaches to support may be needed to help students develop their skills.

The following illustrate questions which students had difficulty with and form the basis for recommendations for areas to target for further support and training for students.

Constructing and implementing effectively designed search strategies

- Did not know how to expand searches or apply them to different databases; identifying additional relevant items from a citation which has already been retrieved.

Refining the search strategy if necessary

- Understanding how phrase searching works and what titles would be retrieved when presented with a specific example and possible results.

- Known item search (journal article): identifying which strategy would retrieve a specific journal article when presented with a number of different possibilities.

- Known item search (book chapter): identifying which strategy would retrieve a specific book chapter when presented with a number of different possibilities.

- Understanding how truncation works and what would be retrieved when presented with a specific example and possible results.

- Understanding how to narrow a search when presented with a number of different possibilities.

- Understanding how to refine a search to suppress irrelevant items when presented with a number of different possibilities.

- Understanding how Boolean operators work and what would be retrieved when presented with a specific example and a range of different possible strategies.

Extracting records and managing the information and its sources, could not recognise different item formats from bibliographic search results presented to them from databases

- Understanding the source of an item from its citation description (journal).

- Understanding the source of an item from its citation description (book).

- Understanding the source of an item from its citation description (chapter in a book).

- Understanding the source of an item from its citation description (newspaper).

- Locating full text of an article from its citation which has a link to 'Full-Text/PDF'.

Certainly, these results provide detailed identification of areas for practitioners to target to improve information literacy – results which we hope the community will find useful. However, in conducting this research other findings have emerged, such that it is posited that:

- there is value in the activity of assessing the information literacy of students;

- it can provide a useful quantitative measure;

- student and tutor feedback provided can be helpful;

- it can provide baselines and progress indicators;

- it can be a cohesive/inclusive activity but could also be negative and we need to be aware of this;

- it can trigger test fatigue and there are task attention issues;

- there are presentation format and question set issues;

- there can be cost and time factors.

Having used a US-based test designed for use in a US context, it is also felt that this may cause bias and/or confusion among UK students. If a UK test were developed then this might prove to be an effective diagnostic tool for students, tutors and library practitioners. Discussions with the LearnHigher Information Literacy Learning Area and the CILIP CSG for Information Literacy has led to initial work to create a UK Information Literacy Question Bank. It is envisaged that this Question Bank may be used by different people in different ways, for example online psychometric tests, printed quizzes or web-based interactive tutorials. This work is now in progress and it is hoped that it will provide the UK with a method to ensure appropriate assessment of information literacy to enable meaningful intervention for students.

References

Alvestrand, V. (2003) 'Support for info literacy certificate grows', *Information World*, 191: 1.

The Association of College and Research Libraries (2000) *Information Literacy Competency Standards for Higher Education*. ACRL

Bainton, T. (2001) *Information literacy and academic libraries: the SCONUL approach*. Proceedings of the 67th IFLA Council and General Conference, August 16–25.

Behrens, S. J. (1994) 'A conceptual analysis and historical overview of information literacy', *College and Research Libraries*, 55(4): 309–22.

The Big Blue: Final Report (2002) *http://www.library.mmu.ac.uk/bigblue/pdf/finalreportful.pdf*.

Bruce, C. S. (1997) 'The relational approach: a new model for information literacy', *The New Review of Information and Library Research*, 3: 1–22.

Doyle, C. S. (1992) *Outcome measures for information literacy. Final report to the National Forum on Information Literacy*. Syracuse, NY: ERIC Clearinghouse, ED 351033. P148.

Glass, B. and Griffiths, J. R. (2009) Online Information Literacy Audits: A Longitudinal Study (Year 2). LILAC 2009, 30 March–1 April, Cardiff University, Cardiff, UK.

Glass, B. and Griffiths, J. R. (2010) Understanding the Information Literacy Levels of Students: The Results of a Three Year Online Information Literacy Audit at Manchester Metropolitan University. LILAC 2010, 29–31 March, Limerick Strand Hotel, Limerick, Republic of Ireland.

Glass, N. R. (2006) *LearnHigher CETL: Information Literacy. The LearnHigher Suite at MMU.* LearnHigher: *www.learnhigher.mmu.ac.uk/learnhigher-suite/.*

Glass, N. R. (2007a) *LearnHigher CETL: Information Literacy. The Project.* LearnHigher: *www.learnhigher .mmu.ac.uk/project/.*

Glass, N. R. (2007b) *LearnHigher CETL: Information Literacy. Resources.* LearnHigher: *www.learnhigher.mmu .ac.uk/resources/.*

Hepworth, M. (2000a) 'Developing information literacy programs in Singapore', in *Information Literacy around the World: Advances in Programs and Research*, C. S. Bruce and P. C. Candy (eds). Wagga Wagga, NSW: Charles Sturt University, pp. 51–65.

Hepworth, M. (2000b). 'Approaches to information literacy training in higher education: challenges for librarians', *New Review of Academic Librarianship*, 6: 21–34.

Open University Library (2003) *Glossary of information terms.* Milton Keynes: Open University, *http://library .open.ac.uk/help/helpsheets/intglossary.html.*

The SCONUL Advisory Committee on Information Literacy (1999) *Information skills in higher education: a SCONUL position paper.* The Society of College, National and University Libraries.

Stubbings, R. and Brine, A. (2003) 'Reviewing electronic information literacy training packages', *Innovations in*

Teaching and Learning in Information and Computer Sciences (ITALICS), 2(1). *http://www.ics.ltsn.ac.uk/pub/italics/issuel/stubbings/010.html.*

Virkus, S. (2003) 'Information literacy in Europe: a literature review', *Information Research*, 8(4). Paper No. 159, *http://informationr.net/ir/8-4/paper159.html* (accessed 2 October 2005).

Wise, S. L. & Yang, S. (2003) *The Adaptex Assessment System (Version 1.5).* US Department of Education Fund for the Improvement of Postsecondary Education.

Wise, S. L., Cameron, L., Yang, S. and Davis, S. (2005) *Information Literacy Test: Test Development and Administration Manual.* Harrisonburg: Institute for Computer-Based Assessment; Center for Assessment & Research Studies, James Madison University.

Appendix

A calendar giving brief details of all the Staffordshire University Information Literacy Community of Practice events from 2006 to 2010. For more detail and linked material see *www.staffs.ac.uk/suilcop*.

2006–7: Information Literacy: Collaboration, Curriculum and Courses

19 July 2006
Speakers:

- **Evans Wema,** PhD research student, Loughborough University
- **Geoff Walton,** Learning & Teaching Fellow, Staffordshire University

Evans Wema gave a presentation on his IL training programme for librarians in Tanzania. Geoff Walton discussed his current research centred on information literacy, online collaborative learning and reflective learning.

1 November 2006
Speakers:

- **Susie Andretta,** Senior Lecturer, London Metropolitan University

- **Alison Pope,** Learning and Teaching Fellow, Staffordshire University
- **Miceal Barden,** Dean of Business School, Staffordshire University

Susie introduced the Six Frames of information literacy, a framework devised by Bruce, Edwards and Lupton (2006) and facilitated a discussion on the findings generated by the workshop run during the Information Literacy Conference, Staffordshire University, 17 May 2006. Alison Pope and Miceal Barden discussed the creation and implementation of an Information Literacy Policy at Staffordshire University.

28 February 2007
Speakers:

- **Lucy Keating,** Netskills, Newcastle University
- **Julie Adams,** Information Services, Staffordshire University

Lucy discussed the work Netskills have undertaken on the JISC i-skills project. Julie discussed approaches to integrating IT training and support into information literacy.

18 April 2007
Speakers:

- **Jo Parker,** Open University
- **Andrea Hatton,** Information Services, Staffordshire University

Jo discussed the rationale behind the Open University's module TU120 'Beyond Google' and using the emerging tools which students are now encountering in their everyday lives to deliver the IL message. Andrea talked about how we learn about the learner and explored the ways in which we teach information literacy.

2007–8: Information literacy: Space, Strategy and Support

7 November 2007: Information literacy and the use of space
Speakers:

- **Bob Glass,** LearnHigher Centre for Excellence in Teaching and Learning, Manchester Metropolitan University (MMU)
- **David Matthews,** Business School Library, Manchester Metropolitan University
- **Julie Adams, Alison Pope and Geoff Walton,** Information Services, Staffordshire University.

Bob described the work of the LearnHigher Centre for Excellence in Teaching and Learning (CETL) at MMU and discussed how the multi-activity learning space used within CETL was developed and their experiences to date in using this space. David Matthews talked about the use of alternative learning spaces in MMU Libraries. Julie, Alison and Geoff discussed the rationale behind the development of the Assignment Survival Kit (ASK) software.

12 March 2008: Information literacy and the strategic agenda
Speakers:

- **John Crawford,** Scottish IL Project, Glasgow Caledonian University
- **Dave Parkes,** Head of Learning Support, Staffordshire University

John Crawford discussed the important of advocacy in 'selling' information literacy to a variety of target groups. He described how this had been done in Finland and the progress made in Scotland with Health Literacy. Dave Parkes unpicked the connection between the Leitch Report and IL and then moved on to ask 'What is information and what is literacy now?'

21 May 2008: Information literacy and the use of learning support materials
Speakers:

- **Cathie Jackson,** Senior Consultant and Information Literacy/Subject Librarian: Law, Cardiff University
- **Paul Johnson,** Learning Support, Information Services, Staffordshire University

Cathie talked about how information literacy is supported at Cardiff University and how it has evolved since 2001. She described how support materials have been developed, including the information literacy Resource Bank and gave details of the recent podcast series on 'A Student Survival Guide to Writing a Good Essay'. Paul talked about selling information literacy to the Web 2.0 generation. In particular he looked at the role that podcasts can play in engaging students.

2008–9 – Information literacy: Development, Dialogue and Design

5 November 2008: Information literacy: Development
Speakers:

- **Debbi Boden,** Deputy Director of ILS, University of Worcester

- **Mark Hepworth,** Senior Lecturer, Department of Information Science, Loughborough University

Debbi discussed some of the challenges in explaining plagiarism to students and engaging their interest in its importance and relevance. She described how Imperial College collaborated with the Royal Academy of Dramatic Art (RADA Enterprises Ltd) to create a number of online resources. Mark led an interactive session where delegates worked to produce a list of metaphors which could be used to help illustrate information literacy.

4 March: Information literacy: Dialogue
Speakers:

- **Gareth Johnson,** University of Leicester
- **Chris Wakeman,** Staffordshire University

Gareth illustrated how carefully planned videos can play a role in helping educate and entertain students and also put over a serious message in a more digestible way. Chris set out a different approach to information literacy from his perspective as an education researcher. He examined how newer approaches to education, such as enquiry-based learning and social constructivism, might be seen to fit within, but also broaden, the traditional definition of information literacy.

29 April: Information literacy: Design
Speakers:

- **Nancy Graham,** University of Birmingham
- **Keith Puttick,** Staffordshire University

Nancy focused on aspects of designing re-usable learning objects (RLOs) to support information literacy (IL) training.

The Birmingham Re-Usable Materials (BRUM) Project had the aim of creating a suite of bite-size learning objects for academics to use with their students to support the teaching of information skills. Keith examined student research skills, and the IL element of student research tasks in the context of Staffordshire University's Enquiring Minds RiT project.

2009–10: Information literacy: Obesity, Overload and Opportunity

4 November: Information literacy: Obesity and overload
Speakers:

- **Andrew Whitworth,** University of Manchester
- **Ben Scoble,** Learning Development and Innovation, Staffordshire University

Andrew's talk explored definitions of information literacy focusing on the fact that much information is filtered out before we get the chance to go through the steps of IL – that is, selecting, evaluating and so on. It explored how this happens; the inbuilt 'cognitive biases' in our mental architecture; and how organisations affect the way we think. Ben looked at learning as a social practice, with an examination of the methods we have available to us to get information, learn and solve our problems.

3 February 2010: **Joint workshop with the Staffordshire University RiT Project**
Speaker:

- **Phil Levy,** University of Sheffield

Phil offered an introduction to Inquiry Based Learning (IBL) across the academic disciplines, and to research and evaluation which has investigated the impact of this approach to learning and teaching on students' learning experiences. Case examples of IBL at the University of Sheffield were presented. This workshop presented a conceptual framework for an undergraduate 'inquiry curriculum', and explored principles and practical ideas for designing and assessing IBL.

Index